STOCKS
BONDS
OPTIONS
FUTURES

Investments and Their Markets

STOCKS
BONDS
OPTIONS
FUTURES

Investments and Their Markets

The Staff of the
New York Institute of Finance

Edited by Stuart R. Veale

NEW YORK INSTITUTE OF FINANCE
Prentice-Hall

Prentice-Hall International (UK) Limited, *London*
Prentice-Hall of Australia Pty. Limited, *Sydney*
Prentice-Hall Canada, Inc., *Toronto*
Prentice-Hall Hispanoamericana, S.A., *Mexico*
Prentice-Hall of India Private Limited, *New Delhi*
Prentice-Hall of Japan, Inc., *Tokyo*
Simon & Schuster Asia Pte. Ltd., *Singapore*
Editora Prentice-Hall do Brasil, Ltda., *Rio de Janeiro*

© 1987 by NYIF Corp.
Simon & Schuster
A Paramount Communications Company

Printed in the United States of America

10   9   8   7   6   5
10   9   8   7   6   5   4   3   2   1   PBK

Library of Congress Cataloging-in-Publication Data

Stocks, bonds, options, futures.

  Bibliography.
  Includes index.
  1. Investments—United States.   2. Securities—
United States.   3. Commodity exchange—United States.
4. Brokers—United States.   I. New York Institute of
Finance.
HG4921.S7945   1987   332.6'78   87-11324
ISBN 0–13–846718–8 (case)
ISBN 0–13–847369–2 (paper)

PRENTICE HALL
A Paramount Communications Company
Englewood Cliffs, New Jersey 07632

Contents

Chapter 13
Underwriting: Raising Capital, 199

Chapter 14
Exchange Markets, 215

Chapter 15

The Over-the-Counter Securities Market, 237

Chapter 16

Operations—Order Processing, 263

Chapter 17

Government Regulations, 291

Chapter 18

Taxation, 311

Foreword

The securities industry is more visible today than at any time in the last fifty years, not only in the United States but around the world. Certainly, more people are employed in this field, directly or indirectly, than ever before. Consequently, the number of people interested in learning about the industry—the products, the markets, the mechanisms, the procedures, the players—grows daily.

Stocks, Bonds, Options, Futures is the long-needed primer for those many people who want or need to know about this exciting and ever-changing business. If you are:

- A securities industry entrant.
- A banking employee.
- A practitioner in a related financial service, such as insurance or accounting.

- An investor, either in the United States or overseas.
- A vendor to the industry.
- Anyone who wants to better understand the financial news—and headlines.

Then this book is the one to read.

The New York Institute of Finance—whose business is to provide the training, publish the books, and design the self-study and custom programs that prepare people to become practicing professionals in the securities industry—is particularly suited to create this book. Behind all its offerings are over sixty years of experience in training more than a quarter-million members of the securities industry.

A special thanks go to the individuals who contributed the extra effort to achieve our objective—a book that is comprehensive, lucid, and fun to read.

- To **Fred Dahl,** our Director of Publishing, who quarterbacked the book from inception.
- To **Bill Rini,** for his valuable critiques on content.
- To **Fred Eickelberg, Bob Gulick** and **Jane Hamingson**—our steering committee—for feedback on presentation and organization.
- To **Dawn Bushey** and **Mary Ann Pietromonaco,** our inhouse readers, whose final review under pressure of the printing deadline proved invaluable.

After the many drafts, reviews, and rewrites, however, it remained for someone to pull it all together into a coherent, enlightening reading experience. That someone turned out to be **Stuart R. Veale,** whose final, word-by-word edit of the manuscript brought it to the point that we were ready to commit it to type. Our thanks go to Stu for that awesome job—as always, under pressure of the printer's deadline.

The people at the Institute hope you find this book informative and pleasant reading. We hope further that you will continue to pursue your training needs with us. Please call us if you have any questions.

STEPHEN P. WININGS
President
New York Institute of Finance

1

The New Financial Marketplace

Up to about ten years ago, the sales representatives for a brokerage firm were commonly called "stockbrokers." For many decades, the name was perfectly suitable. Their job consisted largely of taking orders from their firm's clients to buy and sell stocks. They were the firm's "customer's men."

Nowadays, they go by the title of account executives, financial consultants, investment advisors, or any of a number of names that reflect their greatly expanded role. Today's salespersons (or registered representatives) of a brokerage firm must be familiar with a broad range of investment products, from annuities to zero coupons, and they must be sensitive to their clients' overall financial condition, objectives, and needs.

But if "stockbrokering" was profitable for so many years, why the change? The answer is that no one can survive, much less prosper, as a stockbroker anymore. Salespeople have to work harder, because their employing firms have to work harder to earn profits in today's financial marketplace.

That environment is undergoing a metamorphosis. Up to not so many years ago, people went to the bank to deposit their savings, to open checking accounts, or perhaps to put money into a certificate of deposit. To make an investment, very likely in stock, they called upon a stockbroker. To leave a little something behind them or to provide an annuity for retirement, they bought a whole life insurance policy, probably from an agent who made the presentation at the dining room table.

All that is changing.

First, the roles are changing. Brokerage firms are offering their clients cash management accounts with checking services, and some are selling insurance-type products. Insurance agents are becoming registered to sell securities, and insurance companies are selling stock mutual funds. Banks, too, are selling mutual funds, as well as offering discount brokerage services. No longer does the broker, the banker, or the insurance agent have a lock on any portion of an investor's money. It is all up for grabs.

The product is also changing. Stock and bond issues have proliferated in the 1980s, making for a much wider choice of traditional investments than just ten years aso. In addition, there are many new types of instruments: money market funds, zeros, mortgage-backed securities, stock and index options, futures, options on futures, and so on. Adding to the competition for the investor's dollar are the recent advances in data and telecommunications, which have made trading in foreign securities just as easy as trading in domestic markets.

Finally, the financial environment itself has become increasingly reactive to a number of influences. Consider:

- The size of the U.S. government's debt, whose long-term effect on the financial markets is still unknown.
- The growing use by institutional investors of computers to time their trades, leading to "witching hours" when market prices go wild.
- The super-sensitivity of financial markets to interest rates and foreign currency exchange rates.
- The appearance of "corporate raiders," seemingly everywhere, showing that no company is too big to be taken over if it is perceived as being weak or inefficient.

These are just some of the many changes that make working in the securities industry more challenging than ever.

In short, most of the old ways no longer apply. Securities industry professionals and investors who do not recognize these changes and adapt their investment policies and practices accordingly will find out the hard way that the marketplace has no mercy for the uninformed or the obsolete.

Whether you are a securities industry professional or individual investor, this book provides you with a solid introduction to today's investment instruments, markets, and business from the brokerage firms' point of view. However, if banks and insurance companies continue their forays into the securities business, they will very possibly have to be included in later editions of this book.

THE SECURITIES INDUSTRY

The firms that specialize in creating, trading, and selling "securities" are often referred to as simply *brokerage firms*. Many of these firms have their headquarters in New York's financial district, an area generally referred to as the "Wall Street District" since Wall Street runs right through the center of this section of Manhattan.

Within the financial district are located many of the world's largest exchanges including:

- The *New York Stock Exchange* (NYSE).
- The *American Stock Exchange* (ASE).
- The *New York Futures Exchange* (NYFE).
- The *New York Merchantile Exchange* (NYMEX).

As we shall see, a brokerage firm derives many benefits from having its headquarters close to the exchanges.

ORGANIZATION OF BROKERAGE FIRMS

Like any type of business, a brokerage firm has various departments to perform different functions, all of which are related in one way or another to the creation, trading, and selling of securities. However, not all firms have every department that follows. In fact, many small firms, called *specialty firms* or *boutiques,* perform just one of the functions.

Venture Capital

The venture capital division of a large firm (or a small firm that specializes in venture capital) provides very small companies with "seed money." Newly formed companies often need to research, develop, test, and market new products or ideas—all of which takes money. In exchange for providing the new company with the start-up capital it needs, the venture capital firm usually acquires a partial ownership interest in the new company.

Sometimes a venture capital firm uses its own capital to fund the start-up, and sometimes it offers its clients the opportunity to invest in the start-up. Investing in a small company that grows to become a large company can be both psychologically and financially rewarding. The original investors who backed Lotus Software and Compaq Computer must be very proud (in addition to being very wealthy). Of course, most start-up companies do not survive and grow, making this type of investment very risky.

Corporate Finance

The corporate finance department is responsible for raising capital for more established companies. The highly skilled (and highly paid) professionals who work for this group advise the firm's corporate clients on the most cost-effective way for them to raise the capital needed to finance their growth. Usually, this means selling new shares of stock or bonds of one type or another to investors.

Municipal Finance

The municipal finance department is responsible for assisting state and local governments in raising the money they need to build schools, roads, hospitals, and the like. States and local governments raise capital primarily by selling bonds to investors. The principal attraction of municipal bonds is that the interest they pay can be exempt from federal income tax. These bonds are discussed in greater detail in a later chapter.

THE SYNDICATE DEPARTMENT

The corporate and municipal finance departments do not sell securities. This task falls to the syndicate department, which coordinates the initial sale of new securities to both individual and institutional investors. The work of this department is discussed in greater detail in the chapter on underwriting.

Institutional Sales

The institutional sales department is responsible for dispensing investment advice to, and soliciting securities orders from, the firm's *institutional clients*, such as banks, insurance companies, pension plans, and the like. The professionals who interact with these clients are called *institutional brokers*.

Retail Sales

The retail sales department is responsible for dispensing investment advice to, and soliciting securities orders from, individuals. The professionals responsible for performing this function are called *retail brokers*, *registered representatives*, or *account executives*.

Portfolio Management

Many clients who lack the time and/or the expertise to manage their own investments turn this responsibility over to a *portfolio manager* or *investment advisor*. This "advisor" can be either an individual or a firm. Individuals select portfolio managers on the basis of their investment philosophy and performance record. Because managers have the authority to decide which securities to buy and sell for the client, as well as when to buy and sell them, they are considered to be a *fiduciary*. Under the law, fiduciaries must always place the best long-term interests of the client ahead of their personal interests or the interests of the firm.

Trading Department

The trading department is responsible for executing clients' securities orders. This department effects the actual purchases and sales of securities, in accordance with the clients' instructions. In addition, the trading department tries to buy and sell securities profitably with the firm's own money.

Operations

The operations department is responsible for processing all of the paperwork generated by the firm's other departments, most of it having to do with "clearing" the firm's trades. This department also handles all of the clients' bills and statements.

Compliance

This department is responsible for making sure that all other departments within the firm adhere to the various securities laws and regulations imposed on the industry by federal and state securities agencies.

Research

The research department explores investment opportunities to determine which are the most suitable and beneficial for clients and for the firm's own trading activities. The so-called *full-service brokerage firms* provide their clients with the firm's research at no additional charge. The cost of providing this research is built into the commissions that clients pay when they buy and sell securities. Another type of brokerage firm, called a *discount firm,* does not provide its clients with research. Instead, they charge reduced commission rates for executing orders and clearing trades.

The relationships among these departments will become evident as you read on.

TYPES OF BROKERAGE FIRMS

Most brokerage firms fall into one of four categories:

1. Wire houses.
2. Regional firms.

3. Investment banking firms.

4. Specialty firms.

Wire houses are brokerage firms with numerous offices across the country. The offices are connected by a telecommunications network called a *wire system;* hence the name "wire house." Included in this group are the brokerage firms that are household names, including Merrill Lynch, E. F. Hutton, Dean Witter, Paine Webber, Shearson Lehman, and Smith Barney.

Regional firms are smaller firms that operate in only one region of the country. Some examples are Raymond James & Associates Inc. in the Southeast and W. H. Newbolds and Sons Inc. in the Philadelphia area.

Investment banking firms do the lion's share of the security under-writing, that is, bringing new stocks and bonds to the market (this process is explained in a later chapter). These firms generally have only a few offices located in the world's major financial centers—New York, London, Tokyo, Geneva, and the like. Such firms concentrate their sales efforts on the institutional market. Included in this category are Goldman Sachs, Salomon Brothers, Morgan Stanley, and Bear Sterns.

Specialty firms usually concentrate on just one type of security. They may trade only in U.S. government securities, municipal bonds, or index options. When soliciting clients, these firms stress expertise in their areas of specialty instead of the breadth of their services.

SERVICE COMPANIES

In addition to brokerage firms, numerous companies provide services to the brokerage houses. Included in this category are:

- *Research boutiques* that provide research to the smaller brokerage firms.
- *Law firms* and *accounting firms* that specialize in working in the securities industry.
- *Ratings agencies* (such as Standard & Poor's or Moody's) that evaluate the credit quality of the various publicly traded securities.

• Training companies, such as the New York Institute of Finance, which train brokerage firm personnel in operations and sales.

THE INDUSTRY

The securities industry of the United States is among the largest and most efficient in the world. In the late 1960s, when trading volume began to surge, there was a so-called "paper crunch"—markets closed early each day just to allow the paperwork to catch up with the actual trading. Since that time, automated trading and clearing systems, as well as the hiring and training of hundreds of thousands of workers, has enabled the U.S. markets to attain one trading volume record after another.

To begin explaining how it all works, let's turn to the first investment that people think of when they hear the phrase "Wall Street"—common stock.

2

Common Stock

When they hear the word "investing," most people think of common stock. Indeed, the stock market is extremely popular with Americans. Recent estimates are that one out of four adults over age 25 owns common stock either directly or through a mutual fund.

But what exactly is common stock?

A share of common stock represents a *proportional ownership interest* in a corporation. If a corporation has 100 shares of stock outstanding and you own one of those shares, you own 1/100th of the company. If the company has 1,000,000 shares outstanding and you own 1,000 of those shares, you own 1,000/1,000,000th or 1/1,000th of the company.

A company can change the number of shares outstanding either by selling additional shares or by buying back and canceling some of the shares previously issued. In either case, your proportional interest in the ownership of the company also changes.

Example: If a corporation issues (that is, sells) 100 shares of stock to the public and you buy one of those shares, you own 1/100th of the company. But if the company subsequently issues another 100 shares, your proportional interest drops to 1/200th of the company. In other words, your interest in the company is "diluted" by the issuance of the new shares.

There are fundamentally three types of business entities:

1. The *sole proprietorship* is owned and operated by one person. While the proprietor enjoys great operating freedom, the business literally lives or dies with its owner. In the eyes of the law, the proprietor *is* the business. So the owner's assets are considered one and the same as the business's, and creditors of the business may lay claim to the house, car, and other belongings of the owner, if need be.

2. The *partnership,* owned by more than one person (the partners), may continue to operate after the death of one of the owners. So it has a better chance of staying in business than a proprietorship. Yet, like the proprietorship, it is not a separate legal "person." The partners share the risk of business losses and bankruptcy, but their personal assets are still at risk.

3. The *corporation* is a legal entity. Its owners are shareholders (stockholders), and the people running the company are employees. The owners (shareholders) may also be, and often are, employees. If an employee owns 51% or more of the stock, he or she has a "controlling interest" in the company and, through the stock's voting rights, in effect runs the corporation.

Figure 2-1. *Types of Business Entities.*

On the other hand, suppose a company has 1,000,000 shares of stock outstanding and you buy one share; then the company repurchases and cancels 250,000 of the shares. Your interest rises from owning 1/1,000,000 of the company to 1/750,000th of it.

THE NUMBER OF SHARES OUTSTANDING

In the eyes of the law, a corporation is a separate legal entity—unlike a partnership or proprietorship (see Figure 2-1). A company becomes "incorporated" by filing a copy of its "articles of incorporation" with the secretary of the state that the company wants to be its home state. This is not necessarily the state in which the company will do business. Many corporations incorporate in Delaware because of the favorable tax treatment that the state offers.

Included in a company's articles of incorporation are such things as:

1. The maximum number of shares that a company can issue (to protect current shareholders from excessive dilution). This is often referred to as the number of *authorized shares.*

2. The types of securities that the company may issue.
3. When each year the Board of Director's meeting will be held (discussed later in this chapter).

Example: A company may be allowed, according to its bylaws, to sell up to 1,000,000 shares of common stock. The number of authorized shares generally cannot be exceeded unless the corporate bylaws are changed, an action that often requires a vote by the overwhelming majority of the board of directors.

However, although the company is authorized to sell 1,000,000 shares, it does not have to issue them all. Companies often sell only a portion of their authorized shares at a time. This company, which we will call XYZ, Inc., chooses initially to sell only 250,000 of its 1,000,000 authorized shares to investors for $10 each. The company receives a total of $2,500,000.

When they are sold by the company, the shares are said to be offered in a *primary distribution, primary offering,* or *primary market.* After their initial sale, the shares trade among investors in the so-called *secondary market.* After the initial sale, the company receives no proceeds from any sales of the same shares.

Example: Investor A buys the shares from the company for $10 each in the primary offering. Two years later he sells the same shares to investor B for $15 each, making a profit of $5 per share. One year later investor B sells the shares to investor C for $7 each, taking an $8-per-share loss. The issuing company neither gains nor loses from the sales to investors B or C.

The sole determinant of the market value of the shares in the secondary market is the price that potential buyers are willing to pay and that prospective sellers are willing to accept.

Example: If no current owners of the shares are willing to sell their shares for less than $20 each and you want to buy some shares, you have to pay $20 or more. If you're not willing to pay $20 per share, you will not be able to acquire the shares.

If many current shareholders want to sell and you are the only prospective buyer, you can force sellers to compete to sell their shares to you at the lowest price. The market price of any share is thus determined by the so-called *free market forces*. (The reasons people buy or sell a company's shares are covered in the next chapter.)

There are several classifications of authorized stock:

- Shares that the company sells to investors are said to be *issued*. *Example:* XYZ, Inc. issued 250,000 shares.

- Shares that are issued and not retired are called the number of shares *issued and outstanding*. This number is used to calculate an investor's percentage of ownership. If XYZ, Inc. repurchases and then retires 50,000 of the issued shares, 200,000 shares would remain issued and outstanding. Each share would then represent 1/200,000 ownership interest.

- A company does not have to retire the shares that it repurchases on the open market. Instead, it can elect to hold the shares as an investment, like any other investor, and seek to sell them later at a higher price. Stock that has been repurchased by the issuing company itself is called *treasury stock.*

WHY BUY COMMON STOCK?

Why are investors willing to buy an ownership interest in a corporation? Investors buy common stock for the same reasons that people buy or start their own businesses:

1. They seek *dividends*, that is, they hope the business will generate profits that can be distributed to the owners.
2. They seek *capital gains*, that is, they hope that the business will grow in value and that they will be able to sell their interest in it for more than they paid for it.
3. They seek the *tax benefits* that the tax code provides to business owners.

How important is each of these benefits? The answer depends on the investment objectives of the stockholder. For example, retirees who live on the income generated from their investments place a high degree of importance on a stock's dividend yield. "Yuppies," with no need for current income, place greater emphasis on stocks that are likely to increase in value. All investors benefit from the fact that any increase in the market value of a stock is not taxed until the stock is sold. Thus stock market gains can compound, tax deferred.

Types of Stock

Stocks are generally divided into five categories based on their relative growth versus income potential:

1. Utility.
2. Blue chips.
3. Established growth.
4. Emerging growth.
5. Penny stocks.

Utility Stocks. These stocks represent ownership interests in public utilities. Because most large utility companies are regulated monopolies, there is little risk that they will go out of business. Instead, the risk of owning utility stocks is twofold:

1. The risk that the company may have to reduce or even eliminate its dividend payments because construction expenses (particularly with nuclear plants) have skyrocketed or because the utility regulation board will not allow the utility to raise the price it charges customers for electricity.
2. The risk that market interest rates will rise, making the stock's dividend yield less attractive relative to other investment options, such as money market instruments, certificates of deposit, bonds, and so on. This in turn makes the stock itself less attractive, causing its market value to decline.

Despite these risks, utility stocks are considered the least risky type of common stock.

Blue Chips. These companies are America's largest. They have generally been in business for so long that their names are well known

Figure 2-2a. A Common Stock Certificate (front).

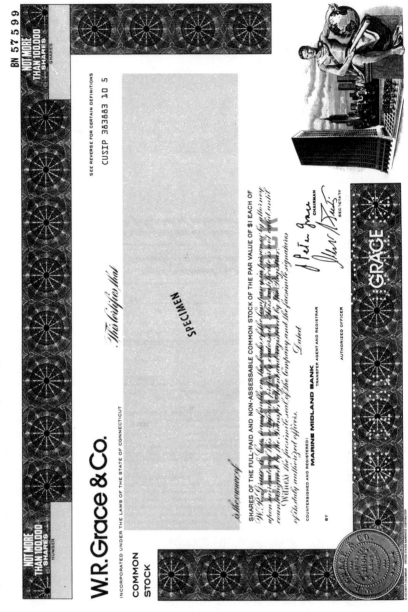

14

W. R. GRACE & CO.

A statement of the designations, terms, limitations and relative rights and preferences of the shares of each class authorized to be issued, any variations in relative rights and preferences between the shares of any series of any class so far as said rights and preferences shall have been fixed and determined and the authority of the Board of Directors of the Company to fix and determine any relative rights and preferences of any subsequent series will be furnished to the holder hereof, without charge, upon request to the Secretary of the Company or to the Transfer Agent named on the face hereof.

The following abbreviations, when used in the inscription of ownership on the face of this certificate, shall be construed as though they were written out in full according to applicable laws or regulations:

JT TEN   —As joint tenants, with right of
                 survivorship, and not as tenants
                 in common
TEN IN COM—As tenants in common
TEN BY ENT—As tenants by the entireties
Abbreviations in addition to those appearing above may be used.

For value received,_____ hereby sell, assign and transfer unto

PLEASE INSERT SOCIAL SECURITY OR OTHER
IDENTIFYING NUMBER OF ASSIGNEE

(PLEASE PRINT OR TYPEWRITE NAME AND ADDRESS OF ASSIGNEE)

SPECIMEN

_____ shares

of the capital stock represented by the within Certificate, and do hereby irrevocably constitute and appoint

_____ Attorney

to transfer the said stock on the books of the within named Company with full power of substitution in the premises.

Dated_____

Notice: The signature to this assignment must correspond with the name as written upon the face of the certificate in every particular, without alteration or enlargement or any change whatever.

Figure 2-2b. A Common Stock Certificate (back).

15

by practically every adult—IBM, GE, GM, or Ford. These companies are firmly established, with experienced boards of directors (to be discussed) and large cash flows from the sale of their products. For this reason, there is little likelihood that any of these companies will go out of business over the short term.

The large sizes of such companies, however, create the risk that increases in their sales and profits will not be great. For example, IBM is not likely to sell twice as many computers next year as it sold last year.

Blue chips, being "mature" companies, usually generate more cash from the sale of their products than they need to support their continued growth. Thus they can afford to pay relatively generous dividends to their shareholders. Consequently, investors who are attracted to blue chips are interested in relatively high dividends and moderate, but consistent, growth.

Established Growth. These growth companies are firmly established ongoing businesses, with at least a few years of solid profitability behind them. Yet they have the potential to achieve significant growth in the future. These companies are financially stable but are generally highly *leveraged* (that is, they have borrowed a lot of money), and so they lack real financial strength. This lack of financial strength makes them more susceptible to economic downturns and competitive pressures.

Since they are still growing fairly rapidly, these companies must reinvest most of their profits in new plants, equipment, and product development. Little money is left over with which to pay dividends, and so, if the company pays them at all, they tend to be small. Investors who buy stock in established growth companies seek above-average growth and are content with minimal dividend income.

Emerging Growth. Emerging growth companies have introduced their products and services into the marketplace, but they are still in the "start-up" phase. They may be profitable but, if so, only barely. All of these companies' revenues must be used to support their continued growth. In fact, many of them need additional financing (from selling more shares of stock or bonds) within the next few years. These companies, being small and financially weak, are very susceptible to competition. Many do not survive, but those that do grow very rapidly, rewarding their investors with substantial capital gains.

Penny Stocks. The so-called "penny stock companies" usually do not yet have a viable product or service. They are still in the development stage and almost always in need of additional financing. They also include companies in bankruptcy that are trying to make a comeback. The failure rate among this group is very high, and investors must be prepared to lose 100% of their investment.

CHARACTERISTICS OF COMMON STOCK

Like all investments, common stock has certain characteristics that distinguish it from other investments:

1. Limited liability.
2. Voting privileges.
3. Priority of claims in bankruptcy.
4. Dividends.

Limited Liability

One of the principal benefits of common stock is that investors cannot lose more than 100% of their investment; that is, the worst is that the value of the stock can go to zero. No matter how much money the company loses or how many of the company's bills go unpaid, the common stockholders, despite being the company's owners, cannot be held personally liable. The reason: A corporation is a separate legal entity under the law.

Voting Privileges

Common stockholders usually have the right to vote on important corporate matters. Most corporations are run as democracies with a "one-share/one-vote rule." If you own 100 shares, you get 100 votes. If you own 5,000 shares you get 5,000 votes. For the sake of efficiency and expediency, the share owners do not vote directly on every issue. Instead, they elect a *board of directors* to represent them—much like U.S. citizens elect members of the House of Representatives to carry out their wishes in running the country. One member of the board is elected *chairman of the board*, who is responsible for running the directors meetings and usually the most powerful individual on the board.

The board, acting on behalf of the shareholders, hires managers to operate the company. In one-person corporations (such as doctors who incorporate their practices), the manager, the shareholder, and the chairman of the board of directors are all the same person. In larger companies the board is usually composed of some of the company's managers and some individuals who are not employed by the company, the so-called *outside directors*.

Company directors are often nominated and elected based on their business acumen and, sometimes, political connections. The people who stand for election as directors are usually suggested by the company's management or its current board.

Most corporate actions require only the approval of a majority of the board of directors. The board can decide to hire a certain management team, make an acquisition (that is, buy a company), divest a division (sell a part of the company), or sell the entire company to another company. Thus any group of shareholders with enough votes to elect a majority of the board of directors has effective control over the entire company. For this reason many family-owned businesses that decide to *go public* (that is, sell shares to investors) still keep 51% of the stock in family hands as a way of retaining control.

One of the major criticisms leveled against some large U.S. companies is that the boards of directors and management teams are too friendly. In some cases, even when the management team is doing a poor job of managing the company, the boards are reluctant to fire them. After all, the very managers to be fired are often members of the board. Even the outside directors may be reluctant to fire a manager if they are personal friends or golfing buddies.

The close relationship between most boards and management teams also makes it difficult for outsiders to get control of the company, even if the company is mismanaged. When a group of the company's shareholders become dissatisfied with the way the management team is running the company, they often try to have the managers fired. The shareholders first appeal to the board. If the board refuses to fire the managers, the shareholders (often referred to as the *dissident shareholders*) nominate their own directors for the board and, at the annual meeting of the shareholders, try to get them elected.

Recently many companies have made it more difficult than usual for dissident shareholder groups by enacting a variety of "takeover defenses." These defenses take many forms, including:

1. Requiring that any decision to oust management require a vote of 75% of a company's board and not just a simple majority.
2. A *poison pill* defense, in which additional shares of stock are distributed to shareholders at a discounted price if an unwelcome shareholder group or individual threatens to seize control of the company.
3. Issuing multiple classes of common stock in which some classes have "multiple votes" per share. Of course, only members of the management team and their allies are eligible to buy the shares that have multiple votes. Thus a small group of shareholders who own only a small percentage of the stock can control the company if they own the shares that offer multiple voting privileges.

Claims in Bankruptcy

Common stock is the most "junior" security that a company offers. In other words, if the company falls on hard times, the first expense that is cut back is the dividend payments to the shareholders. If the company goes bankrupt, all of the company's creditors, all of the company's bondholders, and all of the company's managers are paid off before the common shareholders receive a penny. As an owner, a shareholder is the last to get paid.

Dividend Policy

Corporations make dividend payments (that is, profit distributions) to their common shareholders at the pleasure of the board of directors. They decide whether the company can afford to make a profit distribution and how large a distribution to make. Companies make their dividend payments on a quarterly basis. There are four days that investors need to be concerned with in respect to every dividend payment:

1. On the *declaration date,* the board of directors announces the dividend, its amount, and the day it is to be paid.

2. The *ex-dividend date* is the first day on which the current owner of the stock is *not* entitled to the dividend.

3. On the *record date,* the company examines its current list of shareholders. To receive the dividend, you must be on the company's shareholder list on this day. If you are not, you do not receive the dividend.

4. On the *payment date,* usually about two weeks after the record date, the company mails the checks.

(The dividend cycle is not difficult to understand, but many clients at brokerage firms miss the point of owning the stock on the record date. As a result, many investors who own stock when the checks are mailed do not receive any dividend payments—because they did not own the stock *as of* the record date. The dividend cycle is explained in greater detail later in the book.)

STOCK PRICES

To streamline the trading process, the securities industry has adopted the convention that stock prices are to trade in eighths of a point. For stocks, each *point* is $1, and each eighth is a $1 divided by 8, or 12.5¢. The prices are quoted as ⅛, ¼, ⅜, ½, ⅝, ¾, and ⅞.

Example: A stock, currently trading for $20 per share (or just 20), starts to rise. It may trade at 20⅛, 20¼, 20⅜, 20½, 20⅝, 20¾, 20⅞, and then 21. If the stock is rising quickly, it may bypass certain of these multiples, rising from $20 to 20⅜ in one trade.

While a stock can move by more than an eighth of a point, it cannot move by less than an eighth.

Example: A stock is currently selling for $20 a share. If you want to try to buy it at a cheaper price, you can bid 19⅞ (equal to $19.875) but you cannot bid, say, $19.95.

The only exceptions to this rule are:

- Stocks trading at less than $2 per share, which usually trade with minimum price increments of sixteenths of a point.

3

Analyzing Common Stocks

Over time, the market value of a common stock can either rise, fall, or remain unchanged. Successfully predicting which way stocks will go is the goal of every investor who "plays" the stock market. The process of predicting:

- *which* stocks will appreciate,
- *how much* they will appreciate, and
- *how long* they will take to appreciate

is called *common stock analysis*. As we shall see, this type of analysis is as much an art as it is a science.

Because of the tremendous amount of money invested in the stock market and the large number of stocks owned directly or indirectly by Americans, common stock analysis has become a very big business in and of itself. How much time and money are spent trying to analyze the stock market? There are no accurate answers, but there is no question that the amount is staggering. Consider:

1. Most of the major investment banking firms and commercial banks have entire research departments that often employ hundreds of people. The primary function of these departments is to predict the future market value of various stocks.

2. Numerous magazines and newspapers are dedicated, either primarily or exclusively, to analyzing common stocks. Some of the more popular magazines and newspapers in this category are: *Money, Personal Investor, Forbes, Barrons, The Wall Street Journal, Investor's Daily,* to mention only a few.

3. Over three hundred newsletters deal exclusively with the stock market. In fact, each segment of the market has numerous publications devoted exclusively to it.

4. Hundreds of personal computer-based programs are sold today that are designed to help both small and large investors analyze stocks.

5. In almost every major city, radio shows (or even entire radio stations) commit a large percentage of their programming to analyzing the stock market.

6. The appeal of common stock analysis is so widespread that even nationally syndicated television shows feature stock analysis as a major portion of their programming. A few examples are *Wall Street Week, The Nightly Business Report,* and *Strictly Business.*

7. For investors who can't get enough stock analysis from the preceding sources, there're always the "hot tips" you get from cab drivers.

Regardless of who performs the analysis and what media are used to communicate the results, all common stock analysis basically falls into one of two categories: fundamental analysis and technical analysis.

FUNDAMENTAL ANALYSIS

Fundamental analysis attempts to evaluate a company's future prospects for growth and profitability in light of the expected future outlook for the world economy, the national economy, the company's industry, and the company itself. If approached logically, fundamental analysis is really a three-step process.

- First, a fundamental analyst tries to evaluate what the future business environment is likely to be.

How to Read a Standard & Poor's Stock Report

1. This is the NYSE ticker symbol for this issue.

2. The number 976 is the page number in the book where this particular report is filed.

3. This section provides thumbnail statistics for this stock using earnings reported in the last 12 months and the company's indicated dividend rate.

4. The *Summary* paragraph contains S&P's general comments.

5. This vertical line chart plots the montly highs, lows, and closing prices over the last 6 years.

6. Monthly trading volume is presented for the last 6 years to enable technicians to relate changes in volume subsequent marketplace movements.

7. Net sales statistics are broken down on a quarterly basis for each fiscal year ending in May. They are then presented in a format designed to facilitate comparison between the same reporting periods for each of the preceding 3 years.

8. Earnings per common share (E.P.S.) are recorded in the samed fashion as net sales, that is, quarterly for comparison purposes. From these last two tables and with the number of outstanding shares (49,896,725) taken from the back side of this report in section 16, we can examine management's efficiency by computing an after-tax profit margin for the November quarter. First, multiply the shares outstanding by the $1.53 E.P.S. to arrive at net income ($76,341,989). Then divide net income by net sales ($76,341,989 divided by $1,495,000,000) to arrive at an after-tax profit margin of 5.1%.

9. This is the date on which this report has been prepared.

10. This is S&P's analysis of the company's business plans.

11. Important business and financial news announced by the company since publication of the last Stock Report.

12. Per Share Data isolates six items of statistical information about the company's common shares, normally considered important benchmarks of value by fundamental analysts. The data is presented for the preceding ten-year period to enable interested persons to identify longer-term trends.

13. General Mills' dividend information for the preceding 12 months is listed in this table and will also appear in Standard & Poor's *Dividend Record* book.

14. Relevant details have been culled from the company's balance sheets and income statements over the past 10 years and are presented in the table to facilitate comparisons.

15. *Business Summary* is an analysis of the corporation's operating divisions and its percentage contribution to the consolidated sales and pretax income.

16. Capitalization consists of the total par values of outstanding bonds plus the interest of the common stockholder, as shown on the current balance sheet. There are 28,967 holders of common shares including an unidentified number classified as "institutions" (nonindividuals organized as legal entities) who own 62% of the outstanding stock.

17. This small but important section is often of great interest to analysts and stockholders. It provides (a) the address and phone number of the company's main office, (b) the names of the company's senior officers, (c) the names of directors serving on the board, and (d) transfer agent(s) and registrar(s).

Figure 3-1. *A Report from Standard & Poor's Corp.*

General Mills

976 (2)

(1) **NYSE Symbol GIS**

(3) Price	Range	P-E Ratio	Dividend	Yield	S&P Ranking
Feb. 3'82 34 3/4	1981-2 39 1/2-26 3/4	8	1.64	4.7%	A+

(4) **Summary**

This leading factor in the package food industry has, through aquisitions, established important positions in other consumer-related areas, including crafts, games and toys, furniture, apparel, specialty retailing, and restaurants. Strong established brands, new products, and planned expansion should maintain profits in an upward course.

Current Outlook

(10) **Earnings for fiscal 1981-2 are estimated at $4.45 a share, assuming adoption of FAS 52, up from $3.90 the year before.**

The $0.41 quarterly dividend will probably be raised with the June, 1982 declaration.

Further earnings progress is seen for the second half of fiscal 1981-2, with year-to-year gains in the fourth quarter likely to exceed those of the third. Consumer food operations should account for the bulk of the increase, reflecting strong volume growth and favorable ingredient costs. Restaurant operations will show more moderate progress. Nonfood operations will be impacted by weak economic conditions. Nevertheless, earnings of the fashion and specialty retailing operations should be higher for the year, and specialty retailing profits will be off only slightly from the depressed levels of the prior year. The adoption of FAS 52 would eliminate most of the $0.15 in foreign currency translation losses incurred in the first half.

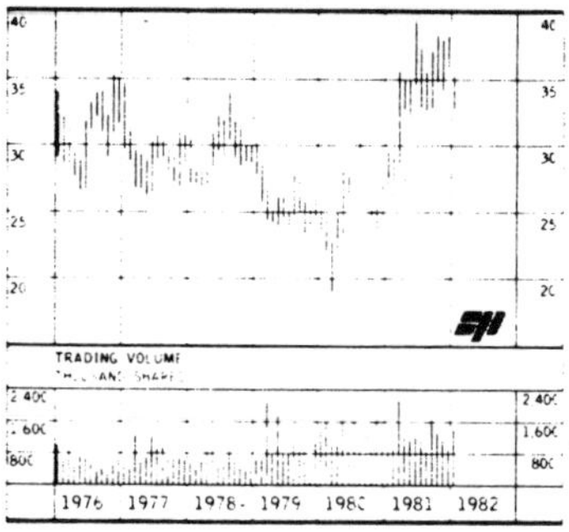

(5) (6)

(7) Net Sales (Million $)

Quarter:	1981-2	1980-1	1979-80	1978-9
Aug	1,345	1,089	973	907
Nov	1,495	1,395	1,205	1,095
Feb		1,105	975	847
May		1,264	1,017	897
		4,852	4,170	3,746

Sales for the 26 weeks to November 29, 1981 rose 14%, year to year. Margins narrowed, largely reflecting heavy advertising and promotional expenditures. Pretax income rose 8.9%. After taxes at 45.4%, versus 46.1%, net income gained 10%, to $2.80 a share from $2.55.

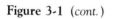

Common Share Earnings ($) (8)

Quarter:	1981-2	1980-1	1979-80	1978-9
Aug	1.27	0.88	0.85	0.86
Nov	1.53	1.67	1.22	1.01
Feb		0.62	0.62	0.45
May		0.73	0.68	0.60
		3.90	3.37	2.92

Important Developments (11)

Jan. '82—The company said that 26 of the 70 new restaurant openings planned for fiscal 1981-2 were in operation by November 29, 1981.

Aug. '81—GIS projected capital expenditures of $1.7 billion for the next five fiscal years, compared with $885 million over the past five years.

Next earnings report due in late March.

(12) Per Share Data ($)

Yr. End May 31[1]	1981	1980	1979	1978	[2]1977	1976	1975	1974	[3]1973	[2]1972
Book Value	NA	18.75	16.75	14.66	12.88	11.37	9.95	8.50	7.49	5.53
Earnings[4]	NA	3.90	3.37	2.92	2.58	2.36	2.04	1.59	1.59	1.40
Dividends	NA	1.44	1.28	1.12	0.97	0.79	0.66	0.58	0.53	0.50
Payout Ratio	NA	37%	38%	38%	37%	34%	32%	37%	33%	33%
Prices[5]—High	39 1/2	30 5/8	30 3/8	34 1/8	34 7/8	35 3/8	30 1/2	29 1/2	33 3/4	32 1/4
Low	26 3/4	19	23 1/2	26 5/8	26 1/4	26 5/8	20 1/4	14	23 1/4	19 1/4
P/E Ratio—	NA	8-5	9-7	12-9	14-10	15-11	15-10	19-9	21-15	23-14

Data as orig reptd. Adj. for stk div(s) of 100% Nov. 1975. 1. Of fol. cal. yr. 2. Reflects merger or acquisition. 3. Reflects merger or acquisition and accounting change. 4. Bef. results of disc. opers. of -0.14 in 1977. 5. Cal. yr. NA-Not Available.

Standard NYSE Stock Reports
Vol. 49 No. 28 Sec. 14

(9) **February 10, 1982**

Standard & Poor's Corp
25 Broadway, NY, NY 10004

Figure 3-1 *(cont.)*

976

General Mills, Inc.

Income Data (Million $)

Year Ended May 31	Revs.	Oper. Inc.	% Oper. Inc. of Revs.	Cap. Exp.	Depr.	Int. Exp.	Net Bef. Taxes	Eff. Tax Rate	**Net Inc.	% Net Inc. of Revs.
1980	4,852	531	11.0%	247	99.5	⁷63.6	⁵374	47.5%	197	4.1%
1979	4,170	446	10.7%	197	81.1	48.6	⁵317	46.3%	170	4.1%
1978	3,745	372	9.9%	159	73.3	38.8	⁵264	44.3%	147	3.9%
²1977	3,243	333	10.3%	152	58.6	29.3	⁵245	47.5%	129	4.0%
1976	2,909	303	10.4%	117	48.1	26.7	⁵230	48.7%	117	4.0%
1975	2,645	276	10.4%	101	46.7	29.4	⁵201	49.6%	101	3.8%
1974	2,309	224	9.7%	112	41.9	36.2	⁵147	48.1%	76	3.3%
³1973	2,000	215	10.8%	92	36.4	28.5	⁵152	50.0%	75	3.8%
⁴1972	1,593	187	11.7%	56	34.7	18.3	⁵135	50.5%	66	4.1%
1971	1,316	156	11.9%	51	32.0	20.4	⁵104	48.7%	52	4.0%

Balance Sheet Data (Million $)

May 31	Cash	Current Assets	Current Liab.	Ratio	Total Assets	Ret. on Assets	Long Term Debt	Common Equity	Total Cap.	% LT Debt of Cap.	Ret. on Equity
1980	39.1	1,076	739	1.5	2,301	9.1%	349	1,145	1,536	22.7%	18.1%
1979	39.1	986	570	1.7	2,012	8.8%	378	1,021	1,423	26.5%	17.6%
1978	97.0	936	495	1.9	1,835	8.5%	385	916	1,326	29.0%	16.9%
1977	19.9	788	503	1.6	1,613	8.4%	260	815	1,092	23.8%	16.7%
1976	22.3	713	415	1.7	1,447	8.4%	276	725	1,021	27.0%	17.1%
1975	81.8	673	378	1.8	1,328	7.9%	282	640	938	30.0%	16.7%
1974	10.0	590	314	1.9	1,206	6.5%	305	560	884	34.5%	14.4%
1973	19.9	581	312	1.9	1,117	7.1%	298	483	796	37.4%	17.1%
1972	16.7	426	247	1.7	906	7.4%	213	357	650	32.8%	19.2%
1971	28.6	342	203	1.7	818	6.6%	231	291	603	38.3%	18.3%

Data as orig reptd. 1. Of fol cal yr. 2. Excludes discontinued operations and reflects merger or acquisition. 3. Reflects merger or acquisition and accounting change. 4. Reflects merger or acquisition. 5. Incl equity in earns of nonconsol subs 6. Bef results of disc opers in 1977 and spec item s in 1971 7. Reflects accounting change

Business Summary

General Mills is a leading factor in the packaged foods industry. and has important positions in other consumer-related areas. Contributions by business segment in fiscal 1980-1 were

	Sales	Profits
Consumer foods	52%	47%
Restaurants	14%	16%
Creative products	14%	15%
Apparel accessories	12%	19%
Spec Retail other	8%	3%

Foreign operations accounted for 11% of 1980-1 sales and 9% of profits

Food operations include Big G ready-to-eat cereals Tom's snack items, GoodMark sausage products. Donruss bubble gum, Betty Crocker cake mixes and packaged products. Hamburger Helper and Tuna Helper, Gold Medal flour Gorton's seafoods, Saluto pizza. Yoplait yogurt, bakery mixes, imitation bacon chips cake decorations, and party favors. Restaurant operations consist mainly of Red Lobster Inns (291 at the end of 1980-1) and York Steak Houses (132)

The Craft, Games and Toys group consists of Parker Brothers. Kenner Products division. and Fundimensions. Other activities include the production of apparel and accessories (mainly jewelry and furniture, and specialty retailing

Employees 71,225

Dividend Data

Dividends have been paid since 1898. A dividend reinvestment plan is available

Amt. of Divd. $	Date Decl.	Ex-divd. Date	Stock of Record	Payment Date
0.37	Mar 23	Apr 6	Apr 10	May 1'81
0.41	Jun 22	Jul 6	Jul 10	Aug 1'81
0.41	Sep 21	Oct 5	Oct 9	Nov 2'81
0.41	Nov 23	Jan 4	Jan 8	Feb 1'82

Capitalization

Long Term Debt: $318,000,000

Common Stock: 49,896,725 shs $0.75 par
Institutions hold about 62%
Shareholders 28,967

Office — 9200 Wayzata Blvd. Minneapolis. Minn 55440 Tel — (612) 540 2311 Chrmn & CEO—H B Atwater Jr Secy—. M. Neville VP-Treas—J L Weaver. Investor Contact—D Bertas Dirs—B Ancker Johnson. H B Atwater Jr. F C Blodgett N B Grossman. S F Keating E R Kinney, L W Lehr L W Menk J W Morrison G A Newkirk. W F Pounds E S Reid W G Smith D F Swanson R L Terrie Transfer Agents—Company s Office Minneapolis Chicago NY C Registrars—Northwestern National Bank Minneapolis Chicago NYC Incorporated in Delaware in 1928

Information has been obtained from sources believed to be reliable but its accuracy and completeness are not guaranteed. R A B

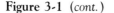

Figure 3-1 *(cont.)*

CAMPBELL SOUP COMPANY

LISTED	SYM.	LTPS•	STPS•	IND. DIV.	REC. PRICE	RANGE (52-WKS.)	YLD.
NYSE	CPB	137.1	103.6	$1.44•	63	69 - 40	2.3%

HIGH GRADE. AS A LEADER IN A COMPARATIVELY STABLE INDUSTRY, WELL ACCEPTED BRAND NAMES HAVE LED TO A GOOD RECORD.

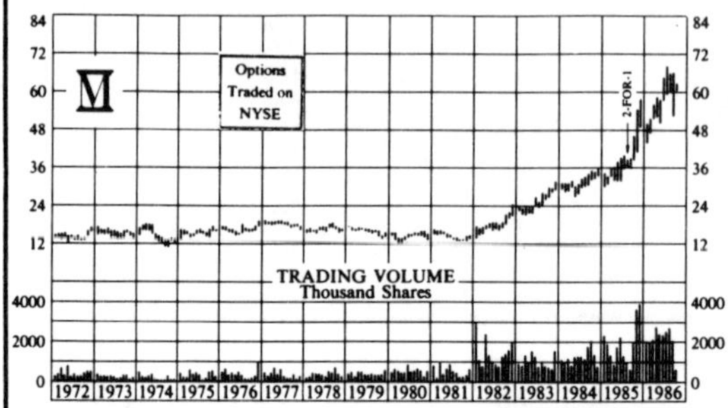

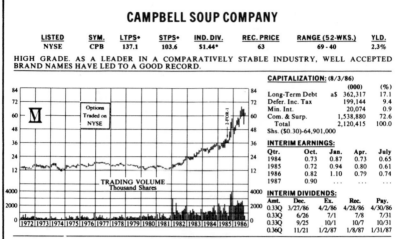

CAPITALIZATION: (8/3/86)

		(000)	(%)
Long-Term Debt	a$	362,317	17.1
Defer. Inc. Tax		199,144	9.4
Min. Int.		20,074	0.9
Com. & Surp.		1,538,880	72.6
Total		2,120,415	100.0

Shs. ($0.30)-64,901,000

INTERIM EARNINGS:

Qtr.	Oct.	Jan.	Apr.	July
1984	0.73	0.87	0.73	0.65
1985	0.72	0.94	0.80	0.61
1986	0.82	1.10	0.79	0.74
1987	0.90	...	...	...

INTERIM DIVIDENDS:

Amt.	Dec.	Ex.	Rec.	Pay.
0.33Q	3/27/86	4/2/86	4/28/86	4/30/86
0.33Q	6/26	7/1	7/8	7/31
0.33Q	9/25	10/1	10/7	10/31
0.36Q	11/21	1/2/87	1/8/87	1/31/87

BACKGROUND:

Campbell is the largest manufacturer of canned soups, spaghetti, and blended vegetable juices and second largest in canned pork and beans and tomato juice. Other areas include pet foods, restaurants and confections. Brand names include CAMPBELL'S, FRANCO-AMERICA, V-8, MRS. PAULS, LE MENU, PREGO, BOUNTY and VLASIC'S. Company operates 63 plants in the U.S. and 32 in foreign countries including Canada, England, Italy, Belgium, France, Mexico and Australia. Campbell manufactures most domestic can requirements. Foreign sales and net income were 20.3% and 11.0%, respectively, of the total. Dividends have been paid since 1902. Insiders own approximately 31% of the common stock.

RECENT DEVELOPMENTS:

For the thirteen weeks ended 11/2/86, net income rose 10% to $58.7 million. Revenues were up 7%. For the year ended 8/3/86, net income climbed 13% to $223.2 million. Sales rose 10%. The soup group achieved volume gains of almost 6%. Strong performers included spaghetti sauce, biscuits, and GODIVA chocolates. FRESH CHEF refrigerated salads and GREAT STARTS FROZEN BREAKFASTS both contributed to sales increases. Results were limited by MRS. PAUL'S KITCHENS and the beverage business unit.

PROSPECTS:

The outlook for near-term earnings and revenue growth is positive. The Company has increased its marketing effort and should also benefit from favorable foreign exchange rates. A reoganization in the soup group is now complete. Prospects are enhanced by CPB's shift to microwaveable plates and trays for its frozen lines. PREGO spaghetti sauce should continue to expand in market share. While CPB is in a competitive industry, its efforts in analyzing consumer eating patterns should keep the Company in a strong position.

STATISTICS:

YEAR	GROSS REVS. ($mill.)	OPER. PROFIT MARGIN %	RET. ON EQUITY %	NET INCOME ($mill.)	WORK CAP. ($mill.)	SENIOR CAPITAL ($mill.)	SHARES (000)	EARN. PER SH.$	DIV. PER SH.$	DIV. PAY. %	PRICE RANGE	P/E RATIO	AVG. YIELD %
7/31													
77	1,769.2	11.7	13.9	107.1	389.6	11.8	65,514	1.64	0.74	45	19¾ - 16⅝	11.1	4.1
78	1,983.7	11.7	14.2	121.4	434.4	43.9	67,662	1.81	0.80	44	19 - 15½	9.6	4.6
79	2,248.7	11.2	14.7	132.7	362.2	36.3	65,934	1.99	0.88	44	18⅞ - 13⅞	8.0	5.5
80	2,560.6	10.5	14.0	134.6	405.6	137.9	65,826	2.04	0.95	47	16⅜ - 12⅝	7.1	6.5
81	2,797.7	9.8	12.9	129.7	368.2	150.6	64,468	2.00	1.05	53	16⅞ - 13⅛	7.6	7.0
82	2,944.8	10.2	14.2	149.6	434.6	236.2	64,462	2.32	1.05	45	24⅝ - 14	8.3	5.4
83	3,292.4	10.5	14.4	165.0	478.9	267.5	64,498	2.56	1.10	43	32 - 21⅞	10.4	4.1
84	3,657.4	9.8	15.2	191.2	541.5	283.0	64,532	2.97	1.15	39	36 - 27⅛	10.7	3.6
85	3,988.7	9.2	14.3	197.8	579.5	297.1	64,644	3.06	1.25	41	58⅛ - 30⅛	14.4	2.8
86	**4,378.7**	**9.5**	**14.5**	**223.2**	**708.7**	**362.3**	**64,901**	**3.45**					

•Long-Term Price Score — Short-Term Price Score; see page 4a. Adjusted for 2-for-1 split, 7/85. STATISTICS ARE AS ORIGINALLY REPORTED. a-Includes capitalized lease obligations.

INCORPORATED:
Nov. 23, 1922 – New Jersey

PRINCIPAL OFFICE:
Campbell Place
Camden, N.J. 08103-1799
Tel.: (609) 342-4800

ANNUAL MEETING:
Friday preceding
Fourth Thursday in Nov.

NUMBER OF STOCKHOLDERS:
32,807

TRANSFER AGENT(S):
Mellon Bank (East), Phila., Pa.

REGISTRAR(S):
Mellon Bank (East), Phila., Pa.

INSTITUTIONAL HOLDINGS:
No. of Institutions: 221
Shares Held: 39,905,314

OFFICERS:
Chairman
W.S. Cashel, Jr.
Pres. & Ch. Exec. Off.
R.G. McGovern
Sr. V.P.-Fin. & C.F.O.
E.L. Harper
Secretary
R.L. Baker
V.P. & Treasurer
D.H. Springer

Figure 3-2. *A Report from* Moody's Handbook of Common Stocks.

- Second, the analyst estimates how well (or how poorly) the company being evaluated will perform in this future business environment (that is, the company's future earnings).
- Third, given the appraisals of the future economy and of the company's future earnings, the analyst estimates how much future investors will be willing to pay for a share of the company's stock (in other words, the stock's future market value).

Step One: The Business Environment

The task of estimating the future business environment falls primarily to professionally trained economists. Starting with the current business setting, economists attempt to project future interest rates, gross national product figures, currency exchange rates, government deficit figures, research and development spending figures, energy prices, money supplies, trade deficits, and many other conditions. Often this analysis entails the use of complex economic models and sophisticated computer programs.

Any discussion of the future business climate usually starts with an evaluation of the global economy. After all, given the increasing globalization of business and finance, what happens overseas can have a dramatic effect on the business climate here in the United States. If interest rates rise overseas, they will probably also rise here. If other countries stimulate their economies, U.S. companies will probably be able to increase their exports. If certain companies default on their debts to U.S. banks, the United States economy could be devastated. And so on.

After completing their projections about the global economy, economists can turn their attention to the national economy. Will it be expanding or contracting? Will the government be raising or lowering taxes? Will unemployment be rising or falling? Will domestic interest rates rise or fall? Will the domestic prices of raw materials rise or fall? Many questions like these must be addressed.

The next phase is to evaluate the industry in which the company operates. Is the size of the industry's market growing (computers) or declining (steel)? How competitive is the company's industry? How quickly do the industry's products become obsolete? Is there a shortage or surplus of skilled people within the industry? How much does government regulate the industry?

Having dealt with these many questions, the economist is ready for the next step.

Step Two: The Company's Performance

Armed with a complete set of economic projections, analysts begin to assess how well or how poorly a company will perform in the projected future business environment. This analysis should include an evaluation of the company's:

- Management.
- Research and development program.
- Liquidity.
- Financial strength.
- Labor relations.
- Efficiency and profitability.
- Growth prospects.
- Good will.

Management. In an evaluation of a company's management, the principal questions are:

1. How much experience does the management team have? Does the management team have the skills necessary to run a company?
2. How well has the management team performed in the past. After all, past performance is one of the best indicators of future performance.
3. How much depth does the management team have? Would the loss of any one individual (or a few of them) be devastating to the company?
4. Is the management team honest and straightforward or shifty and evasive?
5. Does the company's management seem to have well-thought-out plans for the company's future growth? Does senior management anticipate or react to conditions?

Research and Development. If the company is in a business that requires the frequent introduction of new products and/or services, the factors to be considered are:

1. What new products (or services) is the company going to introduce in the near future?
2. How big an impact are the new products likely to have on the size and scope of the company's business?
3. How much money (in both dollars and as a percentage of sales) is the company investing in R&D?
4. Is the company investing more or less in R&D than its competitors?
5. Is the company turning out as many new products as it should be, given its R&D budget?

Liquidity. Liquidity is a measure of a company's cash reserves, which are important for several reasons. Every company needs a cash reserve fund so that it is not devastated by an unexpected expense, or so that it can move quickly to take advantage of business opportunities when they present themselves.

To measure a company's liquidity, most analysts use the current ratio. This ratio is defined as:

$$\text{Current ratio} = \text{Current assets} \div \text{Current liabilities}$$

- *Current assets* consist of cash, short-term receivables, readily sellable inventory, and investments that mature in less than a year.
- *Current liabilities* are the bills the company must pay over the next year including any interest payments on the company's long-term debt).

Some analysts also look at the *quick asset ratio,* which is the same as the current ratio except that the inventory is not included in the numerator. By ignoring the inventory, the quick assets ratio provides a more accurate measure of the company's "cash" reserves relative to its upcoming bills.

As important as liquidity is for a company, the need for liquidity needs to be tempered with a desire for productivity. Ideally, a company should be able to earn a higher return from money invested in its business than from cash reserves committed to its short-term investments. Thus it "costs" a company money to hold cash reserves. Most analysts like to see current ratios of about 2:1 and quick assets ratios of about 0.75:1.

Any evaluation of a company should also include an analysis of whether its liquidity is improving or declining. By calculating the company's current ratio for each of the last few years, you should be able to determine whether the company is becoming more or less liquid.

Financial Strength. Certainly, companies need money, or *capital,* on which to operate: It takes money to make money. Capital comes from two sources: equity and debt.

• *Equity* is the money the company takes in by selling ownership interests (stock offerings), plus the profits earned but not paid out to the owners (known as *retained earnings*).

• *Debt* is the total of the company's long-term borrowings ("long-term" meaning *not* coming due within the next year).

The relationship between the part of a company's capital that comes from borrowing and the part that comes from equity is called the *debt to equity ratio.* This ratio is calculated by dividing the amount of capital made up of debt by the amount made up of equity. The higher this ratio is, the more "leveraged" the company's balanced sheet; that is, the company is using a large percentage of borrowed capital to fund its operation. The more leveraged the company's balance sheet, the better the company's earnings will be during good times and the worse they will be in bad times.

Example: Consider the following *grossly oversimplified* case. Two companies make widgets. One company has $2 of equity and makes a $0.40 profit on its operations. The second company makes the same $0.40 but its capital consists on $1 of equity and $1 of debt, on which it pays 10% interest. Therefore:

• The first company's return on equity is:

$$(\$0.40 \div \$2) \times 100 = 20\%$$

• The second company's return on equity is:

$$[(\$0.40 - \$0.10) \div \$1] \times 100 = 30\%$$

Of course, if there is a business downturn and both companies' profits drop to $0.10, the first company still has a return on equity of 5% ($0.10 ÷ $2), while *all* of the second company's operating profits has to be used to service its debt. If operating profits dropped even lower, the second company would start losing money.

Thus the first company's return on equity is more stable, whereas the second company offers the potential of a higher return on equity. Which company is more attractive? The answer depends on the type of business in which the company is involved, the investment objectives of the investor, the investor's tolerance for risk, and the outlook for the economy and the company's industry.

One of the most important decisions that a company's senior management must make is how leveraged the company should be. This means balancing the conflicting goals of maximizing the investor's return on equity and providing stability. To adjust the company's debt to equity ratio, a company can issue either new equity or new debt, or it can repurchase some of the equity or debt it has outstanding.

Labor Relations. Here are some questions to address in this area:

1. What percentage of the company's work force is unionized?
2. What is the probability of a long and disruptive strike?
3. What is the company's annual employee turnover?
4. Are the company's labor costs above or below those of its competitors?

Efficiency and Profitability. One of the most important factors to analyze is the efficiency of the company's operations. After all, a dollar saved is as good as a dollar earned. Some of the questions relating to efficiency are:

1. What is the company's cost of producing its product or of delivering its service?

2. Are the company's costs above or below the costs of its competitors?

3. Are the company's costs rising or falling?

4. Are the company's plants and facilities modern, or will they have to be replaced shortly?

5. Is the company making use of the latest managerial and administrative techniques to improve its efficiency?

Growth Prospects. Almost every company wants to grow, but growth has its costs. Companies must invest dollars today in the anticipation that the future return will justify the expansion. Also, a company that grows too fast can end up growing itself right into managerial chaos or even bankruptcy. Some of the questions that need to be answered are:

1. Is the market for the company's products large enough to support a high growth rate?

2. Does the company have, or can it obtain, sufficient financing to support a high growth rate?

3. Does the company have, or can it obtain, sufficient plant capacity to achieve a high growth rate?

4. Does the company's management have the time and expertise necessary to manage rapid growth?

5. Does the company have the internal infrastructure necessary to support a high growth rate?

Goodwill. An advantage that an existing company should have over a new competitor is goodwill—goodwill between itself and its customers, its suppliers, its distributors, and others. If a company has the reputation of being a good company with which to do business, potential competitors find it much harder to get started. Some of the factors to be considered are:

1. Does the company have an effective customer support and development program?

2. Does the company have a good working relationship with its suppliers, distributors, and creditors?

3. Does the company have any "name brands" among its product line?

4. Is the company considered a good corporate citizen?

Step Three: The Stock's Future Market Value

Having dealt with all the preceding questions and formed an estimate of the company's future business prospects, the analyst then attempts to predict the future value of the company's stock. Fundamentalists believe that stock prices are based on four interrelated criteria:

1. Dividends.
2. Book value.
3. Cash flow.
4. Earnings.

Dividends. When evaluating a company's dividend policy, a fundamentalist examines:

1. The dividend yield expressed as a percentage of the stock's market value. For example, a $50 stock that pays a $4 dividend offers an 8% return ($4 ÷ $50).

2. Whether the stock's dividend yield is smaller or larger than that of the company's competitors.

3. Whether the stock's dividend is likely to be increased in the near future.

4. Whether the company is earning enough money to continue paying dividends (determining this is explained later in the chapter).

5. Whether the company is paying the "right" percentage of its earnings out to shareholders in the form of dividends (also explained later in the chapter).

Book Value. A company's book value is equal to its assets minus its liabilities, and it is usually expressed on a "per-share basis." In other words, if a company simply stopped doing business, liquidated its assets, and paid off its liabilities, what is left over is the *book value*. A company's book value places no value on the business as a going concern—that is, no value on clients' loyalty to the company, on the employees' expertise, or on new product R&D.

The investors most interested in book value are regarded as *contrarians*. Contrarians buy stocks that no one else seems to be interested in and hold them until they become popular and their prices rise. For example, contrarian investors tend to buy gold and oil stocks when the underlying commodity prices are low, and sell them when the prices of gold and oil soar. One of the best ways to find stocks that are currently out of favor is to look for stocks that are trading at prices near (or even below) their book value.

In addition to simply determining a company's current book value, a fundamental analyst looks at:

1. Whether the company's book value is increasing or decreasing.

2. Whether the company's stock is trading at a higher or lower percentage over book value than its competitors' stock.

3. The price volatility of the company's assets (and liabilities). For example, the price of oil is very volatile, whereas the price of real estate is comparatively stable. Thus the book value of an oil company can change rapidly, while the book value of a real estate holding company is comparatively stable.

4. The degree of certainty in valuing a company's assets and liabilities. It's often difficult to know accurately how many barrels of oil an oil company has in the ground or what the future liabilities of a property and casualty company will be. Other types of companies have assets that are known exactly, such as car dealerships, livestock companies, and the like.

5. Whether the company has any hidden assets. Companies sometimes own real estate that is worth much more than the value at which they carry it on their books. Also, some companies' pension plans have large surpluses, which can be reclaimed at an opportune time.

Cash Flow. The term "cash flow" has nothing to do with the actual number of dollars coming in and flowing out of a company.

Cash flow is defined as net (after-tax) income plus depreciation. Analyzing a company's cash flow is useful because both net income and depreciation can be used to offset the cost of acquiring and/or merging with a company. For this reason cash flow is of particular interest to corporate raiders and corporate officers seeking to acquire other companies. Like book value, cash flow is often expressed on a per-share basis.

Earnings. Of all the factors used to determine what price a share of a company's stock is worth, the company's earnings are the most often used. A company's *earnings* are defined as the difference between its net income (including depreciation) and its expenditures (except for common stock dividends). Again, earnings are often expressed on a per-share basis.

A company may do two things with its earnings. It can either pay them out as distributions of profits, that is, as *dividends.* Or it can reinvest the earnings back into the company, that is, *retained earnings.*

Companies naturally have different policies with regard to disposing of their earnings. Small companies that want to grow quickly generally must reinvest all of their earnings to support their growth, and as a result they pay no dividends to their shareholders. Established companies, which grow at a slower rate, can generally afford to pay a higher percentage of their earnings (if they have any) as dividends. Finally, established utility companies, which have very high cash flows and little need for growth, can afford to pay a high percentage of their earnings to shareholders in the form of dividends (often 80% or more of earnings).

Predicting a Future Price

When valuing a stock, most analysts determine a company's current earnings, predict its future earnings, and estimate (read "guess") the multiple of earnings that future investors will be willing to pay to buy the stock.

Example: XYZ, Inc. is currently earning $1 per share and is selling for $10 per share. After an extensive analysis (like the one already outlined in this chapter), the analyst believes that in two years the company will be earning $2 per share. The question then becomes, what price will investors be willing to pay to buy a share of XYZ two years from now when it should be earning $2 a share? If they are willing to pay 8 times earnings, then the future market value will be about $16 per share. However, if they are willing to pay 20 times earnings, that means a future market value of $40 per share, a very significant difference.

Whether investors are willing to pay 8 times or 20 times earnings depends on two factors: (1) the average multiple for all stocks in the market and (2) whether investors perceive the company as being above average or below average.

Average Multiple of Stocks. In early 1980 the average stock listed on the New York Stock Exchange was trading at a multiple of about 9 times earnings. Stocks that were considered to offer exceptional profit opportunities could be had for 11 to 12 times earnings. By 1986 the average NYSE-listed stock was trading at about 15 times earnings, and the stocks considered to be exceptional were frequently trading at more than 20 times earnings. If the earnings of a company (that the market considered to be average) doubled over this period, the market value of its stock would have increased by over 300%.

1980: $1 of earnings $\times$ 9 = $ 9 market value
1986: $2 of earnings $\times$ 15 = $30 market value

Bull markets are characterized by rising average market multiples, while in bear markets, market multiples are falling. A changing market multiple can leverage (that is, magnify) the effect of a change in the company's earnings on the stock's market value.

By its very nature, fundamental analysis is a long-term approach to stock analysis. Projections are often made years into the future. Since so many variables must be taken into account, and since many of these variables are impossible to know in advance with any degree of certainty, fundamental analysis is at best an inexact science.

The principal drawbacks of fundamental analysis are the fact that it is inexact, that it is very work-intensive, and that it requires access to a tremendous amount of economic and business information.

TECHNICAL ANALYSIS

An alternative to fundamental analysis that is growing in both popularity and complexity is *technical analysis,* which is the study of the market's behavior. Proponents of technical analysis believe that, by studying the stock market's current behavior and trading patterns, they can gain valuable insights into the market's future behavior. (Technical analysis is used primarily to predict short-term trends or price movements.)

Their justification for this belief is that all of the information about a given company (or about a given industry or about the market as a whole) is known by all of the investors participating in the market and it is therefore reflected in the price history and trading pattern of the security. Price movements are therefore believed to "discount" all influences on them. By studying the price history and trading pattern of a stock (or industry or market), you can indirectly obtain the collective knowledge of all the investors in the security, without having to get involved with the "specifics." Indeed, followers of technical analysis often invest in a company without even knowing what products or services the company offers, where it is located, or whether or not it is profitable.

Theories

The term "technical analysis" actually refers to a number of different analytical theories and methods. Some of the more commonly followed technical indicators are:

- Odd lot theory.
- Dow theory.
- Advance-decline theory.
- Cash-futures spread.
- Advance-decline volume theory.

Odd Lot Theory. The odd lot theory is based on the premise that the small investor, who often buys and sells less than 100 shares of a stock at a time, is almost always wrong. Small investors are often financially unsophisticated and have limited access to timely information. Historically, they have often bought stocks at the top of a market cycle and sold stocks at the bottom. So the working principle of this theory is that, the higher the percentage of odd lot *buy* orders (orders for less than 100 shares), the more *bearish* the market outlook is. Conversely, a *bullish* market should be preceded by a large number of odd lot *sell* orders. The relative percentage of odd lot buy orders to sell orders can be found daily in the *Wall Street Journal* and other financial newspapers.

Dow Theory. The Dow theory was first proposed by Charles Dow (founder of Dow Jones & Company, Inc., publisher of the *Wall Street Journal*) in the early 1900s. The Dow theory tries to differentiate true changes in the primary direction of the market from the temporary reversals that inevitably interrupt any major market upswing or downturn.

According to the Dow theory, a major market move is not underway until the Dow Jones Industrial Average (a weighted index of 30 leading industrial stocks), the Dow Jones Transportation Index (a weighted index of 20 leading transportation stocks), and the Dow Jones Utility Index (a weighted index of 15 leading utility stocks) are all moving in the same direction. (See Chapter 2 for a more detailed discussion of stock indexes.) If all three indexes are moving up, the theory holds that a major bull market is underway; if all three indexes are declining, Dow theory concludes that a major bear market has started.

According to the Dow theory, once a major market move has started (the *primary trend*), the periodic reversals (the *secondary trends*) are not important unless the reversals break the primary trend. Frequently the primary trend runs for years while a secondary trend seldom exceeds six months in duration. For example, the chart in Figure 3-3 follows a market with a four-year primary uptrend that is interrupted by four short reversals (secondary trends). None of these reversals represents a break in the primary trend because, after each reversal, the market rallies back to a new high.

If, however, the next high after a reversal fails to exceed the previous high (the dashed line on the chart), then the primary trend would be broken. According to the Dow theory, at this point the market has no clear trend and investors should wait until the three indexes are again headed in the same direction before making any

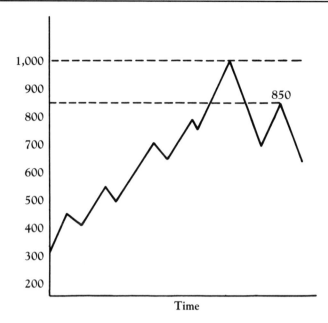

Figure 3-3. *Illustration of the Dow Theory.*

investments. (As you might expect, the Dow theory ignores the intra-day movements—the so-called *tertiary movements*—as irrelevant clutter in the primary market trends.

While the Dow theory has generally proven to be correct, it is often criticized for being too slow to generate buy and sell signals. Consider Figure 3-3: Although the market peaks at 1,000, the Dow theory doesn't give a sell signal until the market drops to 850. Thus a student of the Dow theory never buys at the bottom or sells at the top.

Advance-Decline Theory. The advance-decline theory states that, if the number of stocks rising in price significantly exceeds the number of stocks falling in price, the market is probably bullish. Conversely, if the number of issues in decline exceeds the number on the rise by a significant degree, the market is probably bearish. The number of gainers and losers is readily available in all the business papers.

Short Theory. According to the short theory, the more short positions there are in a given stock (or in a given industry or in the market), the more bullish the outlook for the stock (industry or market). The reasoning is that every shorted share must eventually be bought back. So the larger the short position, the greater the number of shares that have to be purchased in the future. The more shares to be purchased in the future, the more bullish the outlook for the stock (industry or market). In other words, the stock's price can drop only so far before short sellers start to take their profits. The short theory is also called the *cushion theory* since the eventual future buying acts as a "cushion" under the stock's future market value.

The figures for the short interest for the overall market can again be found in major business newspapers.

Cash Futures Spread. A relatively new technical indicator is the spread between the value of the major stock indexes (see Chapter 2) and the futures contracts on those same indexes (see Chapter 12). Although these vehicles are covered in greater detail later, for now just remember that, as these spreads widen, the probability of a short-term rally increases; when these spreads narrow, the probability of a short-term decline increases.

Advance-Decline/Volume Theory. When the average daily trading volume of either a single stock, the stocks of a certain industry, or the market as a whole increases, the current trend of the stock (industry or the market) continues. However, if the average daily trading volume declines, then the direction of the current trend will likely reverse itself. Thus, if the market's trend is up and the average daily volume is increasing, the market will probably continue its advance. If the market is declining and at the same time the average daily trading volume is also declining, the probability is that the market is close to reversing itself, that is, starting a new uptrend.

Charting

One of the tools that technical analysts often use to chart the performance of a stock, an industry, or the market as a whole is simple graph paper. Many technical analysts believe that certain price "patterns," when graphed, are indicative of a stock's (or industry's or market's) future market performance.

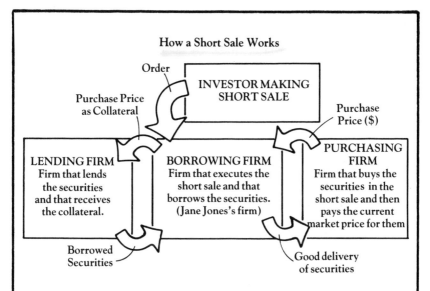

How a Short Sale Works

Order

INVESTOR MAKING
SHORT SALE

Purchase Price
as Collateral

Purchase
Price ($)

LENDING FIRM
Firm that lends
the securities
and that receives
the collateral.

BORROWING FIRM
Firm that executes the
short sale and that
borrows the securities.
(Jane Jones's firm)

PURCHASING
FIRM
Firm that buys the
securities in the
short sale and then
pays the current
market price for them

Borrowed
Securities

Good delivery
of securities

Investor Jane Jones has analyzed XYZ stock, selling at $25 per share, and concluded that its market price will go *down* over the next few weeks. Given her expectations, she reverses the time-honored dictum to, "Buy low, sell high." Instead, she sells high and *then* buys low.

She does that by *selling short*.

Jane calls her broker to place an order to sell 100 shares of XYZ short at $25. The brokerage firm executes the order like a normal sale, selling 100 XYZ to another firm at $25. The difference between a normal sale and a short sale, however, is that Jane does *not* own any shares of XYZ.

The buyer's brokerage firm delivers $2,500 ($25 × 100 shares), but how does Jane deliver securities to her brokerage firm for delivery to the buyer's firm? The answer is that, since Jane entered an order for a "short" sale, she indicated to the broker that she does not intend to furnish the certificates. (The reason may be that she does not own them, but it might also be that she owns them and does not want to surrender them.)

For a short sale, therefore, the seller's brokerage firm borrows 100 shares of XYZ, either from another firm or from one of its other customers, and delivers the borrowed securities to the buyer (in return for the $2,500 purchase price). The lender of the stock is paid for the "use" of the stock, and the short seller pays the fee.

Several weeks later, XYZ stock drops to $18 per share—this is as low as Jane thinks the stock will go. So she calls the broker again, this time to buy the 100 XYZ at 18. This stock is then used to close out her short position: The 100 shares are paid for by deducting $1,800 ($18 × 100 shares) from the $2,500 proceeds of the short sale, and the certificates are "paid back" to the lender.

Jane's gross profit is $700 (ignoring commissions and other expenses)—$2,500 less $1,800. As you can see, a short sale eventually has to be offset by a purchase.

You should also be able to see what Jane's predicament would be if the price of XYZ stock were to rise sharply!

Figure 3-4. *The Short Sale.*

Example: A pattern that many analysts believe is indicative of a trend reversal is the "head and shoulders" pattern (see Figure 3-5). To the technical analyst, the pattern in Figure 3-5 suggests that the stock is about to start rising.

Trends. A basic principle of technical analysis is that, once a stock has established a trend, the trend continues until something happen's to change it. (Objects that are in motion tend to stay in motion.) Look at Figure 3-6a. In the chart of XYZ stock's uptrend, the bottom line connecting all the low points is the *trendline* (always drawn below the price movement in an uptrend.) The *parallel* upper line, connecting the high points, is called a *channel line.* Between the trendline and channel line is the *trading range,* the area in which the stock is likely to trade until the trend is reversed.

Similarly, in Figure 3-6b, the *trendline* is the upper line, connecting all the price peaks. (Trendlines are drawn above the price action in a downtrend.) The parallel channel line is drawn along the price lows, or *troughs.* Again, the S&P 500 is likely to trade within the range between these two lines until something reverses the trend.

In Figure 3-6c, it is difficult to distinguish the trendline from the channel line, because the oil industry is moving *sideways,* or *horizontally.*

Resistance and Support. Prices change direction for many reasons, not all of which can be identified, much less foreseen. Perhaps the

Figure 3-5. *The Head and Shoulders Pattern—One of Many Used by the Technical Analyst.*

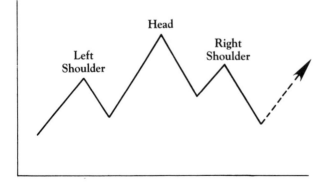

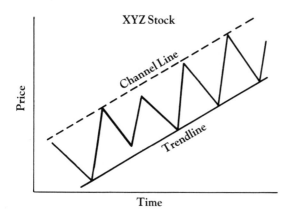

Figure 3-6a. *XYZ Common Stock in an Uptrend.*

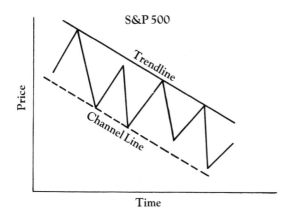

Figure 3-6b. *S&P 500 Index in a Downtrend.*

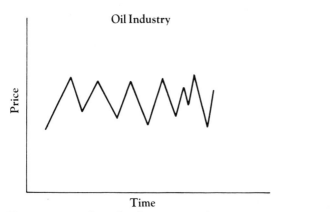

Figure 3-6c. *The Oil Industry in a Sideways (or Horizontal) Market.*

greatest influence on price behavior, however, consists of the expectations and desires of the market participants, who fall into three basic
categories:

1. The longs (those who own stock).
2. The shorts (those who have sold short).
3. The uncommitted (those who have no position in the market).

Any of these participant groups can affect price movements.
For example, with prices in an uptrend, the longs are delighted but
wish they had bought more. The shorts are coming to the conclusion
that they were wrong and would like to get out without losing too
much. Of the uncommitted group, some never opened a position
but wish they had, and others liquidated positions and wish they
had not. All four of these groups are watching the market for a dip.
If prices break downward, they are all liable to become buyers, that
is, "buy the dip." As a result, should prices begin to drop for any
reason, these would-be buyers respond by buying, thereby creating
demand and forcing prices up again.

When declining prices meet with such demand and "bounce
back," they are said to have hit *support*. The price dip, as plotted
on the chart, is known as a *trough* or *reaction low*. Support is therefore
a level or area below the market where buying interest is strong
enough to overcome selling pressure.

Resistance is the opposite of support. It is a level or area, above
the market, at which selling pressure overcomes buying interest. In
this case, the market is trending downward. The longs are looking
for a chance to sell, while the shorts are waiting for the opportunity
to increase the size of their positions. The uncommitted are likely
to go short. Should the market turn upward, all these participants
are primed to sell, thereby creating supply and eventually causing
prices to turn downward again. (The upturn and drop in prices, once
charted, are referred to as a *peak* or *reaction high*.)

Support and resistance often reverse their roles once they are
significantly penetrated by price movements. Penetrated by upward
movement, resistance becomes support (Figure 3-7). Support, after
being penetrated, becomes resistance (Figure 3-8). What constitutes
"significant" penetration, however, is arguable. Some chartists say

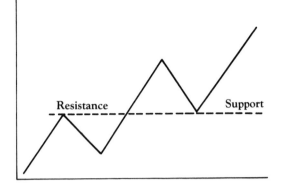

Figure 3-7. *Resistance, Once Penetrated, Can Become Support.*

10%, others 3 to 5%. In practice, each technician must set an individual criterion for a "significant" penetration.

Price Patterns. In addition to trendlines and channel lines, technicians are able to identify a number of *price patterns*. These are price movements that, when charted, describe a predictable pattern. Some price patterns indicate a trend reversal, and they are therefore called *reversal patterns*. Others, called *continuation patterns*, reflect pauses or temporary reverses in an existing trend and usually form more quickly than reversal patterns.

When a resistance or support line is violated, the reason is often

Figure 3-8. *Support, Once Penetrated, Can Become Resistance.*

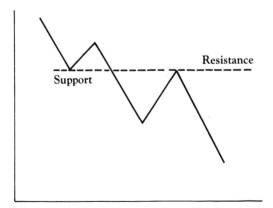

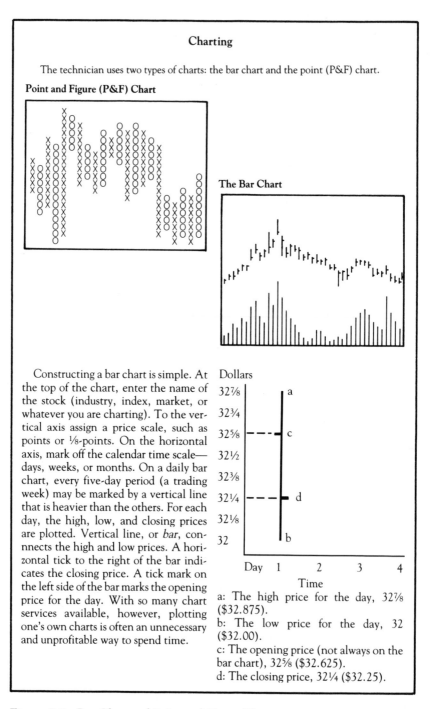

Charting

The technician uses two types of charts: the bar chart and the point (P&F) chart.

Point and Figure (P&F) Chart

The Bar Chart

Constructing a bar chart is simple. At the top of the chart, enter the name of the stock (industry, index, market, or whatever you are charting). To the vertical axis assign a price scale, such as points or ⅛-points. On the horizontal axis, mark off the calendar time scale—days, weeks, or months. On a daily bar chart, every five-day period (a trading week) may be marked by a vertical line that is heavier than the others. For each day, the high, low, and closing prices are plotted. Vertical line, or *bar*, connects the high and low prices. A horizontal tick to the right of the bar indicates the closing price. A tick mark on the left side of the bar marks the opening price for the day. With so many chart services available, however, plotting one's own charts is often an unnecessary and unprofitable way to spend time.

a: The high price for the day, 32⅞ ($32.875).
b: The low price for the day, 32 ($32.00).
c: The opening price (not always on the bar chart), 32⅝ ($32.625).
d: The closing price, 32¼ ($32.25).

Figure 3-9. *Bar Chart and Point and Figure Chart.*

48

Unlike bar charts, point and figure charts record only price movements; if no price change occurs, the chart remains the same. Time is not reflected on a P&F chart, although time reference points, such as "Mon," are sometimes used. Volume is indicated only by the number of recorded price changes, not as a separate entity.

Box Size. In a P&F chart, a rising price change is represented by an X, a declining price movement by an O. Each X or O occupies a box on the chart. One of the first decisions in constructing a P&F chart is therefore how great a price change each box should represent. For example, a chart might have a box size of a ¼-point ($0.25). On a less sensitive chart, a box might equal a point ($1); price movements of less than $1 would not be registered. On a more sensitive scale of, say, ⅛-point per box, more detailed price action would be visible. Obviously, the smaller the value assigned to the box, the movement the chart will reflect—and the more tedious it is to construct.

Reversal Criterion. On a P&F chart, the analyst moves one row of boxes to the right every time prices change direction. The question is what constitutes a reversal? If prices move ⅛-point against the trend, is that a significant enough reversal to warrant recording? Or is a 1-point reversal sufficient? Whatever the chartists decides to use as the occasion to move to the next row becomes the *reversal criterion* for the chart.

Example: A stock trades at the following prices:

25⅛	25⅜	25⅛	24¼
25⅛	25	25	
25¼	25½	24⅞	
25⅜	25⅛	25⅛	

If we want to chart these movements, the box size should probably be equal to ⅛-point. A box size that is only slightly larger—¼-point—would not include most of these movements. The reversal criterion should probably be ⅛-point also; otherwise, again, most of the reversals would not be reflected on the chart. The movements, as charted, would look like this (the dot represents the first transaction):

25½		X			
25⅜	X		X	O	
25¼	X	O	X	O	
25⅛	●	O	X	O	X
25		O		O	X	O
24⅞				O		O
24¾						O
24⅝						O
24½						O
24⅜						O
24¼						O

As you might suspect, box size and reversal criterion play a great role in how sensitive the chart is to price movements and in how the price movement data is represented. A "1x1" chart, for example, presents data so that every box is equal to a point and every point reversal is recorded. This would be a much more sensitive—and very different-looking chart—than a "2x3" chart, in which only two-point price changes and three-box reversals are reflected.

Figure 3-9 (*cont.*)

a dramatic increase in the amount of buying pressure or selling pressure (respectively). For this reason, the penetration of a resistance line is considered to be a very bullish technical indicator, and the violation of a support line is considered a bearish technical indicator.

The Role of Technical Analysis

At first, much of technical analysis appears to be illogical. A stock's past performance would seem to be of little consequence in predicting how it will perform in the future. Yet the success of technical analysis in predicting short-term trends and price movements is undeniable. Figure 3-9 illustrates two tools used by technical analysts.

Part of the reason for this success, some would argue, is that in many cases prediction becomes a self-fulfilling prophecy. Fundamentalists claim that, if thousands of investors buy a stock because it penetrates a resistance line, the value of the stock rises sharply due simply to the demand for it; after a brief upward spurt, the price may very well simply settle back to its previous trading range. In response, the technical analyst maintains that many investors can simultaneously recognize a previously hidden underlying value in the stock. Nevertheless, technical analysis is not considered to be an especially useful analytical method for determining long-term trends.

ROLE OF ANALYSIS

Different investors, looking at the same information, often come to different conclusions about the relative attractiveness of an investment. This disagreement is, after all, what makes a market a market. If a given investment was universally attractive, there would be no sellers. Very often, in practice, different technical theories give contradictory results, or the conclusions of technical and fundamental analyses are at odds with one another. Perhaps the best rule of thumb is to invest only when fundamental analysis and most of the technical theories lead to the same conclusion about the direction of a stock and the market itself.

4

Preferred Stocks

Distinct from common stock, preferred stock is similar to bonds in that the company issuing the stock pays the stockholder a fixed number of dollars per year.

Example: A company pays the owners of its preferred stock $10 per year per share. The investors who own this preferred receive four *quarterly* dividend payments of $2.50 each.

Because the investor receives a *fixed* return every year, preferred stock is very similar to bond investments. In fact, preferreds are included in the *fixed income* marketplace with bonds. Investors who find bonds attractive usually also find preferred stocks attractive.

Preferreds are different from bonds, however, in three ways:

First, preferred stockholders are considered to be owners, and not creditors, of the issuing company. Consequently, if the issuing company is financially unable to make a scheduled payment to a creditor (that is, a bondholder), the creditor can force the company into bankruptcy court. But if the issuing company is financially unable to pay the scheduled dividends on its preferred stock, the investors in the stock have no such right. Instead the investors must simply hope for the best.

Second, all bonds are "senior" to the company's preferred stock.

The company pays the bondholders their scheduled interest before it pays the preferred stockholders. Even in the event of bankruptcy, the bondholders are paid off before the preferred stockholders.

Third, because a company's preferred stocks are junior to a given company's bonds, the preferreds generally offer investors a higher return than the company's bonds. In addition, companies with poor credit ratings or weak balance sheets have to offer investors higher yields than strong companies in order to entice investors into investing.

Given their backseat treatment to bonds, why are preferreds called "preferreds"? The reason is that they are senior to the issuing company's common shares. Thus preferred shareholders generally receive their dividends before the common shareholders receive theirs.

Preferred stocks generally do not offer the voting rights that common stockholders have, unless the company is financially unable to make its scheduled dividend payments. In such a case, the preferred shareholders generally get very generous voting rights (5 to 10 votes per share) so that they have the "leverage" to protect their investment.

RETURNS

The return that an investor receives on preferred stock is equal to the annual dividend payment divided by the stock's market price.

Example: A company issues a new preferred for $100 per share, and the stock pays $8 in dividends per year. The investor's initial return is 8% [$8 ÷ $100) × 100].

As market interest rates change, the market value of the preferred also changes.

Example: If market interest rates rise to the point that new, comparably rated preferred stocks are being issued with a 10% return, the market value of the preferred in the preceding example drops to $80 per share. At $80.00 per share, the $8 per year of dividends that the investor receives nets the stockholder a 10% return ($8 dividend ÷ $80 cost).

If market interest rates for comparably rated preferreds fall to

4%, the value of the preferred shares rises to [$200 ($80/$00) × 100].

Thus investors who buy preferred stocks prior to a decline in market interest rates usually have a capital gain (a rise in the market value of their investment) in addition to the dividend income. Investors who purchase preferreds prior to a rise in market interest rates usually have a capital loss offsetting their dividend income.

TYPES OF PREFERRED

In addition to "straight" preferred, as just described, there is great diversity in the preferred market. Additional types of preferreds include:

Prior Preferreds

Many companies have several different issues of preferred stock outstanding at the same time. Usually one issue is designated "senior" to all other issues. If the company has only enough money to meet its dividend schedule on one of the preferred issues, it makes the dividend payments on the prior preferred.

Also, if the company should go bankrupt, the prior preferred shareholders are paid off (at the stock's par value) before the other preferred shareholders receive a dime. Thus the company's prior preferred has less credit risk than the company's other preferred issues. As a result, the prior preferred also usually offers a lower yield than the company's other preferreds.

Preference Preferred

Ranked behind the company's prior preferred (on a seniority basis) are the company's various preference issues. These issues receive "preference" over all other classes of the company's preferred except for the prior preferred. If the company issues more than one issue of preference stock, then the various issues are ranked by their relative seniority. One issue is designated first preference, the next senior issue is second preference, and so on.

53

Convertible Preferred

Convertible preferreds are preferred stocks that the investor can exchange for a predetermined number of the company's common shares. This exchange can occur at any time the investor chooses regardless of the current market price of the common stock. Convertible securities are discussed in detail in the chapter on special bond investments.

Participating Preferred

Participating preferreds offer their investors the opportunity to receive extra dividends if the company achieves some predetermined financial goals. The investors who purchase these stocks receive their regular dividends regardless of how well or how poorly the company performs—assuming, of course, the company does well enough financially to make the dividend payments. If the company achieves a predetermined sales, earnings, or profitability goal, however, the investors receive an additional dividend.

Example: XYZ, Inc. offers a new preferred stock that makes regular dividend payments of $6 per year when other comparably rated preferreds are being issued paying $8. However, if the company reports earnings of $10 million or more in a given year, the participating preferred stock owners receive an extra dividend of $4 per share.

If the company does well, the investor in the participating preferred receives an exceptional return, whereas if the company doesn't do well the investor receives a below-average return. Thus participating preferreds share some of the business risk with the common stock holders.

Cumulative Preferred

If a dividend payment on a cumulative preferred is missed, it is not forgotten. Instead, it accumulates and must be paid off before any dividend payments can be made to the common stockholders.

Example: A company issues a new cumulative preferred for $100 that is supposed to pay its investors $8 per year in dividends. One year later, however, the company gets into financial trouble and cannot make the scheduled dividend payments. For the next two years the company omits the dividend payments on its cumulative preferreds. Before the company can make any dividend payments to its common stockholders, it must first pay off the $16 in back dividends to the cumulative preferred shareholders.

A company can also issue cumulative preference preferred, participating prior preferred, or any other combination of preferred stock.

5

Equity-Related Investments

In addition to the traditional equity investments (common and preferred stocks), other types of investment vehicles are closely related to equities but are *not true equities*. These vehicles include subscription rights, warrants, American depository receipts, convertible bonds, equity options, stock index futures, and options on stock index futures. Like all investment vehicles, each of these has its advantages and its disadvantages.

SUBSCRIPTION RIGHTS

When a company issues additional shares of stock, its existing shareholders run the risk of having their ownership percentage "diluted."

Example: If XYZ, Inc. currently has 1,000,000 shares of stock outstanding and Ms. Green owns 100,000 of those shares, she effectively owns 10% of XYZ, Inc. If, however, XYZ, Inc. issues another 200,000 shares of common stock, then, to retain her 10% interest, Ms. Green will have to buy another 20,000 shares of XYZ. If she elects not to purchase any additional shares, her ownership percentage would be "diluted" after the offering to 8.3% [(100,000/1,200,000) × 100].

Figure 5-1a. A Rights Certificate (front).

A COPY OF THE RIGHTS AGREEMENT SETTING FORTH IN FULL THE RIGHTS OF THE HOLDER HEREOF AND THE QUALIFICATIONS, LIMITATIONS OR RESTRICTIONS OF SUCH RIGHTS MAY BE OBTAINED WITHOUT CHARGE FROM THE RIGHTS AGENT, 400 CALIFORNIA STREET, SAN FRANCISCO. CALIFORNIA 94104.

ABBREVIATIONS

The following abbreviations, when used in the inscription on the face of this instrument, shall be construed as though they were written out in full according to applicable laws or regulations:

TEN COM — as tenants in common
TEN ENT — as tenants by the entireties
JT TEN — as joint tenants with right of survivorship and not as tenants in common

UNIF GIFT MIN ACT — .... Custodian.....................
(Cust)   (Minor)
under Uniform Gifts to Minors
Act ....
(State)

Additional abbreviations may also be used though not in the above list.

FORM OF ASSIGNMENT

(To be executed by the registered holder if such holder desires to transfer the Rights Certificate.)

FOR VALUE RECEIVED _____

hereby sells, assigns and transfers unto _____

_____
(PLEASE PRINT NAME AND ADDRESS OF TRANSFEREE)

_____

this Rights Certificate, together with all right, title and interest therein, and does hereby irrevocably constitute and appoint

_____ Attorney,
to transfer the within Rights Certificate on the books of the within-named Company, with full power of substitution.

DATED: _____, 198___

_____
SIGNATURE

Signature Guaranteed:

NOTICE: THE SIGNATURE TO THE FOREGOING ASSIGNMENT MUST CORRESPOND TO THE NAME AS WRITTEN UPON THE FACE OF THIS RIGHTS CERTIFICATE IN EVERY PAR-TICULAR, WITHOUT ALTERATION OR ENLARGEMENT OR ANY CHANGE WHATSOEVER

FORM OF ELECTION TO PURCHASE

(To be executed if holder desires to exercise the Rights Certificate.)

To the Rights Agent

The undersigned hereby irrevocably elects to exercise _____ Rights represented by this Rights Certificate to purchase the shares of Common Stock issuable upon the exercise of such Rights and requests that certificates for such shares be issued in the name of:

_____
(PLEASE INSERT SOCIAL SECURITY OR OTHER IDENTIFYING NUMBER)

_____
(PLEASE PRINT NAME AND ADDRESS)

_____

If such number of Rights shall not be all the Rights evidenced by this Rights Certificate, a new Rights Certificate for the remaining balance of such Rights shall be registered in the name of and delivered to:

_____
(PLEASE INSERT SOCIAL SECURITY OR OTHER IDENTIFYING NUMBER)

_____
(PLEASE PRINT NAME AND ADDRESS)

_____

I certify under penalty of perjury that the social security and other identifying numbers indicated above are correct.

DATED: _____, 19___

_____
SIGNATURE

Signature Guaranteed:

(SIGNATURE MUST CONFORM IN ALL RESPECTS TO NAME OF HOLDER AS SPECIFIED ON THE FACE OF THIS RIGHTS CERTIFICATE)

Figure 5-1b. *A Rights Certificate (back).*

As a way of assisting its existing shareholders to maintain their ownership percentages, some companies give their existing shareholders *subscription rights* whenever they issue new shares of stock. These subscription rights allow existing shareholders to purchase additional shares of the company at a lower price than the one at which the new shares will be offered to the general public.

Whether a given company issues subscription rights when it has a new stock offering is usually specified in the corporation's charter. Investors generally consider the stocks of companies that offer subscription rights to be more attractive than the stocks of companies that don't, all other factors being equal.

Example: XYZ, Inc. stock is trading for $100 a share when the company announces that it will be selling the additional 200,000 shares (mentioned in the previous example). As part of this stock offering, XYZ will give their existing shareholders *one subscription right for every share each shareholder already owns.* For every *five* subscription rights an investor receives, he or she is able to purchase *one* additional share of stock for $70 per share instead of the public offering price of $100 per share.

Since Ms. Green owns 100,000 shares of XYZ, she receives 100,000 subscription rights. These rights give her the option of acquiring up to an additional 20,000 (100,000/5) shares at $70 per share. To acquire the additional shares, all Ms. Green has to do is have her broker send her rights (and a check for $1,400,000) to the right department at XYZ, Inc. If Ms. Green exercises her rights, she will buy $2,000,000 worth of stock (20,000 shares × $100 market value) for $1,400,000.

If investors do not want to purchase any additional shares of the corporation, they can still generate a return from their rights distribution by selling their rights in the open market to investors who do want to acquire shares of the company. After all, these rights have "value" since they entitle holders to buy stock at a discount from the price offered to the public.

The *theoretical market value* of a right is determined by the following formula:

$$\text{Theoretical market value} = \frac{\text{Market value of stock with right} - \text{Subscription price}}{\text{Number of rights required to buy one share } plus \ one}$$

Example: In the case of Ms. Green:

$$\text{Theoretical market value} = \frac{\$100 - \$70}{5 + 1}$$

$$= \$5 \text{ Value per right}$$

The $100 market value of the stock *includes* the value of the right that the existing shareholders will receive, so we have to add "one" to the denominator. If the stock is offered for sale without the right (that is, *ex-rights*), then the stock's price would be $5 lower and the denominator would be 5 instead of 6. Performing this calculation on an ex-rights basis yields the same theoretical value for the rights.

Remember that, while it's easy to calculate the theoretical value of a right, the actual value of a right, like any investment, is worth only what someone else is willing to pay for it. That price may be more or less than the stock's "theoretical value."

Rights have *very* short lives, usually three weeks or less. If Ms. Green did not sell her rights or use them to acquire additional shares within three weeks, they would expire worthless and Ms. Green would lose $500,000 ($5 per right × 100,000 rights). For this reason decisions about whether to exercise or sell rights must be made quickly.

WARRANTS

A *warrant* is a security that entitles its owner to buy a share of the issuing company's stock at a predetermined price—regardless of the stock's current market value. If the stock's market value is higher than the warrant's predetermined price, then the investor can generate an immediate profit. By using the warrant to buy the stock from the

Figure 5-2a. A *Warrant* (*front*).

WARRANT

THIS WARRANT WILL BE VOID IF NOT EXERCISED ON OR PRIOR TO MARCH 15, 1981

No. W

McCARRY CORPORATION

FOR THE PURCHASE OF

________ SHARES

COMMON STOCK PURCHASE WARRANT

THIS CERTIFIES that, for value received, Corporation, a Delaware corporation (hereinafter called the "Company"), upon the surrender of this Warrant, as hereinafter provided, to the Company at the corporate trust office in the City of New York of the Warrant Agent hereinafter mentioned (or of its successor as Warrant Agent), provided, and only if, this Warrant shall be so surrendered on or before March 15, 1981, will sell and deliver, or cause to be sold and delivered, to

or assigns, the number of fully paid and non-assessable shares set forth above of the Company's Common Stock, par value fifty cents per share, as constituted on the date of the Warrant Agreement hereinbelow mentioned, upon payment of the warrant price for the number of shares in respect of which this Warrant is exercised; *provided, however,* that under certain conditions set forth in said Warrant Agreement the number of shares of the Company's Common Stock purchasable upon the exercise of this Warrant may be increased or reduced and the warrant price may be adjusted, or securities other than shares of said Common Stock may become purchasable in lieu thereof upon the exercise of this Warrant. Subject to adjustment as aforesaid, the warrant price shall be $20 per share to and including March 15, 1976 and $22.50 from March 16, 1976 to and including March 15, 1981 (herein called the "warrant price"). As provided in said Warrant Agreement, the warrant price is payable, upon the exercise of this Warrant, either in cash or by certified check or bank draft payable in New York funds. No adjustment shall be made for any dividends on any shares of stock issuable upon exercise of this Warrant. The right of purchase represented by this Warrant is exercisable, at the election of the registered holder hereof, or his assigns, either as an entirety or from time to time for part only of the shares specified herein and, in the event that this Warrant is exercised in respect of less than all of such shares, a new Warrant for the remaining number of such shares will be issued on such surrender in accordance with instructions set forth in the election to purchase on the reverse hereof.

Upon the exercise of this Warrant the form of election to purchase on the reverse hereof must be duly executed by the registered holder hereof, or his assigns, and the accompanying instructions for the registration and delivery of stock must be filled in.

This Warrant is issued under and the rights represented hereby are subject to the terms and provisions contained in a Warrant Agreement dated as of March 15, 1966, between the Company and CHEMICAL BANK NEW YORK TRUST COMPANY, as Warrant Agent, to all the terms and provisions of which the holder of this Warrant, by acceptance hereof, assents. Reference is hereby made to said Warrant Agreement for a more complete statement of the rights and limitations of rights of the registered holder hereof and his assigns, the rights and duties of the Warrant Agent and the rights and obligations of the Company thereunder. Copies of said Warrant Agreement are on file at the corporate trust office of said Warrant Agent. The Company shall not be required to issue fractions of shares of Common Stock on the exercise of this Warrant but shall make adjustment therefor in cash on the basis of the current market value of any fractional interest (computed as provided in said Warrant Agreement) or, at its option, shall issue scrip in lieu thereof, all as provided in said Warrant Agreement.

In the event that this Warrant shall not be exercised on or before March 15, 1981, this Warrant shall become void and all rights hereunder shall cease.

This Warrant is transferable at the corporate trust office in the City of New York of the Warrant Agent (or of its successor as Warrant Agent) by the registered holder hereof or his assigns, in person or by attorney duly authorized in writing, but only in the manner and subject to the limitations provided in the Warrant Agreement, and upon surrender of this Warrant. Upon any such transfer, a new Warrant, or new Warrants of different denominations, of like tenor and representing in the aggregate the right to purchase a like number of shares of the Company's Common Stock will be issued to the transferee in exchange for this Warrant.

This Warrant when surrendered at the corporate trust office in the City of New York of the Warrant Agent (or of its successor as Warrant Agent) may be exchanged, in the manner and subject to the limitations provided in the Warrant Agreement, for another Warrant, or other Warrants of different denominations, of like tenor and representing in the aggregate the right to purchase a like number of shares of the Company's Common Stock.

Certificate or certificates for shares of the Company's Common Stock shall be deemed to have been issued (pursuant to the provisions of this Warrant and of the Warrant Agreement) and any person so designated to be named therein shall be deemed to have become a holder of record of such shares as of the date of the surrender of this Warrant, and payment of the Warrant price and any applicable taxes; *provided, however,* that if, at the date of surrender and payment of such Warrant price and taxes, the transfer books for the Company's Common Stock or other class of stock purchasable upon the exercise of this Warrant are closed for any purpose, the certificate for the shares in respect of which this Warrant is then exercised, shall be issuable as of the date on which such books shall next be opened and until such date, the Company shall be under no duty to deliver any certificate for such shares.

Nothing contained in this Warrant shall be construed as conferring upon the holder hereof any rights whatsoever of a Stockholder of the Company.

This Warrant shall not be valid unless countersigned by the Warrant Agent.

WITNESS the facsimile seal of McCrory Corporation and the facsimile signatures of its duly authorized officers.

SPECIMEN

Dated:

COUNTERSIGNED:
CHEMICAL BANK NEW YORK TRUST COMPANY,
WARRANT AGENT,
BY

SPECIMEN

AUTHORIZED SIGNATURE

CORPORATE SEAL 1915 DELAWARE

McCARRY CORPORATION

ATTEST:

BY

SPECIMEN

Seymour Greene

SECRETARY

CHAIRMAN OF THE BOARD

SECURITY-COLUMBIAN BANKNOTE COMPANY

ELECTION TO PURCHASE

(To be executed if owner desires to exercise the Warrant.)

To **McCarry Corporation**

The undersigned hereby irrevocably elects to exercise the right of purchase represented by the within

Warrant for, and to purchase thereunder, ... shares of the stock provided for

therein, and requests that certificates for such shares shall be issued in the name of ....

PLEASE INSERT SOCIAL SECURITY OR OTHER
IDENTIFYING NUMBER

....
(Please print name and address)

....
and, if said number of shares shall not be all the shares purchasable thereunder, that a new Warrant

for the unexercised portion of the within Warrant be registered in the name of ....

....
(Please print name and address)

....

Dated: ...., 19.......

Signature: ....

NOTE: The above signature must correspond with the name as written upon the face of this Warrant or with the name of the person to whom this Warrant has been duly assigned in every particular, without alteration or enlargement or any change whatever, and if signed by an assignee, or if shares and/or Warrants are to be issued in a name other than that of the registered holder of the Warrant, the form of assignment hereon must be duly executed. If shares and/or Warrants are to be issued in a name other than that of the registered warrant holder, this election to purchase must be accompanied by appropriate documentary stamp taxes.

ASSIGNMENT

(To be executed if owner desires to transfer Warrant Certificate.)

FOR VALUE RECEIVED ....hereby sell, assign and transfer unto

....

....
the within Warrant, together with all right, title and interest therein, and do hereby irrevocably constitute
and appoint

.... Attorney,
to transfer said Warrant on the books of the within-named Corporation, with full power of substitution
in the premises.

Dated: ...., 19.......

....
(Signature)

NOTE: The above signature must correspond with the name as written upon the face of this W   at in every particular, without alteration or enlargement or any change whatever. The signature to the Assignment must be guaranteed by a commercial bank or trust company having an office or correspondent in New York City or by a firm having membership in the New York Stock Exchange or in the American Stock Exchange Clearing Corporation.

Signature Guaranteed:

....

Figure 5-2b. *A Warrant (back).*

company at the predetermined price and then selling the stock at the higher current market price, the investor makes a profit equal to the difference between the two prices.

Example: Mr. Brown owns a warrant issued by XYZ, Inc. The warrant entitles Mr. Brown to buy one share of XYZ common stock for $10. If XYZ common is currently trading at $25 in the open market, Mr. Brown could obtain an immediate $15 profit. All he does is use his warrant to purchase one share of XYZ stock from the company for $10, and then sell that share in the open market for $25.

It stands to reason that a warrant that entitles Mr. Brown to receive an immediate $15 profit would be worth *at least* $15. In fact, this warrant would probably trade in the open market for more than $15.

The market value of a warrant is composed of two components: the "intrinsic value" and the "premium."

- In the previous example, the warrant would save the investor $15 if he used it to buy a share of the stock at $10 instead of at the $25 market value. Thus we can say that the warrant has $15 worth of *intrinsic value,* or immediately realizable value.
- The difference between the market value of the warrant and its intrinsic value is the *premium.* Thus, if the XYZ warrants were trading in the open market at $17.50 each, the price would consist of $15 of intrinsic value and $2.50 of premium—that is, a premium of 16.67% [($2.50/$15.00) × 100]. Investors are usually willing to pay a premium in order to buy warrants because warrants are "leveraged" investment vehicles, that is, they enable holders to obtain higher percentages of return than is possible by buying the stock itself.

Example: Mr. Brown has the choice of buying either XYZ warrants for $17.50 or XYZ common for $25. He expects that the value of XYZ common will rise to $50 a share in the near future. If it turns out that Mr. Brown's prediction is correct, the warrants would be a better investment than the common stock. If Mr. Brown buys the common stock, he will have a profit of $25 per share or, expressed as a percentage, a profit of 100% on his original investment.

Sale price	$50
Purchase price	−25
Profit	$25

$$\text{Return on Investment} = \frac{\text{Profit}}{\text{Purchase Price}} \times 100$$

$$= \$25.00/\$25.00 \times 100$$
$$= 100\%$$

However, if Mr. Brown buys the warrants, he will realize a much higher profit margin percentage. If XYZ common rises to $50 a share, then each warrant will have an intrinsic value of $40. Assuming that when the stock is trading at $50 the warrant's premium is still at the same 16.67%, then the warrant's market value would be:

$$\$40.00 + (\$40.00 \times 0.1667) = \$46.69$$

This represents a return of 267% [($46.69/$17.50) × 100) on Mr. Brown's original investment.

Thus the warrants would clearly be a better investment if Mr. Brown's $50-a-share prediction turned out to be correct.

Unfortunately, this is not the whole story. If Mr. Brown was wrong and the market value of XYZ's stock dropped sharply, then Mr. Brown would be better off—*relatively speaking*—by buying the stock instead of the warrants.

Example: If the market value of the stock drops to $5 a share, then Mr. Brown loses 80% of his original investment if he buys the stock. However, if Mr. Brown buys the warrants, he would probably lose close to 100% of his investment. After all, the ability to buy a stock at $10 a share isn't worth much when the stock is selling in the open market for $5. (Of course, if the warrant, although long-termed, should expire before the stock price returns to a profitable level, then the warrant becomes useful only as scrap paper. A stock certificate does *not* expire unless the issuing company does.)

Thus warrants, like any *leveraged* investment vehicle, are a two-edged sword, increasing both the potential return and the potential risk to the investor.

Valuing Warrants

Valuing a warrant is as much an art as it is a science. The principal factors that investors need to consider when determining how much of a premium to pay for a given company's warrants include:

1. The underlying stock's appreciation potential.
2. The time remaining until the warrant expires.
3. The investor's tolerance for risk.

Generally, the greater the underlying stock's potential for capital appreciation, the higher the premium. From the investor's point of view, it's worth a high premium to be able to buy an asset that's expected to appreciate sharply on a "leveraged basis."

Length of time until the warrant expires is also a critical factor in determining the amount of premium. A warrant's "life" is fixed when it is first issued. Most warrants have lives of between five and ten years from the date they are first issued, although some warrants are perpetual. The longer a warrant's remaining life, the more time a warrant has to become a profitable investment. The more time a warrant has to become profitable, the higher the premium that investors will be willing to pay to own it.

Lastly, the more "speculative" the investor, the more appealing the higher risk/reward ratio of a warrant becomes relative to the underlying company's stock. Thus investors who have a high tolerance for risk will be more attracted to, and consequently willing to pay a higher premium for, warrants.

Why Corporations Issue Warrants

When warrants are first issued, the predetermined price at which the stock can be purchased is usually slightly higher than the stock's current market price. The investor who purchases warrants cannot make an immediate profit from using them to buy stock. For the warrants to become valuable, the common stock must appreciate in value. Warrants are therefore issued to enhance the *future* value of the stock to the holder. Corporations issue warrants to make best use of their future value.

When a company first goes public, the investment banking firm that handles the underwriting often receives warrants as part of its fee for handling the transaction. (Underwriting is explained more fully in a later chapter.) Thus, as the company grows and the value of the company's common stock rises, so does the market value of its warrants. Thus the investment banking firm that originally brought the company public will share in the corporation's growth.

Shareholders are also sometimes issued warrants. If a company is very young, it may have trouble finding potential investors to buy its stock. As an enticement to prospective stockholders, the company might elect to issue warrants to investors who buy its shares. Often it packages a share of stock with a few warrants and sells the resulting "units" to investors as a way of raising capital. By attaching one or more warrants to each common share, the company increases the potential return for the shareholders if the company survives and grows.

Also, sometimes a large company provides a small company with financial assistance if the small corporation is working on a product that the large company wants to buy or market. As part of the "financing package," the large company often demands warrants for the small company's stock.

AMERICAN DEPOSITORY RECEIPTS (ADRs)

As part of the increasing "globalization" of the financial industry, more and more U.S. investors are buying the securities of foreign companies and vice versa. Unfortunately, however, buying and selling in foreign markets can be complicated, frustrating, and dangerous. Different time zones, foreign exchange problems, different operational systems, different settlement procedures, language barriers, regulatory problems, high transaction fees, and the lack of effective avenues of legal recourse—all combine to make buying and selling securities overseas unattractive to many American investors.

To circumvent many of these problems, the financial community developed American depository receipts (ADRs). To create an ADR, a commercial bank buys a large number of shares of a foreign security and places them into a trust account. The bank then issues U.S. securities—ADRs—representing partial ownership of the pool of foreign securities. Since the bank-issued ADRs are U.S. securities, they trade just like other U.S. securities even though they (indirectly) represent ownership of foreign securities. This eliminates many of the usual problems of foreign trading.

Example: MNO Company is a car-manufacturing company in West Germany. A U.S. commercial bank purchases 500,000 shares of MNO's common stock and deposits them in a trust account. Then the commercial bank firm issues 250,000 MNO ADRs. Each ADR is sold for a U.S. dollar price equal to the German mark price of two of the foreign shares. The price of the U.S. securities will, of course, fluctuate in response to the price of the German shares and the current U.S. dollar/German mark exchange rate.

Remember, however, that the MNO ADRs are equity "one step removed." While their market value usually rises and falls in tandem with the value of the foreign shares, they do not represent direct ownership in the MNO Car Company. Instead they represent equity in a trust that, in turn, has direct ownership in the car company.

CONVERTIBLE BONDS

Convertible bonds (CBs) are bonds that are convertible into a fixed number of shares of the issuing company's common stock at any time, at the option of the investor. The relationship that determines how many shares of common stock is received for each convertible bond is called the *conversion ratio.* It can be expressed as a ratio or as a conversion price.

Example: XYZ, Inc. has a 9% bond that's convertible into 100 shares of XYZ, Inc. Mr. Smith buys the bond for par in the open market. As long as Mr. Smith owns the bond, he collects $90 a year in interest.

Mr. Smith can also return the bond to the company and receive 100 shares of XYZ common stock. The 100 shares is the *conversion ratio*—100 shares per bond. The conversion feature can also be expressed as a price by dividing the ratio into the face value of the bond: $1,000 face value ÷ 100 common stock shares = $10 *conversion price.*

be calculated by multiplying the number of shares that the bond converts into by the current share price of the common.

$$\frac{\text{Conversion}}{\text{value}} = \frac{\text{Number of shares}}{\text{for convertible bond}} \times \frac{\text{Market value}}{\text{of share}}$$

Example: GHI Corp. has a bond that's convertible into 50 shares, and the stock is trading for $12.50. The conversion value of the GHI bond is $625 (50 shares × $12.50).

As you can see, as the market value of the common stock changes, so does the conversion value of the convertible bond.

Also, the *market value* of a convertible bond is always equal to or greater than its conversion value. No one would sell a bond that could be converted into, say, $1,200 worth of stock for less than $1,200. Almost all convertible bonds therefore trade for more than their conversion value. The difference between a bond's conversion value and its market price is called the *conversion premium.* Investors are generally willing to pay a premium to own convertible bonds, in lieu of owning the common stock, because convertibles offer a number of advantages relative to the common, including:

1. Convertible bonds generally pay investors higher interest rates than the underlying stocks pay in dividends.
2. The bond is "senior" to the common in the event the issuing company goes into bankruptcy, and so it is less risky from a credit risk point of view.
3. The bond is exposed to less market risk because the stream of coupon payments that the bond makes establishes a floor price for the bond (barring a default). Thus, even if the value of the company's stock drops to $0.50 per share, the value of the bond will not drop below the value of nonconvertible bonds with the same credit rating and maturity.
4. The bond will eventually mature and return its face value to the investor (again barring a default); the stock comes with no such guarantee.

When convertible bonds are first issued, their conversion value is usually 15% to 25% below the bond's face value. So investors

When convertible bonds are first issued, their conversion value is usually 15% to 25% below the bond's face value. So investors who buy new offerings of convertible bonds are not able to effect a profitable conversion unless the market value of the underlying company's common stock rises by at least 15% to 25%.

Example: DEF, Inc. issues a convertible bond that's convertible into 80 shares of DEF common. If, when the bond is issued, DEF common is selling for $10 a share, the bond has an initial conversion value of $800 (80 shares × $10). This means that the value of the stock has to rise *by 25% before the conversion value of the bond would equal the bond's purchase price.*

$$\text{Conversion premium} = \text{Bond value} - \text{Conversion value}$$
$$= \$1,000 - \$800 = \$200$$

$$\text{Premium \%} = (\text{Conversion premium} \div \text{Purchase price}) \times 100$$
$$= (\$200 \div \$800) \times 100 = 25\%$$

If the market value of the common shares increases from $10 to $12.50 per share, the conversion value then equals the bond's purchase price.

DETERMINING HOW MUCH PREMIUM TO PAY

Any investor who considers investing in convertible bonds soon faces this question: How much of a conversion premium is justified to own a given convertible bond, instead of the underlying common stock? While owning convertibles offers advantages over owning the underlying common, these advantages are not free. Investors must pay for these advantages in the conversion premium. The question therefore becomes how much of a conversion premium is "too much"?

There is no pat answer to this question. When presented with the same choice, different investors with different objectives and expectations will come to different conclusions. Some questions to ask include:

1. *Which way do you expect interest rates to move?* If you expect interest rates in general to decline, then you must take into account that the convertible bond will probably appreciate in value in response to the decline in market interest rates. Therefore anyone who expected interest rates to move down might be tempted to pay a higher premium to own the convertible bond instead of the stock.

2. *What is the spread between the bond's yield to maturity and the stock's dividend return?* The higher this yield spread is, the more attractive the bond becomes relative to the stock. Investors might pay a higher premium for a relatively high yield spread than they would for a convertible bond that offered a low yield spread over the common's dividend yield.

3. *How quickly do you expect the market value of the underlying stock to appreciate?* The shorter the period over which the stock is expected to appreciate, the more attractive the convertible bond becomes relative to the stock. The longer the investor's time horizon, the lower the premium level an investor would be tempted to pay in order to own the bond.

4. *How is the underlying company's financial strength?* If a company is weak financially (many emerging growth companies and turn-around situations fall into this category), the bond becomes more attractive than the stock. If the company goes bankrupt, bondholders stand a better chance of recouping at least a portion of their investment, since stockholders' claims are junior to those of bondowners.

5. *What are your investment objectives and tolerance for risk?* If your investment objectives are balanced and you have a low tolerance for risk, then you might be willing to pay a higher premium to buy convertible bonds instead of stocks. If, however, your objectives are to maximize capital gains, then you may not be willing to pay a high conversion premium.

Remember that the market value of a convertible bond is determined by how attractive investors perceive the investment to be both as a bond *and* as an equity surrogate. Thus the market value of a convertible bond depends on the performance of both the equity market and the bond market. If both markets are bullish, convertible bonds generally do very well. But if both markets are bearish, convertibles generally do very poorly. During those periods when the stock market is moving up but the bond market is moving down (or vice versa), convertibles generally provide a mediocre overall return to their investors.

6

Corporate Bonds

In addition to selling stock, there is another way to raise capital: selling bonds. A *bond* is a certificate that represents a loan *from* the institutions or individuals buying the bonds (the investors or bond-holders) *to* the entities selling the bonds (the issuers). Because bond-holders have, in effect, made loans to the issuer, they are legally the issuer's "creditors" and not "owners," as stock investors are.

Bonds are sold to investors by a wide variety of issuers, including U.S. corporations, the U.S. government and its agencies, state and local governments, and foreign governments and companies.

CORPORATIONS ISSUE BONDS

Corporations issue bonds for a variety of reasons:

1. Issuing bonds provides corporations with a way to raise capital without diluting the current shareholders' equity.

2. By issuing bonds, corporations can often borrow at a lower interest rate than the rate available from their banks. By issuing bonds, corporations borrow directly from the investors and eliminate the banks as intermediaries in the transactions. By eliminating the

Figure 6-1a. A Bond Certificate (front).

W.R. Grace & Co.

REGISTERED

12⅝% NOTE DUE 1990

NUMBER

DOLLARS

SEE REVERSE FOR CERTAIN DEFINITIONS

CUSIP 383883 AC 9

12⅝%
DUE
1990

DOLLARS

12⅝%
DUE
1990

or registered assigns,
the principal sum of

SPECIMEN

W.R. Grace & Co., a Connecticut corporation (hereinafter called the "Company," which term includes any successor corporation under the Indenture hereinafter referred to), for value received, hereby promises to pay to

on September 15, 1990, and to pay interest thereon from September 15, 1980, to the most recent Interest Payment Date to which interest has been paid or duly provided for, semiannually on March 15 and September 15 in each year, at the rate of 12⅝% per annum, until the principal hereof is paid or its payment duly provided for. The interest so payable, and punctually paid or duly provided for, on any Interest Payment Date will, as provided in such Indenture, be paid to the Person in whose name this Note is registered at the close of business on the Regular Record Date for such interest which shall be the March 1 or September 1 (whether or not a Business Day), as the case may be, next preceding such Interest Payment Date. Any such interest not so punctually paid or duly provided for, and any interest payable on a Special Record Date for the payment of such Defaulted Interest to be fixed by the Trustee, notice whereof shall be given to Holders of Notes not less than 10 days prior to such Special Record Date, or may be paid at any time in any other lawful manner not inconsistent with the requirements of any securities exchange on which the Notes may be listed, and upon such notice as may be required by such exchange, all as more fully provided in such Indenture. Payment of the principal of and interest on this Note will be made at the office or agency of the Company maintained for that purpose in the Borough of Manhattan, The City of New York, in such coin or currency of the United States of America as at the time of payment is legal tender for payment of public and private debts; provided, however, that payment of interest may be made at the option of the Company by check mailed to the address of the Person entitled thereto as such address shall appear in the Note Register.

Reference is hereby made to the further provisions of this Note set forth on the reverse hereof, which further provisions shall for all purposes have the same effect as if set forth at this place.

Unless the certificate of authentication hereon has been executed by the Trustee referred to on the reverse hereof by manual signature, this Note shall not be entitled to any benefit under the Indenture or be valid or obligatory for any purpose.

In Witness Whereof, the Company has caused this instrument to be duly executed under its corporate seal.

W.R. Grace & Co.

BY

PRESIDENT

ATTEST:

SECRETARY

GRACE

DATED:

TRUSTEE'S CERTIFICATE OF AUTHENTICATION.
THIS IS ONE OF THE NOTES REFERRED TO IN THE
WITHIN-MENTIONED INDENTURE.

BANKERS TRUST COMPANY,
AS TRUSTEE

BY   SPECIMEN

AUTHORIZED OFFICER

74

W. R. GRACE & CO.
12⅜% NOTE DUE 1990

This Note is one of a duly authorized issue of Notes of the Company designated as its 12⅜% Notes Due 1990 (herein called the "Notes"), limited (except as otherwise provided in the Indenture referred to below) in aggregate principal amount to $100,000,000, issued and to be issued under an indenture (herein called the "Indenture") dated as of September 15, 1980 between the Company and Bankers Trust Company, Trustee (herein called the "Trustee", which term includes any successor trustee under the Indenture), to which Indenture and all indentures supplemental thereto reference is hereby made for a statement of the respective rights thereunder of the Company, the Trustee and the Holders of the Notes, and the terms upon which the Notes are, and are to be, authenticated and delivered.

The Notes are subject to redemption, upon not less than 30 nor more than 60 days' notice by first-class mail, at any time on or after September 15, 1986, as a whole or from time to time in part, at the election of the Company, at a Redemption Price equal to 100% of their principal amount, together with accrued interest to the Redemption Date (but interest instalments whose Stated Maturity is on or prior to the Redemption Date will be payable to the Holders of such Notes, or one or more Predecessor Notes, of record at the close of business on the relevant Record Date referred to on the face hereof), all as provided in the Indenture.

In the event of redemption of this Note in part only, a new Note or Notes for the unredeemed portion hereof shall be issued in the name of the Holder hereof upon the cancellation hereof.

If an Event of Default, as defined in the Indenture, shall occur and be continuing, the principal of all the Notes may be declared due and payable in the manner and with the effect provided in the Indenture.

The Indenture permits, with certain exceptions as therein provided, the amendment thereof and the modification of the rights and obligations of the Company and the rights of the Holders of the Notes under the Indenture at any time by the Company and the Trustee with the consent of the Holders of 66⅔% in aggregate principal amount of the Notes at the time Outstanding, as defined in the Indenture. The Indenture also contains provisions permitting the Holders of specified percentages in aggregate principal amount of the Notes at the time Outstanding, as defined in the Indenture, on behalf of the Holders of all the Notes, to waive compliance by the Company with certain provisions of the Indenture and certain past defaults under the Indenture and their consequences. Any such consent or waiver by the Holder of this Note shall be conclusive and binding upon such Holder and upon all future Holders of this Note and of any Note issued upon the transfer hereof or in exchange herefor or in lieu hereof whether or not notation of such consent or waiver is made upon this Note.

No reference herein to the Indenture and no provision of this Note or of the Indenture shall alter or impair the obligation of the Company, which is absolute and unconditional, to pay the principal of and interest on this Note at the times, places, and rate, and in the coin or currency, herein prescribed.

As provided in the Indenture and subject to certain limitations therein set forth, this Note is transferable on the Note Register of the Company, upon surrender of this Note for registration of transfer at the office or agency of the Company in the Borough of Manhattan, The City of New York, duly endorsed by, or accompanied by a written instrument of transfer in form satisfactory to the Company and the Note Registrar duly executed by, the Holder hereof or his attorney duly authorized in writing, and thereupon one or more new Notes, of authorized denominations and for the same aggregate principal amount, will be issued to the designated transferee or transferees.

The Notes are issuable only in registered form without coupons in denominations of $1,000 and any integral multiple thereof. As provided in the Indenture and subject to certain limitations therein set forth, Notes are exchangeable for a like aggregate principal amount of Notes of a different authorized denomination, as requested by the Holder surrendering the same.

No service charge shall be made for any such transfer or exchange, but the Company may require payment of a sum sufficient to cover any tax or other governmental charge payable in connection therewith.

The Company, the Trustee and any agent of the Company or the Trustee may treat the Person in whose name this Note is registered as the owner hereof for all purposes, whether or not this Note be overdue, and neither the Company, the Trustee nor any such agent shall be affected by notice to the contrary.

The Notes are hereby designated as Superior Indebtedness for the purposes of (a) the Indenture covering the Company's 4¼% Convertible Subordinate Debentures Due March 1, 1990 issued pursuant to the Indenture dated as of March 1, 1965 between the Company and Chemical Bank New York Trust Company, Trustee, within the meaning of, and as defined in, Section 3.01 of such Indenture and (b) the Indenture covering the Company's 6½% Convertible Subordinate Debentures Due 1996 issued pursuant to the Indenture dated as of November 15, 1971 between the Company and The Chase Manhattan Bank (National Association), Trustee, within the meaning of, and as defined in, Section 3.01 of such Indenture.

Terms used herein which are defined in the Indenture shall have the respective meanings assigned thereto in the Indenture.

ABBREVIATIONS

The following abbreviations, when used in the inscription on the face of this Note, shall be construed as though they were written out in full according to applicable laws or regulations—

TEN COM —as tenants in common
TEN ENT —as tenants by the entireties
JT TEN —as joint tenants with right of survivorship and not as tenants in common

UNIF GIFT MIN ACT—........ Custodian.........
　　　　　　　　　　(Cust)　　　　　(Minor)
under Uniform Gifts to Minors
Act.................
　　　　(State)

Additional abbreviations may also be used though not in the above list.

FOR VALUE RECEIVED, the undersigned hereby sells, assigns and transfers unto

PLEASE INSERT SOCIAL SECURITY OR OTHER IDENTIFYING NUMBER OF ASSIGNEE

PLEASE PRINT OR TYPEWRITE NAME AND ADDRESS OF ASSIGNEE

the within Note of W. R. GRACE & CO. and does hereby irrevocably constitute and appoint

_____Attorney

to transfer the said Note on the books of the within-named Corporation, with full power of substitution in the premises.

Dated_____

Figure 6-1b. *A Bond Certificate (back).*

"middle men," the borrowing process becomes more efficient and less expensive.

3. By issuing bonds, a corporation can often borrow money at a fixed rate for a longer term than it could at a bank. Most banks will not make fixed rate loans for longer than five years because they fear losing money if their cost of funds (raised by selling CDs, savings accounts, and the like) rises to a higher rate than their long-term loans. Many companies want to borrow money for long terms and so elect to issue bonds.

4. The bond market offers a very efficient way to borrow capital. This efficiency stems from the fact that, by issuing bonds, the borrower is spared the task of undergoing numerous separate negotiations and transactions in order to raise the capital it wants. Just consider the chaos that would result if a large company, which borrows money from thousands of investors, had to negotiate separate loan terms and conditions with every potential investor.

Instead, when a corporation issues bonds, it creates one *master loan agreement* and offers investors the opportunity to participate in the loan on a "take-it-or-leave-it" basis. (Exactly how bonds are created and sold to investors is explained in a later chapter.) Thus, if a company wants to borrow $10,000,000 for ten years and is willing to pay the investors who buy the bonds a 7% interest rate for the use of the money, the company offers the identical deal to all investors regardless of whether they are individuals interested in buying one bond each or insurance companies each interested in buying 5,000 bonds.

If investors think the bond is attractive, they buy some. If they don't feel the bond is attractive, they pass. If the company cannot find enough investors to buy all the bonds it wants to sell, it either has to cancel the bond offering or make the terms more attractive for all investors.

The master loan agreement between the corporation and the investors is called the *bond indenture*. The indenture contains all the information that you would expect to find in any loan agreement for a substantial loan, including:

1. The amount of money the company is borrowing.

2. The interest rate the company will pay.

3. The collateral for the loan (if any).

4. When the company will make its interest payments.

5. Whether the company will be subject to any limitations with regard to issuing additional debt, called *restrictive covenants.*

6. When the company will pay off the loan, that is, when the bonds will mature.

7. Whether the company and/or the investor will have the option of shortening the bond's original maturity.

To ensure meeting all of the terms and conditions spelled out in the bond indenture, the company's actions are monitored by a *corporate trustee* (usually a commercial bank), which is responsible for protecting the rights of the bondholders.

DESCRIBING CORPORATE BONDS

Before you can analyze and trade corporate bonds, you must learn the nomenclature and jargon used to identify and describe the many types of corporate bonds available in the marketplace.

A broker, a trader, or an investor must list the following in order to identify a bond:

• The name of the issuer.
• The months and dates when interest is paid.
• The bond's coupon (its interest rate).
• The year the bond matures.

Example: A bond might be described in the following way:

IBM–JJ15–7% of '01

"Translated," this describes the bond issued by IBM corporation that pays its interest on January 15 and July 15 of each year, offers a 7% annual interest rate, and matures in the year 2001.

Let's look more closely at the second part of the description, when the bond pays its interest. Almost all corporate bonds pay

NEW YORK EXCHANGE BONDS

Tuesday, March 17, 1987

Total Volume $33,610,000

SALES SINCE JANUARY 1

1987	1986	1985
$2,085,513,000	$2,589,837,000	$1,841,393,000

	Domestic		All Issues	
	Tue.	Mon.	Tue.	Mon.
Issues traded	802	784	806	789
Advances	320	289	323	289
Declines	280	292	280	295
Unchanged	202	203	203	205
New highs	35	37	36	37
New lows	6	10	6	10

Dow Jones Bond Averages

–1985–		–1986–		–1987–			---Tuesday---					
High	Low	High	Low	High	Low		–1987–		–1986–		–1985–	
83.73	72.27	93.65	83.73	95.51	93.43	20 Bonds	94.77	+0.06	89.89	–0.02	72.32	–0.11
82.88	68.62	95.79	81.85	98.23	95.64	10 Utilities	97.08	+0.19	90.43	–0.07	68.97	–0.20
84.58	75.61	91.64	84.82	93.10	91.21	10 Industrial	92.46	–0.07	89.36	+0.03	75.68	–0.02

Bonds	Cur Yld	Vol	High	Low	Close	Net Chg.
Hutton 12s05	11.3	24	106⅝	106	106	– ⅝
IBM Cr 9⅞88	9.7	10	102	102	102	+ ⅜
IBM Cr 9⅝90	9.3	140	103¾	103¾	103¾	...
ICN 12⅞98	12.7	30	101⅝	101	101	– ¾
IdelB 9¼00f	...	25	92	89	92	+ 3
IllBel 8s04	8.3	15	96¾	96¾	96¾	– 1½
IllPw 10½04	10.0	10	105½	105½	105½	+ ½
IllPw 8⅝06	8.9	1	97	97	97	– 1
IllPw 9⅜16	9.2	25	102	102	102	...
Inco 12⅜10	12.0	20	103	103	103	...
IndBel 8⅛11	8.5	15	96	96	96	– ¾
IndBel 8⅛17	8.5	10	95⅛	95⅛	95⅛	– 1⅜
Inexc 8½00	cv	32	91	90⅝	90⅝	...
InldStl 9½00	10.1	5	93⅞	93⅞	93⅞	+ 1¾
InldStl 7.9s07	10.3	36	76½	76½	76½	...
InldStl 11¼90	11.2	292	100¾	99⅝	100½	– 1½
ItgRs 10¾96	10.8	33	99½	99¼	99½	+ ¼
Intlgc 11.99s96	12.8	15	94	93⅞	94	+ ⅛
Intrfst 7¾05	cv	30	69	68½	69	...
IBM 9⅜04	8.9	111	105⅛	105	105	...
IBM 7⅞04	cv	414	122¼	121	122	+ ¾
IBM 10¼95	9.1	8	113	113	113	– 1
IPap 8.85s95	8.7	10	102	102	102	...
IntRec 9s10	cv	8	86	85	86	...
Intnr 10½08	cv	90	135	131½	135	+ 3¾
Intnr 11s95	10.2	10	108	108	108	+ 2¼
Ipco 5¼89	5.6	4	94½	94½	94½	...

Bonds	Cur Yld	Vol	High	Low	Close	Net Chg.
Mobil 13.76s04	12.0	27	115⅛	115⅛	115⅛	...
Monog 10s99	11.0	10	91	91	91	...
Mons 8¾08	8.7	75	100¾	100¾	100¾	– ¼
MonW 4⅞90	5.2	57	93	92½	93	...
MonW 9⅜00	9.3	4	100½	100½	100½	+ ⅛
MntWC 6½87	6.5	2	99½	99½	99½	...
MntWC 9¼90	9.2	5	101	101	101	– ½
MntWC 9.6s95	9.1	15	105⅜	105⅜	105⅜	...
Morgn 4¾98	cv	10	234	234	234	...
MtSTI 9¾12	9.2	34	106	105½	106	+ ½
MtSTI 9⅝15	9.1	9	105¼	105¼	105¼	...
MtSTI 8⅝18	8.7	10	99¼	99¼	99¼	+ ¼
NBD 8¼10	cv	40	134	134	134	...
NBI 8¼07	cv	1	77	77	77	+ ½
NLInd 7½95	9.0	145	83	82	83	+ 2
NWA 7½10	cv	31	126	126	126	– 1
NConv 9s08	cv	15	90¾	90¾	90¾	– ¼
NtEdu 6½11	cv	30	115½	115	115	...
NEnt 4¾96	cv	3	58	58	58	+ 1
NtGyp zr04	...	757	61½	60	61½	+ 1
NMed 9s06	cv	113	114¾	114½	114⅝	+ ⅛
NMed 8s08	cv	187	103⅞	103½	103½	– ⅜
NMed 12¾99A	11.8	5	107⅞	107⅞	107⅞	+ 2⅝
NMed 12⅛99B	11.5	5	105⅛	105	105	– ⅛
NMEd 12s00	11.4	10	105	105	105	...
NMed 12½00	11.8	25	106½	106	106	– ½
NMed zr04	[illegible]	252	[illegible]	[illegible]	[illegible]	[illegible]

Figure 6-2. *Reading the Bond Quotations.*

Understanding Bond Quotations

The investor who wants to enter orders to buy or sell stock needs to know only the name and current price of the stock. Bond investors need additional information: namely, the rate of interest the bond is paying and its maturity.

Let's look at the IBM 9⅜04 in the left-hand column. The description "IBM 9⅜04" means that the issuer of the bond is International Business Machines, that the bond has a 9⅜% coupon (or nominal rate), and that it matures in 2004. Bond investors and brokers would refer to this bond as "nine and three-eighths of oh-four." This information tells you that each year this bond pays holders 9⅜% of $1,000 (the face value), or $90.38. Although not so stated in the description, the interest will be paid twice a year in equal amounts of $45.19, and at maturity it will pay holders the face amount of $1,000.

Skip the next column, labeled "Cur Yld," for now.

The column headed "Vol" tells you the number of IBM bonds traded that day. In this case, 111 bonds traded.

The "High," "Low," and "Close" columns provide a record of price fluctuations during the trading day. The highest price at which IBM traded for the day was 105⅛, and the lowest was 105—the same price at which it closed.

Remember that bond quotations are not read the same as stock quotations. In stock trading, "95⅛" means

"$95.125." In bond trading, "95⅛" means "$951.25." In other words, a "point" in a stock price is $1, but a "point" in bond trading is $10.

The "Net Chg." (net change) column marks the change in the closing price from the last day's closing price. The IBM 9⅜04 did not change in price from yesterday. The IBM 7⅞04, on the next line down, went up ¾-point ($7.50), as indicated by the plus sign. So yesterday's closing was 121¼ (122 − ¾). The IBM bond below the 7⅞04 went down a full point ($10), so that yesterday's close was 114 (113 + 1).

Now let's go back to the "Cur Yld" (current yield) column. Because the price of the IBM 9⅜04 bond (105, or $1,050.00) is higher than the face value ($1,000), it is said to be trading at a *premium*. Because the seller has to pay more to own the bond, the yield on the investment is reduced. So if you apply the current yield formula to this bond, you will find that the current yield for the IBM 9⅜04 is 8.9%—just the figure shown in the column.

A bond that is selling for less than the face amount, such as the IntRec 9s10 a little farther down the column, is said to be trading at a *discount*. Because the discount in the price represents less of an investment outlay for the buyer, the percentage return is higher than if the bond were trading at *par*, that is, at its face value.

Figure 6-2 *(cont.)*

their interest on either the first or the fifteenth of two months that are six months apart; that is, interest payments are semiannual. Thus there are only twelve possibilities:

| | Abbreviations | |
Months Interest Is Paid	On the 1st*	On the 15th
January–July	JJ	JJ–15
February–August	FA	FA–15
March–September	MS	MS–15
April–October	AO	AO–15
May–November	MN	MN–15
June–December	JD	JD–15

* By convention, if interest is paid on the first of the months, the date is omitted.

The next component, the interest rate, is always expressed as a percentage of the bond's $1,000 face value. The final component, the year the bond matures, is usually expressed without the first two digits. Thus 1991 is expressed as '91 and 2014 is expressed as '14.

If a corporate bond is trading in the market for a price other than par, its price is expressed in points and eighths of a point. Each point equals $10.

Example: A price of 86⅜ means:

$$(86 \times \$10.00) + (⅜ \times \$10.00) = \$860 + \$3.75 = \$863.75$$

And a price of 123⅛ means:

$$(123 \times \$10.00) + (⅛ \times \$10.00) = \$1,230 + \$1.25 = \$1,231.25$$

CATEGORIZING CORPORATE BONDS

Corporate bonds are divided into categories based on the type of company that issues the bonds and the type of collateral backing the bonds. Four types of companies issue corporate bonds: utilities, industrials, transportations, and bank and finance companies. The justification for dividing bonds into such groups is that these categories are often subjected to different accounting conventions, methods of analysis, and other types of financial treatment. Therefore, when grouped, bonds become easier to analyze and trade.

Another way of categorizing bonds is to organize them according to the type of collateral that secures the bonds. Again, bonds backed by different types of collateral are subjected to different types of analysis; so categorizing them in this manner is both useful and logical. Grouped by type of collateral, the categories of corporate bonds are:

- First mortgage bonds.
- Second mortgage bonds.
- Third mortgage bonds.
- Collateral bonds.
- Equipment trust certificates.
- Senior debentures.
- Subordinated debentures.
- Income bonds.

Mortgage bonds are secured by property and/or buildings. Companies with poor or nonexistent credit ratings often *have to* secure their debt with real estate in order to make their bonds safe enough to attract investors. Companies with good credit ratings often *elect to* issue mortgage bonds so that they can borrow at a lower interest rate. Because the bonds are secured by real estate, they have less chance of defaulting (that is, their credit risk is reduced), and so investors are willing to accept a lower interest rate.

Sometimes a company issues several bond issues secured by the same piece of real estate. In this case one of the issues is designated as the first mortgage bonds, another as the second mortgage bonds, and so on. In the event the issuing company files for bankruptcy, the property will most likely be sold so that the bondholders can recoup their investments. The first investors that will be paid off are the holders of the first mortgage bonds; then the second mortgage bondholders will be paid—and so on. For this reason the first mortgage bonds always have less credit risk than the subsequent mortgage bonds and therefore offer a lower yield.

Collateral bonds are secured by other (usually high-quality) securities that are owned by the issuing company.

Example: A company owns $100 million (face amount) of U.S. government securities. It issues $75 million (face amount) worth of corporate bonds secured by the government bonds.

Or a subsidiary of a large company may issue bonds that are secured by some of its parent company's securities.

Equipment trust certificates are bonds secured by liens against a company's equipment. This type of bond is often issued by airlines and railroad companies. When an airline wants to acquire a new jet, it usually makes a deposit equal to approximately 20% of the purchase price, and finances the balance of the purchase by issuing bonds called equipment trust certificates. Should the company ever default on its bonds, the corporate trustee exercises its right to seize and sell the jet for the benefit of the bondholders.

Debentures are bonds that are secured not by any specific collateral or guarantees, but instead by only the full faith and credit of the issuer (that is, the issuer's good name). If a company issues several series of debentures, the different series are ranked according to which issue will be paid off first in the event the company goes bankrupt. The first series to be paid off is called the *senior debentures,* and the subsequent classes are called *subordinated debentures.*

In the past only companies with the highest credit ratings were able to issue debentures. Recently, however, bonds issued by companies with poor credit ratings, otherwise known as *junk bonds,* have become more popular. The theory behind junk bonds is that, although they will have a higher default rate than bonds issued by stronger issuers, the higher interest rate they offer more than offsets the losses due to defaults *if the investor owns a well-diversified portfolio of these lower-quality bonds.* This theory has yet to be proven.

Income bonds are different from other types of bonds in that the company makes the promised interest payments only if it can afford to do so. If the company is losing money, it can omit making its interest payments. However, if the company is operating profitably, as defined in the bond indenture, it cannot omit making the interest payments.

If the company can't make the interest payments on its income bonds, the missed payments accrue at a predetermined interest rate and must be paid off before any dividends can be paid to the common shareholders. If a company misses an interest payment on any type of bond other than an income bond, the bondholders have the right to force the company into bankruptcy so as to protect their interests. Holders of income bonds, however, cannot force a company into bankruptcy for missing interest payments. In exchange for forfeiting this right, investors earn a higher rate of return on an income bond *when and if* the company makes interest payments.

VALUING CORPORATE BONDS IN THE SECONDARY MARKET

After the issuer sells the bond to investors, they may in turn resell it to other investors. When one investor sells the bond to another, the trade is said to occur in the *secondary market*. Secondary market bond transactions can take place either on an exchange or in the over-the-counter market. (Later chapters discuss both these areas.)

Secondary market transactions can take place at a price that is either substantially below or above the bond's original issue price. In other words, the first investor may very well sell the bond at either a profit or a loss. Three principal factors determine the resale value of a bond:

1. The relative change in market interest rates.
2. The change in the credit quality of the bond.
3. The relative supply of, and demand for, bonds.

Changes in Interest Rates

If, after a bond is issued, interest rates should rise, then the market value of the bond falls.

Example: XYZ, Inc. issues an "A-rated," 30-year, 8% bond (a bond that pays $80 of interest per year). Michael Bennet, an investor, buys one of the bonds. Five years later, Bennet wishes to sell the bond (which now has 25 years left to maturity) *but* newly issued A-rated, 25-year bonds are now yielding 10%. If Bennet tries to sell the bond for its full face value, he will soon find that his bond's lower yield makes it uncompetitive relative to the new 25-year bond offerings.

To make the bond attractive to potential investors, Bennet must price it so that it offers a competitive return. Since the bond pays $80 in interest and must yield 10% to be competitive, the price must be around $800 for it to be attractive to potential investors [($80/$800) × 100 = 10%].

On the other hand should interest rates go down, the first investor can sell the bond at a profit.

Example: If, after five years, the interest rate offered by the newly issued A-rated, 25-year bonds falls to 6%, then the investor can price the bond so that $80 a year of interest offers only a 6% return. [($80/$1,333) × 100 = 6%].

Fluctuations in market interest rates are probably the most important factor in determining the market value of a bond. Unfortunately, since no one can accurately predict future interest rates, no one can accurately forecast future bond prices.

Credit Rating

If, after a bond is issued, its credit quality should either improve or decline, the market value of the bond will be adjusted accordingly by the market. Unfortunately, most investors lack the resources and/or the expertise to accurately assess the credit quality of individual corporate bond issues. Fortunately, investors do not have to assess the credit quality of most corporate bonds by themselves.

Several companies do this for investors by assessing the credit quality of various bond issues outstanding in the marketplace. The two best known companies in the credit rating business are Standard & Poor's, Inc. and Moody's, Inc. Table 6-1 lists the credit ratings that these companies assign to bonds and what the ratings mean.

Supply and Demand

From time to time, the relative supply of bonds changes with respect to the demand for them. During a period when bonds are in relatively short supply, investors wishing to sell get a better price than when there is a surplus of bonds on the market. Often tax

Table 6-1. *Ratings of Bonds.*

Investment Bracket	Fitch	Moody's		Standard & Poor's
Top quality	AAA	Aaa		AAA
	AA	Aa		AA
	A	A ⎫		A
Medium quality	BBB	Baa⎟ 1–2–3*		BBB
to speculative	BB	Ba ⎬		BB
	B	B ⎭		B
Poor quality	CCC	Caa		CCC
	CC	Ca		CC
	C	C		C
Value is	DDD			DDD
questionable	DD			DD
	D			D

* The number 1 added to these ratings indicates the *high* end of the category—number 2 the *mid-range* ranking—number 3 the *low* end.

changes bring a flood of new bond offerings that temporarily depress the bond market.

BOND TRADING AND SETTLEMENT

When two investors want to enter into a secondary market bond transaction, they have to agree not only on the price at which the transaction will occur, but also on when the actual exchange of bond certificates and cash will occur. Thus, if on a Monday two parties (in separate parts of the country) agree to enter into a bond transaction, they have to agree not only on the price at which the transaction will occur but also on which day the bonds and the cash will actually change hands. Tuesday? Wednesday? The following Monday? Perhaps the seller has to get the bonds out of a safe deposit box. Or the buyer may need to liquidate some money market investments before making payment.

By convention, the transaction may take place, or *settle*, in one of four common ways, each involving a different day. These four dates are called the *settlement options*.

1. *Regular way:* A regular way trade settles on the fifth business day after the trade date. Only business days are counted—no weekends or holidays. Usually this results in a trade that settles one calendar week after the trade. Regular way settlement is assumed for all corporate bond trades unless the parties specify a different settlement option at the time they enter into the trade.

2. *Cash settlement:* A cash settlement trade settles on the same day on which the trade is made. Obviously, both parties have to agree to, and be prepared for, a cash settlement. By convention any cash trade that occurs at or before 2:00 P.M. settles at 2:30 P.M. Any trade that occurs after 2:00 P.M. settles one half-hour later.

3. *Next-day settlement:* A next-day settlement settles on the first business day after the trade date.

4. *Seller's option:* A seller's option trade settles *up to* 60 days after the trade date. This kind of settlement is usually chosen if the seller is not able to deliver the bonds within the time required by the other settlement options. For example, a seller may be on vacation when she wants to sell some bonds. If the bonds are in her safe deposit box at home, she has to opt for a seller's option settlement. When she returns home, she can deliver the bonds to the buyer at any time up to the 60-day limit, providing that she gives the buyer a one-day written notice of when the bonds will be delivered. Sellers who need to settle via this option usually get a slightly lower price from buyers than they would if they were able to use one of the other settlement options.

ACCRUED INTEREST

When bonds trade, the buyer must usually pay the seller "accrued interest"—in addition to the purchase or sale price. *Accrued interest* is the interest that the buyer must pay the seller in compensation for the time the seller owned the bond since the last interest payment date.

Example: Consider a regular way trade of 10 XYZ, Inc.–FA–10% of '99 bonds at 96⅜ on April 5. The total proceeds that the buyer has to pay the seller is equal to the trade price *plus* the accrued interest.

The purchase price is equal to 96⅜ or $963.75 per bond. Since the trade is for 10 bonds, the trade price is $9,637.50.

You must calculate the accrued interest, which takes two steps. The first step is to determine the number of days that the seller has owned the bond from the last payment date. Interest accrues to the seller until *the day before* the trade settles (*regardless* of which settlement option is used). For corporate bonds, the convention is to assume that each whole month has 30 *days* regardless of the actual number of days in the month. Since each month is assumed to have 30 days, then each year must contain 360 days (12 months × 30 days per month).

Thus, if the trade was made on April 5 with a regular way settlement, it settles on April 12, five *business* days after the trade date. The number of days of accrued interest in April would therefore be 11 days—*up to and including the day before the settlement date.*

April*

S	M	T	W	T	F	S
					1	2
3	**4**	**5**	6	7	8	9
10	**11**	12	13	14	15	16
17	18	19	20	21	22	23
24	25	26	27	28	29	30

* Boldface days are accrued days.

Since the bond last paid interest on February 1, the seller is also entitled to receive interest for the entire month of February and the entire month of March (30 days for each month by convention), in addition to 11 days accrued in April, for a total of 71 days accrued.

The second step is to solve this equation:

$$\text{Accrued interest} = \text{Principal} \times \text{Rate} \times \text{Time}$$

The *principal* is $10,000 because the trade is for 10 bonds. (Note that the purchase price makes no difference.) The *rate* is the bond's coupon yield expressed as a decimal. The *time* is equal to the number of days accrued divided by 360.

The formula for accrued interest for this bond therefore becomes:

$$\frac{\text{Accrued}}{\text{interest}} = \$10,000 \times 0.10 \times (71/360) = \$197.22$$

So the total number of dollars due to the seller from the buyer for this trade is:

Purchase Price	$9,637.50
Accrued interest	$ 197.22
	$9,834.72

Let's now look at a more unusual example.

Example: Consider a next-day settlement trade of 20 XYZ, Inc. MS–15 8% bonds at a price of 61⅛ with a July 3 trade date. The purchase price is equal to 20 times $611.25 or $12,225. The formula for calculating the accrued is:

$$\text{Accrued interest} = \text{Principal} \times \text{Rate} \times \text{Time}$$
$$= \$20,000 \times 0.08 \times T$$

The value of T is equal to the number of days over which interest accrues divided by 360

On the following calendar, the trade settles on July 7. The day after the trade, July 4, is a legal holiday, and the fifth and sixth are weekend days. So the next business day is the seventh, and the trade settles on that day. Therefore, in July there will be 6 days accrued.

July

S	M	T	W	T	F	S
		1	2	3	4	5
6	7	8	9	10	11	12
13	14	15	16	17	18	19
20	21	22	23	24	25	26
27	28	29	30	31		

Since the last interest payment is on March 15, we now have to compute the number of days from March 15 to July 6.

Month of March (starting on March 15)	16 days
Month of April	30 days
Month of May	30 days
Month of June	30 days
Month of July	6 days
	112 days

So the accrued interest calculation becomes:

$$\frac{\text{Accrued}}{\text{interest}} = \$20{,}000 \times 0.08 \times (112/360) = \$497.78$$

and the total dollars due the seller on settlement day become: $\$12{,}225.00 + \$497.78 = \$12{,}722.78$.

While almost all bonds trade with accrued interest, bonds that are in default or income bonds that are not currently paying interest will trade *flat*, that is, without accrued interest. If a bond is trading flat, the seller must disclose that fact to the buyer before the trade is consummated.

YIELDS

Investors need to be very careful when they are quoting bond yields because most bonds have more than one type of "yield." To avoid misunderstandings when talking about yield, always specify which kind of yield you are quoting. The three most commonly used yields are:

1. Coupon yield.
2. Current yield.
3. Yield to maturity.

Coupon Yield

Coupon yield is the yield, expressed as a percentage, that the issuer pays on the bond's face value. Thus a bond that pays $80 of interest per $1,000 of face amount has a coupon yield of 8% ($80 ÷ $1,000). This yield never changes and is usually printed right on the bond certificate. In the case of the preceding bond, the yield quoted is the coupon yield.

$$\text{Coupon yield} = \frac{\text{Number of dollars of interest the bond pays}}{\text{Bond's face value}} \times 100$$

(Multiplying the yield by 100 converts it to a percentage.)

Current Yield

Since bond prices are constantly changing, the "cash-on-cash" return on the bond is also changing all the time. The bond's current yield takes the bond's changing market value into account. Current yield is the yield, expressed as a percentage, calculated by dividing the number of dollars of interest that a bond pays by its *current market value*. In effect this yield represents the annualized *cash-on-cash* return of a bond.

$$\text{Current yield} = \frac{\text{Number of dollars of interest a bond pays}}{\text{Bond's current market value}} \times 100$$

Example: If the bond pays $80 a year in interest and its market value is $800, its current yield is 10%:

$$\text{Current yield} = \frac{\$80}{\$800} \times 100$$

If the same bond had a market value of $1,250, then:

$$\text{Current yield} = \frac{\$80}{\$1,250} \times 100 = 6.4\%$$

Yield to Maturity

If a bond is purchased in the secondary market for a price that is *higher or lower than the bond's face value,* and if the investor holds the bond until it matures, then the investor will have a gain or loss in addition to the interest earned.

Example: The investor buys the 8% bond for $800 and will therefore have a $200 gain when the bond matures because it pays its face value of $1,000. However, the investor who buys the bond for $1,250 and holds it to maturity will have a $250 loss.

Of course, this profit or loss doesn't occur all at once. As a bond that is selling below or above its face value gets closer to maturity, its market value approaches its face value. The yield that takes this into account is called the yield to maturity (YTM).
The formula to approximate the YTM is:

$$\text{Yield to maturity} = \frac{\text{Number of dollars of interest per year} \begin{cases} + \text{ Prorated gain} \\ - \text{ Prorated loss} \end{cases}}{\text{Average of the purchase price and the maturity value}} \times 100$$

The prorated gain or loss is equal to the total gain or loss divided by the number of years remaining until the bond matures. A gain is added to the interest income, and a loss is subtracted from it.

Example: Assume that the bond in the preceding example has *ten years left* until it matures. If you buy the bond for $800, the approximate YTM is:

$$\text{Yield to maturity} = \frac{\$80 + (\$200/10)}{(\$800 + \$1,000)/2} \times 100$$

$$= \frac{(\$80 + \$20)}{\$900} \times 100 = 11.11\%$$

For the bond purchased at $1,250, the YTM is:

$$\text{Yield to maturity} = \frac{\$80 - (\$250/10)}{(\$1,250 + 1,000)/2} \times 100$$

$$= \frac{\$80 - \$25}{\$1,125} \times 100 = 4.89\%$$

CONCLUSION

Bonds may be issued by the U.S. government, by federal agencies, by state or local governments, and even by foreign countries. These types of bonds are the subjects of the next few chapters.

7

U.S. Government
and Agency Securities

The largest debtor in the world is the United States government. The U.S. government borrows primarily to finance its annual budget deficits which, in recent years, have routinely exceeded $100 billion. Despite the incredible size of its accumulated deficit (currently over $1 trillion), U.S. government securities are still considered to have less "credit risk" (that is, risk of default) than any other bonds in the world.

Part of the reason these bonds are held in such high esteem by investors is the sheer strength and size of the underlying American economy. Since these bonds are paid off with tax dollars, the stronger the economy, the greater the potential taxing power of the government. Also, the U.S. government has something to ensure that its debts can be paid when they come due—a printing press that prints legal currency, the most widely accepted currency in the world.

Because of these factors the interest rate that the U.S. government has to pay on its bonds to attract investors is one of the lowest of any country in the world with a free market economy. Since U.S. government bonds are considered to have no credit risk, there is no need for a bond indenture or for Uncle Sam to collateralize the bonds.

THE VARIETY OF U.S. GOVERNMENT DEBT INSTRUMENTS

Uncle Sam issues a variety of debt instruments to finance its debt, of which the major types are:

- Treasury bills.
- Savings bonds.
- Treasury notes.
- Treasury bonds.

Treasury Bills

Treasury bills (T-bills) are unquestionably the safest and most liquid investment vehicle in the world. Twenty-four hours a day, three hundred and sixty-five days a year, in markets all over the world, investors buy and sell U.S. Treasury bills. They are short-term securities originally issued with maturities of 3 months (91 days), 6 months (182 days), and 12 months (364 days). (For purposes of calculating yield, however, a T-bill's "year," like a corporate bond's "year," is considered to have 360 days.)

Treasury bills are sold on a *discount basis,* meaning that they are sold for less than their face value. The difference between their purchase price and face value represents the investor's return.

Example: An investor buys a $10,000, 6-month T-bill for $9,661.84 and holds it to maturity. The return, in dollars, is $338.16 ($10,000 − $9,661.84). This represents a return of $338.16/$9,661.84 = 3.50% over the six months.

To annualize this return, you must multiply it by 360 (the number of days in the T-bill year) and divide it by the actual number of days the investor holds the security.

Example: The investor holds the T-bill for 182 days. By performing this calculation, the investor finds that the annualized return is:

$$3.50\% \times 360/182 = 6.92\%$$

Savings Bonds

U.S. savings bonds have recently experienced a surge in popularity because their rate has become competitive with the rates of other investment options. U.S. savings bonds are currently offered in two different series: series EE and series HH.

Like T-bills, *series EE bonds* are sold at a discount to their face value. Unlike T-bills, however, EE bonds are long-term investments and "pay" a floating interest rate. "Pay" is actually a misnomer in that series EE bonds do not make periodic interest payments; instead, the imputed interest payments accrue and are added to the value of the bonds. The interest rate they "pay" is adjusted quarterly and is set so as to yield 85% of the rate offered by the Treasury's five-year note. (Treasury notes are explained later in the chapter.)

To earn this high rate, investors must hold the savings bond at least five years. If they sell the bond prior to owning it for five years, investors receive a lower interest rate. To make series EE bonds even more attractive, these instruments offer an interest rate floor (6% at the time of this writing). Thus, even if the yield offered by the five-year Treasury note drops to a very low level, the series EE savings bonds will still yield at least 6%. Series EE bonds are sold in denominations as low as $50.

Series HH bonds can be exchanged for Series EE bonds. They make interest payments on a semiannual basis just like other bonds. They are available in denominations starting at just $500. The rate that newly issued HH bonds pay is adjusted periodically to reflect the current market rate. However, once an HH bond is issued, its interest rate never changes.

Many employers encourage their employees to invest in U.S. savings bonds by sponsoring payroll deduction purchase plans. In these programs the employee sets aside a portion of each paycheck to buy savings bonds. For many people who have trouble saving money, this out-of-sight/out-of-mind approach to accumulating wealth is very practical.

Treasury Notes and Bonds

Treasury notes and Treasury bonds represent Uncle Sam's longer-term borrowings. These so-called T-notes and T-bonds differ only with regard to their initial maturity. Notes, by definition, have initial maturities of one to ten years, while bonds have initial maturities longer than ten years.

Initial Distribution. The responsibility for creating and distributing U.S. government T-bills, T-notes and T-bonds belongs to the Federal Reserve Bank of New York, affectionately (or not so affectionately) known as the "Fed." To distribute these securities, the Federal Reserve Bank holds "auctions" among securities and banking firms called *primary dealers* because they are authorized to deal in the primary offerings of government securities. Naturally, since the government wants to keep its financing costs as low as possible, the bidders that are willing to accept the lowest yield will end up winning the auction and getting the securities.

Pricing

Because U.S. government bonds are so actively traded, the prices move in 32nds of a point, instead of eights of a point like corporate bonds. Thus the minimum variation for long-term government securities is $0.3125 ($10 ÷ 32), smaller than the trading variation for corporate bonds, $1.25 ($10 ÷ 8).

Example: A price of 94.05 means 94$^{5}\!/_{32}$ or:

$$(94 \times \$10) + (5\!/_{32} \times \$10) = \$941.5625$$

A price of 68.28 means 68$^{28}\!/_{32}$ or:

$$(68 \times \$10) + (28\!/_{32} \times \$10) = \$688.7500$$

The spread between a dealer's *bid price* (the price at which a dealer will buy a bond) and *ask price* (the price at which a dealer will sell it) is often just a 32nd of a point. For example, a dealer might bid a bond at 94.05 and offer it at 94.06. That is just a little over 31 cents per bond.

Settlement and Accrued Interest

Government notes and bonds usually settle on the next business day after the trade day, although the other settlement options outlined in the previous chapter can also be used. Accrued interest on government bond transactions is calculated differently than it is for corporate bonds. The formula remains the same:

$$\text{Accrued interest} = \text{Principal} \times \text{Rate} \times \text{Time}$$

While the principal component remains the same, the rate and time components are different.

The rate component used to calculate accrued interest for government bonds is the *semiannual interest rate* expressed as a decimal.

Example: For a 7% bond, the figure used in the formula is 3.5%, or 0.035 (0.07/2).

The time component is the *actual* number of days from the last interest payment date to the day before settlement date, divided by the *actual* number of days between the last interest payment and the next interest payment. A month with 28 days or 31 days is computed as such; there is no assumption that every month has 30 days (as is the case with corporate bonds).

Example: Use the following calendar and assume that January has 31 days, February has 28, and March has 31. The number of days of accrued interest for a JJ bond that is traded on April 3 is:

April

S	M	T	W	T	F	S
			1	2	3	**4**
5	6	7	8	9	10	11
12	13	14	15	16	17	18
19	20	21	22	23	24	25
26	27	28	29	30		

January	31 days
February	28 days
March	31 days
April	5 days (the day before the next business day after trade date)
	95 days

If the number of days between the two interest periods is 183 (it can be as low as 181 or as high as 185 depending on the 6-month period), then

97

the time component becomes: 95/183. If the trade is for $250,000 face amount and the bond's coupon yield is 9%, the amount of accrued is:

$$\text{Accrued interest} = P \times R \times T$$
$$= \$250,000 \times 0.045 \times 95/183$$
$$= \$5,840.16$$

This accrued interest would have to be added to the bond's purchase price to determine the total amount that the buyer must pay the seller on the settlement date.

U.S. AGENCY SECURITIES

In addition to the U.S. Treasury, many federal agencies borrow money directly from investors for their own purposes. Some of these agencies are:

- *Banks for Cooperatives:* The twelve district Banks for Cooperatives borrow money by issuing bonds that are fully collateralized by cash, government securities, or other collateral. The funds raised by this agency are then lent to farming cooperatives to support their activities.
- *Federal Intermediate Credit Banks:* The twelve Federal Intermediate Credit Banks provide short-term financing for the seasonal production of crops and livestock. To support their lending activities, these banks issue bonds that are collateralized by cash, Treasuries, or loans.
- *Federal Land Banks:* The twelve Federal Land Banks make first mortgage loans of up to 65% of the appraised value of farm properties. To finance its activities, the Federal Land Bank issues bonds secured by cash, Treasuries, or first mortgages on farm properties.
- *Federal Home Loan Banks:* The Federal Home Loan Banks are twelve regional banks that are owned by the nation's Savings & Loan Institutions (S&Ls). The Federal Home Loan Banks issue bonds and then lend the proceeds to S&Ls so that they, in turn, can make more residential mortgage loans.

• *Student Loan Marketing Association (Sallie Mae)*: This agency provides loans to banks that make student loans; it also buys students' loans, repackages them, and sells them to investors. To support its activities, Sallie Mae issues a wide variety of different types of bonds. Sallie Mae is considered one of the most creative agencies with regard to its own financing.

Issuing Agency Securities

Agency securities are not as popular as Treasury securities and therefore cannot be successfully auctioned. Instead, when one of the agencies wants to sell securities, it usually hires one or more investment banking firms to distribute the securities. For their services the investment banking firms earn commissions on the bonds they distribute.

Because the agencies issue securities by authority of an act of Congress, the securities are exempt from the registration requirement to which corporate securities are subjected. However, because the securities are not issued directly by the U.S. Treasury, investors who buy new issues of agency securities must be provided with a prospectus.

Trading Agency Securities

Since there are fewer agency securities than Treasury securities, the market for them is not as active, and the spread between the bid and the asked price tends to be wider. With their wider spread, agency securities are less liquid and therefore generally offer a higher yield than Treasury securities.

U.S. agency securities are backed by either the full faith and credit of the U.S. government or by its moral obligation. Regardless of whether the securities are fully backed by Uncle Sam, it is inconceivable that the federal government would allow the securities issued by one of its agencies to go into default. For this reason agency securities are considered to have a negligible amount of credit risk.

MONEY MARKETS

Prior to the late 1970s and early 1980s, most individuals were content to leave their ready cash in the local bank or savings and loan (S&L).

In effect, they lent it to the bank, which in turn lent it to borrowers at a higher rate. After all, the bank offered safety, paid between 4% and 5¼% interest (which was a fairly competitive rate of return), and offered immediate liquidity (to get your money back anytime, just fill out a withdrawal slip).

The relative attractiveness of putting surplus cash into the bank changed in the late 1970s and early 1980s as interest rates skyrocketed. The combination of high inflation, the rapid rise in oil prices, and the tight money policies enacted by the Federal Reserve Board all combined to push short-term interest rates up over 20%. Even financially strong borrowers were willing to pay more than 20% a year to borrow money.

Unfortunately for investors, banks and S&Ls were legally restricted from paying their depositors an interest rate higher than 5¼%. To many investors this seemed unfair. After all, if borrowers were willing to pay 20% a year and you had money to lend, why settle for 5¼%?

Soon investors found a number of vehicles that offered sharply higher interest rates but that also required substantially higher minimum investments (often exceeding $100,000). Since this was more than most people could afford to invest, many investors could not take advantage of the higher rates offered by these vehicles.

To solve this problem, many mutual fund companies started offering money market mutual funds (see Chapter 9 on mutual funds). In these money funds investors could pool their resources, hire a professional manager, and enjoy the higher rates of return offered by the so-called "money market." As the popularity of these money market funds spread, more and more people withdrew their money from banks and S&Ls, creating a severe liquidity crisis for many banks and S&Ls.

Although many investors bought (and are still buying) shares in money market funds, few really understand the vehicles that make up the "money market."

Money Market Vehicles

Traditionally, *money market* vehicles are defined as relative risk-free debt securities that mature in less than a year. Included in this definition are:

- Treasury bills.
- Commercial paper (CP).
- Banker's acceptances (BAs).
- Most negotiable ($100,000 and over) certificates of deposit (CDs).
- Repurchase agreements (repos).

Let's examine each of these vehicles in more detail (except for T-bills which were already covered).

Certificates of Deposit. The certificate of deposit (CD) is one of the most popular investment vehicles in America—for several reasons:

1. *Various maturities* allow investors to select the term that best suits their needs and objectives. The shortest-term CDs mature just 7 days after they are issued, although CDs with maturities of 30, 60, 90, 180, and 360 days are more popular with investors.

2. *Various forms* allow investors to select the one to best meet their needs and objectives. These forms include not only traditional fixed-rate, fixed-term CDs (that are bought and redeemed at par, but also zero coupon CDs (that are bought at a discount and par at maturity) and variable-rate CDs (that are bought at par but pay an interest rate that is periodically adjusted to reflect changes in market rates).

3. *CDs' competitive returns* rival the returns offered by other secure, fully taxable, short-term investment vehicles.

4. *The credit risk is minimal* because deposits in a banking institution in one name are insured up to $100,000 by the Federal Deposit Insurance Corporation (FDIC) or by the Federal Savings and Loan Insurance Corporation (FSLIC).

5. *Liquidity* is a feature if the CD is issued by one of America's leading banks. Investors more interested in liquidity than in yield generally invest only in CDs issued by the top-tier money center banks. The reason is that the secondary market is fairly well developed. It is possible to buy and sell these instruments at almost any time at a fair price and with minimal transaction costs.

The price investors pay for this liquidity is a lower yield. Investors who are more yield-conscious generally hire a CD broker to place their CDs with banks and savings and loans (S&Ls) offering the highest yield, regardless of where the banks and S&Ls are located. Because there is no secondary market for CDs issued by small banks and S&Ls, investors needing their funds prior to the CD's maturity date have to redeem them with the issuing institution and incur a six-month interest penalty.

Commercial Paper. Commercial paper (CP) is an unsecured promise by the issuing company to pay the investor a certain number of dollars on a stated maturity date. If the proceeds are used to finance current transactions (that is, not added to capital) and mature in less than 270 days, the issuers are exempted from registering the issue as a security offering.

Commercial paper is sold on a discounted basis like a zero coupon bond. CP can be divided into two main classifications based on the type of issuer: direct issue paper and dealer paper.

Direct issues are sold directly by the issuing companies. These companies are so large, and they are in the commercial paper market so often, that it is cost-effective for them to build and maintain a dedicated in-house CP sales force. Examples of direct issuers are the large finance companies and the largest public corporations. Smaller companies, on the other hand, use dealers to sell their CP when they are in the market. For this service they generally pay a fee to the dealer of approximately .125% of the offering proceeds.

CP, regardless of the issuer, is always unsecured debt. It is backed only by the full faith and credit of the issuing corporation but not by a specific lien against any of the issuer's assets or collateral. For this reason, investors need to pay close attention to the credit ratings of CP issues. CP is rated 1, 2, 3, or 4 by the major rating services. Number 1 paper is the safest, and number 4 paper is either already in or well on its way to default. A typical CP rating is expressed as "A1-P2"—meaning that Standard & Poor's rates it a "1" and Moody's rates it a 2.

Often a company with a low credit rating gets its bank to issue a letter of credit guaranteeing the paper or an insurance company to issue a financial guarantee bond covering it. This way, paper that would have been rated 3 can come to market with a 1. Even after paying the bank or insurance company a fee for providing the guarantee, the company's net cost of borrowing is often reduced by obtaining these third party guarantees.

CP trades in pieces as small as $50,000 or as large as several $100 million. Recently, municipalities have beg··n to enter the CP market by selling short-term paper to investors who can benefit from the exemption from federal income taxes that this paper offers. Foreign companies have also begun tapping this relatively low-cost source of funds.

Most of the CP purchased by investors is held to maturity. Part of the reason for this is that on average CP has a very short duration (less than 30 days). The other reason is that, while dealers and issuers usually buy back paper from investors who need to sell it to raise cash, the secondary market for CP is not nearly as well developed as it is for other money market instruments. Thus CP is not suitable for trading.

Banker's Acceptances. A *banker's acceptance* (BA) is an obligation of a bank to pay to the holder a certain number of dollars on a certain day. A bank creates BAs in a variety of ways, but usually they are created to finance trade.

Example: A wine merchant in New York wants to import $950,000 worth of wine from a winery in Italy. The merchant would like to buy the wine, sell it, and pay the winery in Italy from the sale proceeds. This cycle he feels will take him approximately six months from the date the wine is delivered to New York. First, he presents his proposal to the winery but, for whatever reason, the winery is either unwilling or unable to finance him for six months. The winery informs the merchant that they cannot extend him a trade credit and that they require prompt payment if they are going to do business.

Because the merchant has an excellent credit rating, he is able to go to his bank in New York and get a $1 million line of credit (LC) for a term of 9 months. This done, the merchant sends a purchase order to the winery in Italy and instructs his bank to send a letter of credit (LC) to the winery's bank in Italy. Upon receipt of the LC, the winery's bank notifies the winery that the LC has been received and that the wine can be shipped.

The wine merchant then ships the wine and provides proof of shipment to his bank (bills of lading and the appropriate shipping documents).

The Italian bank then forwards these same documents to the merchant's bank in New York.

Assuming the paperwork is completed properly, the merchant's bank then forwards the funds ($950,000) to the bank in Italy, which credits the funds to the winery's account. Thus *the winery has been paid before the merchant has sold (or probably has even received) the wine. At the same time, the merchant has received proof that the wine has been shipped prior to releasing any funds to the winery.* This somewhat complicated process, with the two banks acting as intermediaries, protects both parties to the transaction.

The merchant's bank then delivers the shipping documents to the merchant so he can take delivery of the wine upon its arrival in America. If four weeks have elapsed, the merchant has eight months left on his LC, after which the bank can expect to receive $1 million. In the meantime, it has paid out $950,000. The difference between the $950,000 that the bank sends to Italy and the $1 million that it collects from the merchant covers the bank's fees, expenses, and profit.

Should the bank have a better use for those funds it may elect *to sell the right to receive the $1 million on a discounted basis to an investor.*

Example: The bank sells the note to an investor when it has four months left to maturity for the sum of $982,000. In so doing, the bank, determining that it can make better use of its funds elsewhere, has sold the right to the $1 million in four months for $982,000. The purchasing investor receives $1 million in four months, the difference between the $982,000 purchase price and the $1 million maturity value representing the return on the investment.

To make the note salable to the investor, the bank has to guarantee that it will pay the investor $1 million in four months regardless of whether the wine merchant honors his obligation to the bank. It does so by stamping the word "ACCEPTED" on the note.

Hence the name: banker's acceptance.

Because investors must rely on the bank for payment, they generally prefer to deal with either local banks that they are familiar with or with the strongest money center banks. No American has lost a penny of principal in a banker's acceptance since they became popular over sixty years ago.

Banker's acceptances trade in million dollar pieces, but most dealers break BAs into smaller pieces for smaller investors. Banker's acceptances have maturities of up to 270 days and are always sold on a discount basis. Generally BAs are held in bearer form and are fully negotiable. They are an attractive investment alternative for investors who are very safety conscious.

REPURCHASE AGREEMENTS

A *repurchase transaction* (*repo*) is the sale of a security from a seller to a buyer with the simultaneous agreement from the seller to repurchase the security at a fixed price (or pricing rate) on a specified future date. Thus, while a repo is technically a "sale," functionally it represents a loan from the buyer to the seller with the security used as collateral.

The most common repurchase transaction is a U.S. government bond dealer selling U.S. government bonds to an investor and at the same time agreeing to repurchase the bonds the next day at a slightly higher price. The difference in price represents the return to investors. In this type of transaction the dealer is able to use the investor's money to finance its bond inventory at a lower cost than what a bank would charge to finance it. Investors, on the other hand, are able to lock in a fixed return on an overnight investment, generally at a higher rate than they could get from a money market fund.

Although most repos are overnight transactions, corporate investment officers frequently enter into longer-term repo transactions (up to a month or more) if the rate offered them by a dealer is particularly attractive, or if they expect interest rates to decline and wish to lock in a fixed rate. Further, the repo market is not limited to government securities. Repo transactions can also be done against certificates of deposit, banker's acceptances, high-quality corporate bonds, U.S. government agencies, mortgage securities, or other high-quality, liquid securities.

105

High-quality liquid securities are needed because, in the event the seller is either unable or unwilling to repurchase the securities on the agreed-upon date and at the agreed-upon price, the buyer must then sell the securities in the open market to recoup the investment. Only high-quality, liquid securities offer repo investors real protection in this situation.

If the transaction is done properly, investors should not have any market risk. If, over the course of the transaction, the market value of the collateral should either rise or fall, the market gain or market loss *accrues to the seller and not to the investor.* The investor, by agreeing *in advance* to a specific repurchase price (or pricing rate), effectively locks in a return regardless of how changing market conditions affect the market value of the collateral.

The principal risks to the investor are therefore twofold:

1. In the event the seller fails to repurchase the securities, the buyer must have clear and unencumbered access to the securities in order to sell them.

2. The securities, when sold, must bring a high enough price in the open market to allow the investor to recoup not only the initial investment, but also any incurred costs and a fair return on the investment.

To limit the first risk—access to the securities—repo investors must try to take delivery of the securities themselves. When this is either impractical or uneconomical (as in the case of a small dollar volume or an overnight transaction), they must make sure that the securities are properly escrowed for their benefit at an appropriate financial intermediary, such as a commercial bank or clearing house. Either way, if they do need to sell the securities, they are free to do so.

Stories sometimes appear in the financial press about repo investors who either lost money or had to sue a seller to recoup an investment because they neglected to stringently follow this rule—Lombard Wall, Drysdale, ESM securities, and so on. In some of the more bizarre cases, investors have entered into repos with dealers *who did not even own any securities,* much less have them properly escrowed for the investors' benefit.

To protect against the second risk—recouping their investment plus costs and a profit in the event of a forced sale—buyers need to be sure that they have sufficient "margin" in the transaction. *Margin,* in repo transactions, is defined as requiring the seller to transfer enough securities to the buyer to slightly *over*collateralize the loan. In the event that the dealer defaults on his obligation to repurchase the securities at the same time that the market value of the securities drops, the investor has a "cushion" against any loss of principal during the forced liquidation.

The amount of the margin in a given transaction is negotiable. When negotiating margin requirements, investors should take into account the reputation and financial strength of the dealer, as well as the quality, volatility, and liquidity of the securities involved. Top dealers often offer no margin at all, believing that their good name offers investors sufficient security. However, with smaller dealers, obtaining sufficient margin is a must.

Naturally, margin should be a two-way street. If, during a longer-term repo transaction, the market value of the securities being used as collateral should rise appreciably, then the seller should be allowed to recall some of the "excess" collateral.

Recently, at the urging of the Fed and members of the securities industry, the bankruptcy code was modified and "clarified" to protect repo investors in certain types of repo transactions involving Treasury securities, government agencies, certificates of deposit, and banker's acceptances. In the event that an investor is involved in a repurchase transaction with a dealer who files for bankruptcy, and the investor is thus forced to sell the securities, the code helps to protect the investor from the bankruptcy trustee, should he or she attempt to attach the sale proceeds.

MUNICIPAL INVESTMENTS

Investors in high tax brackets invest in tax-exempt municipals because the interest paid by such municipal securities is exempt from federal income tax. Also, if the issuer and investor are from the state, the interest can be *double tax exempt,* that is, exempt from federal and state taxation. If issuer and investor are from the same issuing city or municipality, the interest can be exempt from city tax too, that is, *triple tax exempt.*

Every municipal security with less than a year to either its maturity date or its "put" date can be considered a money market instrument. Generally, however, when investors refer to the municipal money market, they are referring to *tax anticipation notes* (TANs), *revenue anticipation notes* (RANs), *bond anticipation notes* (BANs), or *muni low-floaters* (MLFs). TANs, RANs, and BANs are distinguished by the source of funds that will be used to pay off the notes when they mature.

- If a city needs money immediately but does not collect its taxes for six months, it might issue a six-month tax anticipation note, using the tax revenues, when they are collected six months hence, to pay off the TANs.

- If a state is going to float a 20-year municipal bond offering but feels that interest rates will be lower in nine months, it might elect to issue nine-month BANs. Thus, the state raises the money it needs now, but it doesn't have to issue its long-term fixed rate debt for nine months. In this situation, the state is betting that interest rates will be lower in six months, and thus the cost of its long-term financing, when issued, will also be lower. If, instead of moving lower, interest rates should move higher over the next nine months, the state might elect to issue a second series of BANs, using the sale proceeds of the second BAN offering to pay off the first BAN offering. When the second series of BANs come due, interest rates are then expected to be low enough so that the state can float its long-term bonds without the need for a third series of BANs!

- Revenue anticipation notes rely on a future revenue source—such as tolls, federal revenue sharing funds, and the like—to pay off the note holders. The specific revenue projections, as well as detailed information on the expected revenue source, can be found in the offering memorandum.

- Muni low-floater notes are rated by the major credit agencies in a manner very similar to the ones the agencies use to rate CP. After evaluating all the relevent information about an issuer's financial strength and ability to meet its financial obligations on a timely basis, the agencies assign it a rating from P1 to P3 (Standard and Poor's) or MIG1 to MIG4 (Moody's).

Also like CP, municipal issuers with low credit ratings commonly have a bank issue a letter of credit or an insurance company issue a financial guarantee bond, so that the issue can come to market with a top credit rating.

Unlike the negotiable CD market, where only about a dozen banks are considered prime, there are thousands of issues and issuers in the muni note market. Most issues trade only locally, although the better known ones, such as State of California or New York City, trade nationwide. Muni notes are offered in both coupon and discount form. The coupon notes are available in both fixed-rate and variable-rate form.

An additional vehicle that you should be familiar with is the municipal lease. Many county and municipal governments have restrictions against borrowing money for terms of more than one year without first holding a public referendum. This is to prevent an outgoing administration from saddling an incoming administration with a high debt load. Because of these restrictions, many municipal purchases are technically made as a series of renewable one-year leases.

Example: If a municipality wants to purchase a fire truck, it might structure the deal as a series of five one-year renewable floating rate leases with the option to purchase the truck for $1 at the start of the sixth year.

These leases are written with such onerous cancellation clauses that they are almost never terminated; so the investor is well protected. (Additionally, a municipality will go to almost any length before it will default on its fire truck payments.) These leases offer substantially higher rates of return (although less liquidity) than other short-term municipal investments. Brokers offering municipals to their clients and prospects should become familiar with municipal leases.

While the preceding vehicles represent the traditional domestic money market instruments, any longer-term bond or note can be included in this definition if it's scheduled to mature in the coming year.

Example: If you want to make a six-month investment, a 20-year Treasury bond, that was originally issued 19½ half years ago and thus has a remaining life of 6 months, is as much of a candidate for your investment dollars as a newly issued six-month T-bill. Both are backed by the full faith and credit of Uncle Sam, both mature in six months, and both are very liquid (that is, easy to buy and sell at a fair price). Yet the 20-year bond frequently offers a higher yield.

The same reasoning applies to any longer-term bond or note that can be put (that is, sold) back to its issuer within a year, even if the maturity date is farther off than one year.

8

Municipal Bonds
and Special Bond Types

MUNICIPAL BONDS

Municipal bonds are issued by state and local governments and their agencies—state highway departments, turnpike authorities, industrial development agencies, airport authorities, and the like. The principal attraction of municipal bonds is that the interest they pay is generally exempt from federal income tax (just as interest on Treasury securities is exempt from state and local taxation). This reciprocal tax immunity stems from the wording of the U.S. Constitution itself, which states that the federal government cannot interfere with the operation of the states, and the states may not interfere with the operation of the federal government. Taxing each other's debt instruments is considered "interfering."

In addition, many states and cities also exempt the interest their residents receive from municipal bonds—providing that the bonds are from an issuer within the state. Thus, for a New Jersey resident, bonds issued by the state of New Jersey, or by any other municipality within New Jersey, are also exempt from any New Jersey state and/ or any city income tax. Thus in certain states, the interest paid by municipal bonds is truly *triple tax free.*

Historically, federal tax rates have been higher than state tax rates and/or local tax rates (or even the combination of states and local rates). As a result, municipal bonds have been able to attract investors with a lower coupon rate than either corporate bonds or Treasury bonds with comparable maturities.

Example: A New Jersey investor is in the 28% federal income tax bracket, the 3% state income tax bracket, and the 2% local tax bracket. An investor has a choice between a corporate bond, a U.S. Treasury bond, and a New Jersey state bond, all of which have an 8% coupon, are priced at par, and are equal in every other way. In such a case, the investor would *always* choose the municipal bond because it offers the highest after-tax yield.

The corporate bond is fully taxable and thus the investor has to pay taxes totaling 33% (28% federal, 3% state, 2% city) on the interest received, leaving only 67% (100% − 33%) of the 8% income stream on an after-tax basis.

$$8\% \text{ pre-tax} \times 0.67 = \underline{5.36\%}$$

The Treasury bond is subject only to federal tax, and thus the investor has 72% (100% − 28%) of income left on an after-tax basis.

$$8\% \text{ pre-tax} \times 0.72 = \underline{5.76\%}$$

However, the municipal bond is not subject to any tax and thus the pre-tax and after-tax yield are the same.

$$8\% \text{ pre-tax} \times 1.00 = \underline{8.00\%}$$

Given this choice, every investor would choose the municipal bond because it offers the highest after-tax yield. Municipalities, like other borrowers, are interested in keeping their borrowing costs as low as possible.

Example: If corporations are able to attract investors by offering bonds that yield an 8% pre-tax return (which is, as we've seen, the equivalent of 5.36% after-tax return), then a New Jersey municipality's bond only has to offer a New Jersey resident a 5.36% return to be an equally attractive investment opportunity. (This assumes, of course, that both bonds are of equal maturities and credit worthiness.)

Thus, if corporate bonds are yielding 8% and municipal bonds are paying more than 5.36%, the municipal bond is a better buy. But if the municipal bond is yielding less than 5.36%, then the investor is better off buying the corporate bond.

Denominations

Municipal bonds are issued in $5,000 denominations unlike Treasuries and corporates, which are usually issued in $1,000 denominations. Thus investors are limited to buying multiples of $5,000 in face amount—$5,000, $10,000, $15,000, and so on. The logic behind making the denomination so large is that investors who find municipals to be attractive are generally in the higher tax brackets, which means they generally have more money to invest.

Investors interested in buying municipals in other amounts can do so through the use of mutual funds and/or unit trusts (see Chapter 9 on mutual funds).

Types of Municipals

Municipal bonds fall into one of two broad categories: general obligation bonds and revenue bonds. These bond types differ with regard to the source of funds used to make the interest payments and to retire the bonds.

General Obligation Bonds. General obligation (GO) bonds are backed by the full faith, credit, and taxing power of the issuer. If the state of California issues a general obligation (GO) bond, the security is fully backed by the state. If the state needs to raise taxes to pay the bondholders the principal and interest to which they are entitled, then it raises taxes. If the state needs to sell off assets (such as state lands) to honor its obligations to bondholders, then the state must do so. In other words, the state must do whatever it takes to honor its obligations.

Because these bonds have such a strong guarantee, they are often very highly rated by the credit agencies.

Revenue Bonds. Revenue bonds, on the other hand, are generally backed only by revenue generated by the project funded by the bond issue.

113

UNITED STATES OF AMERICA
STATE OF CONNECTICUT
COUNTY OF NEW LONDON

CITY OF NORWICH

GENERAL IMPROVEMENT BOND, ISSUE OF 1970

KNOW ALL MEN BY THESE PRESENTS that the **CITY OF NORWICH**, a municipal corporation organized and existing under and by virtue of the laws of the State of Connecticut, situated in the County of New London in said State, for value received hereby promises to pay to the bearer, or, if this Bond be registered, to the registered holder hereof, the principal sum of

FIVE THOUSAND DOLLARS ($5,000)

in lawful money of the United States of America, at the principal office of the Hartford National Bank and Trust Company, in the City of Hartford, State of Connecticut,

ON THE FIRST DAY OF JULY,

and to pay interest thereon at the rate of six per centum (6.00%) per annum, from the date hereof, payable semi-annually, on the first day of January and the first day of July of each year, until it matures, upon presentation and surrender, as they severally become due, of the coupons attached hereto.

This Bond may be registered as to principal only by the holder in his name on the bond register of the City kept in the office of the Comptroller of said City, and such registration shall be noted hereon by said Comptroller. If so registered, this Bond may be transferred on said bond register by the registered owner in person or by attorney, upon presentation of this Bond to the Comptroller with a written instrument of transfer in a form approved by said Comptroller and executed by said registered owner. If this Bond be so registered, the principal shall thereafter be payable only to the person in whose name it is registered unless this Bond shall be discharged from registry by being registered as payable to bearer. Such registration shall not affect the negotiability of the coupons, which shall continue to pass by delivery.

This Bond is one of an authorized issue, the aggregate principal amount of which is $700,000, the Bonds of which are of like tenor, except as to number and date of maturity, and are issued pursuant to the Constitution and Statutes of the State of Connecticut, including the Charter of said City and other provisions of law applicable thereto, and a bond ordinance entitled: "AN ORDINANCE AUTHORIZING THE ISSUANCE OF $700,000 GENERAL IMPROVEMENT BONDS, ISSUE OF 1969, OF THE CITY OF NORWICH TO FINANCE THE COST OF THE CONSTRUCTING OF ACQUIRING VARIOUS CAPITAL IMPROVEMENTS FOR SAID CITY; PRESCRIBING THE FORM AND DETAILS THEREOF AND SECURITY THEREFOR; AND AUTHORIZING THE SALE THEREOF," duly enacted by the Council of said City on the 5th day of August, 1968, as amended, and approved by the qualified electors of said City at an election held in the City of Norwich on the 5th day of November, 1968.

It is hereby certified and recited that all acts, conditions and things required to exist or be done precedent to and in the issuance of this Bond by the Constitution and Statutes of the State of Connecticut, exist, have happened and have been performed; that provision has been made for the levy and collection of a direct annual tax upon all the taxable property within the City of Norwich sufficient to pay the interest on and principal of this Bond as the same become due; and that the total indebtedness of said City, including this Bond, does not exceed any constitutional, statutory or charter debt limitation or restriction.

The full faith and credit of the City of Norwich are hereby irrevocably pledged for the punctual payment of the principal of and interest on this Bond according to its terms.

IN WITNESS WHEREOF the **City of Norwich** has caused this Bond to be signed by its City Manager and Comptroller under its corporate seal and the interest coupons hereto attached to be authenticated with the facsimile signatures of said City Manager and Comptroller as of the 1st day of July, 1970.

CITY OF NORWICH

By _____

By _____

SPECIMEN

SPECIMEN

Comptroller

City Manager

Figure 8-1. *The Front of a Municipal Bond.*

Example: A city wants to build a new airport, believing that the new facility will attract industry to the area. To finance the construction of the airport, the city issues revenue bonds. The money for the periodic interest payments and eventual retirement of the bonds comes from airplane landing fees, ticket counter and concession rentals, hanger rentals, airline fuel surtaxes, and other revenues associated with the facility.

In other words, only revenue generated by the airport can be used to service the airport revenue bonds. If the airport generates enough revenue to pay off the bonds, then bondholders receive their interest and principal in full and on time. However, if the airport does not generate enough revenue, bondholders either receive their interest and principal late or nothing at all. The bondholders have no recourse to the city's general treasury fund.

Because revenue bondholders are solely dependent on the revenue generated by the project being financed, revenue bonds typically have more credit risk than GO bonds. For this reason, investors should pay especially close attention to the project's projections and economics.

Serial Issues

Many municipalities issue bonds in *serial* fashion, that is, within the bond offering are different bonds with different maturities and different coupon yields.

Example: A $50-million bond offering may be structured as follows:

Dollar Amount	Maturity	Coupon
5 million	2 years	4.5%
5 million	4 years	5.0%
5 million	6 years	5.5%
5 million	8 years	5.7%
5 million	10 years	5.9%
5 million	14 years	6.0%
20 million	20 years	6.3%

Thus, a total of $30 million worth of the bonds will mature prior to when the last bonds mature. The bonds that mature early are called "serial bonds" because they mature in series, ranging in this example from 2 to 14 years. Each series, when considered separately, usually represents a fairly small percentage of the entire bond offering (10% in our example).

The long-term bonds, which represent the larger portion of the issue, are called the *term bonds*. Thus investors can pick the maturity that best meets their needs.

Municipalities often issue their bonds with this staggered maturity so that they do not have to borrow any money for longer than necessary.

Example: In our airport revenue bond issue, the airport authority may project that, in two years, they will have a $5 million cash surplus that they can use to retire $5 million worth of bonds. By shortening the maturity, the issuer not only has to pay interest for fewer years, but also has the benefit of being able to offer a lower interest rate (short-term bonds generally pay less than longer-term bonds).

Competitive Bidding

When a state wants to issue bonds, it usually posts a "request for bids" in some of the major business and bond publications (*The Bond Buyer*, the *Wall Street Journal*, and the like). This request for bids states how much money the municipality wants to borrow and what term it wants to borrow the money for, as well as any other restrictions or conditions for its borrowing. For example, a municipality may put a cap on the maximum interest rate it is willing to pay for certain years. Also included in the ad are the date, time, and location at which sealed bids for the business will be accepted.

Investment banking firms interested in competing for the municipality's business contact the municipality to obtain any other information that they need. On the auction day, representatives of the investment banking firms submit their proposals on how, if awarded the financing contract, they will structure the municipality's financing. The proposals submitted by the firms are binding. Naturally, the firm awarded the contract is the one that comes up with the proposal costing the municipality the lowest overall financing cost.

"Taxable" Municipals

Because of the favorable tax treatment that municipal bonds receive, there is an ever-present temptation for municipalities to borrow money from investors for no purpose other than to invest in Treasuries.

Example: A municipality might be able to issue bonds to investors that pay a 6% interest rate and then invest the sales proceeds in Treasuries that yield 8%—and in the process make a 2% "spread."

Other municipalities have used the guise that their "industrial development authorities" were issuing bonds for the sole purpose of making below-market-rate loans to profitable and established companies—often companies with strong local political connections. Needless to say, these bond issues did not always qualify as a legitimate "operation" of state or local government.

To prevent such abuses, Congress passed legislation in 1986 limiting the amount of industrial development bonds that a municipality can issue. Congress has also sharply restricted the practice of reinvesting municipal bond sales proceeds in Treasuries to earn the spread. If a municipality wants to issue bonds above this amount, it may do so, but the interest on such bonds is *not* exempt from federal income tax.

SPECIAL BOND TYPES

In addition to the traditional types of bonds—those that pay interest twice a year and their face value upon maturity—investors should be familiar with two other types of bonds: mortgage-backed securities and zero coupon bonds.

- *Mortgage-backed securities* are bonds that are collateralized with pools of mortgages. They make monthly payments of both principal and interest as the homeowners pay down their mortgages—that is, as homeowners' mortgage payments indirectly pay off the bonds.
- *Zero coupon bonds* pay no interest at all but instead have face values that are substantially above the security's original purchase price.

The difference between these two prices represents the investor's return.

Mortgage-Backed Securities (MBSs)

In days gone by, local savings and loans and other financial institutions originated mortgages in their local markets, held the mortgages in their investment portfolios (as assets on their balance sheets), serviced the mortgages (by collecting the monthly payments, and so on), and accrued to their income statements any profits or losses that resulted from making the mortgage loan.

No more! While this way of doing mortgage business is very profitable when interest rates are stable, it creates real problems for the lending institutions when interest rates become volatile because during times of volatile interest rates, institutions originating and holding mortgage loans frequently find themselves with a mismatch of assets and liabilities. Savings and loans (S&Ls) raise money by offering savings accounts, NOW accounts, checking accounts, and short-term certificates of deposit, all of which are sources of *short-term funds*. Mortgage loans, on the other hand, are long-term loans (30 years being the most popular term). Thus institutions making mortgage loans often borrow short-term funds and then relend those funds at a higher long-term interest rate.

Example: A financial institution can borrow money at 6% by offering its CDs to investors. It might lend money to home buyers at 9%, initially making a 3-point spread over its cost of funds. As time passes, however, interest rates go up sharply. The financial institution then finds itself paying 12% to borrow money through its short-term sources of funds (CDs, NOW accounts, and the like) to support a 9% outstanding mortgage loan made several years previously. Thus the institution is losing 3 points per year on this mortgage loan.

The dramatic increase in short-term interest rates in the late 1970s and early 1980s caught many financial institutions in this type of asset/liability mismatch. This mismatch was, in turn, a major reason that a record number of S&Ls closed (and are still closing) their doors.

In response to this problem, the mortgage institutions looked for ways to mitigate the risk of asset/liability mismatches. The solutions they have devised have taken two principal forms:

1. Issuing adjustable rate mortgages.
2. Securitizing mortgage loans.

Adjustable Rate Mortgages. An *adjustable rate mortgage* (ARM) differs from a traditional mortgage in that the interest rate charged to the homeowner is periodically adjusted to reflect market interest rates. Thus the interest rate on the mortgage loan is allowed to float up and down in line with the institution's cost of funds. The rationale is that, when the bank has to pay more to its depositors to attract funds, it can in turn pass the higher costs on to the homeowners and thus maintain its *positive yield spread.*

The adjustable rate mortgage, however, is not a perfect hedge. For one thing, how much the interest rate charged on a given mortgage can be increased over a one-year period and over the life of the mortgage loan is limited—usually 2% and 5%, respectively. Also, the hedge is further weakened by timing differences between when the bank's cost of funds increase and when it can pass those costs on to the homeowners.

Aside from being an imperfect hedge, ARMs also have problems from a marketing point of view. Borrowers, except for those who have difficulty qualifying for a mortgage, have shown a clear preference for traditional fixed rate mortgages. Thus ARMs are not the ideal answer to the mortgage institutions' asset/liability mismatch problem.

Securitizing Mortgages. The second alternative available to a mortgage institution is to sell the mortgages it originates to investors. By doing so, the financial institution can keep the lucrative mortgage origination fees and the very profitable mortgage servicing business, while gaining two benefits:

- Transferring *both* the interest rate risk and credit risk to the investor.
- "Recycling" its capital by selling the mortgage as soon as it is issued. The institution uses the capital to make another mortgage loan, earn another origination fee, and add another mortgage to its lucrative servicing business.

However, selling individual mortgages is very difficult because they are an unattractive investment to many potential investors for the following reasons:

1. *A high minimum investment:* Most individual mortgages are for many tens of thousands of dollars, making them too large for many potential individuals.

2. *Unusual loan amounts:* Mortgage loans are often made in unusual amounts (such as $83,765.34), which makes them cumbersome and unattractive to many.

3. *Assessing the credit risk involved:* Most investors lack the time, resources, and expertise to do the property appraisals, employment verifications, credit checks, and other things necessary to accurately assess the credit risk inherent in an individual mortgage.

4. *Illiquidity:* There is no ready market for individual mortgages. An investor who purchases a mortgage and later wants to resell it might have a problem reselling it quickly at a fair price.

5. *Accounting headaches:* A traditional mortgage is a *self-amortizing* investment; in other words, each *monthly* payment is part principal and part interest. Adding complexity is the fact that the percentage of each varies from month to month. An MBS is also a *self-liquidating* investment in that investors receive their principal back as part of the monthly payments. The self-liquidating nature of MBSs makes many investors uncomfortable with them.

6. *Prepayment problems:* Almost all mortgages can be prepaid by the borrower at any time without penalty, and so investors in an MBS can never be sure of their investment's "maturity."

For these reasons a liquid market for individual mortgages never developed until the mortgage institutions started "securitizing" their mortgage portfolios. *Securitizing* mortgages means taking individual mortgages and turning them into readily marketable securities that are easier to analyze and trade. In the case of mortgages, the securitization process begins when an institution sells mortgages to a sophisticated financial *intermediary* (a process that will be explained later). By selling the mortgage to the intermediary, the institution effectively recycles its capital.

Participating Certificates. The intermediary combines various mortgages into pools and resells *undivided* interests in the pools to investors (just as owners of a co-op apartment buy percentages of interest in the whole building). These undivided interests are called *participating certificates* (PCs). The intermediary then receives the mortgage payments from the homeowners (from the servicing organizations) and passes them through to the investors on a proportional basis. The intermediary also guarantees investors that, if any of the underlying mortgages should go into default, the intermediary will pay investors all the principal and interest to which they are entitled.

By having the intermediary create these certificates, several of the problems associated with investing in individual mortgages are solved:

1. The minimum investment is reduced to $25,000. In addition, numerous mutual funds that invest in participation certificates allow investors to participate in this market with a minimum investment as low as $1,000.

2. These mutual funds also allow investors to invest any amount of money (over the minimum) in this market. No longer are investors limited to irregular investment sums.

3. Investors do not have to check the credit rating of the homeowners. The intermediary performs all the necessary credit checks and backs up its work by guaranteeing all of the mortgages it uses to back its PCs. Thus, from the investor's point of view, the credit strength of the PC comes not from the homeowner and the property involved, but from the credit strength of the intermediary. This is probably the biggest advantage that investing in PCs offers relative to investing in individual mortgages.

4. After these PCs started to be issued in large numbers, a very liquid market developed. Today, they are some of the most liquid securities available.

However, pooling individual mortgages into PCs does not solve all of the problems associated with investing in mortgages:

1. The accounting problem is not solved in that both principal and interest are still passed through to the investors on a monthly

basis, and the percentage of each changes from month to month. Participation certificates are also self-liquidating.

2. The prepayment problem also remains unsolved in that the underlying mortgages can still be prepaid at any time. So the investor still does not know the weighted maturity of the underlying mortgage portfolio.

Collateralized Mortgage Obligations. A *collateralized mortgage obligation* (CMO) goes one step further than a PC. In a CMO offering, the intermediary buys a portfolio of individual mortgages. Instead of combining the mortgages into pools and selling participating interests in those pools, however, the intermediary uses the mortgages as collateral for a more traditional bond offering, that is, bonds that pay interest every six months and return all principal at maturity.

Bonds issued as a CMO generally come in different *tranches* or *classes,* usually three to five per offering. The classes differ with regard to their *interest rate* and *maximum maturity date.* When the yield curve is positively sloped, the class of bonds with the shortest maximum maturity (usually called the "class A" bonds) offer the lowest coupon. Each subsequent class has a longer maximum maturity and a higher coupon.

Example: If an intermediary assembles a $1 billion portfolio of mortgages yielding 10%, it might structure a CMO offering so that it includes five classes of bonds, each of which includes $2 billion face amount of bonds, with the following yields and average maturities:

Hypothetical CMO Class Maturity and Yield Schedule		
Class A: Yielding 8.00%	To be fully paid off in	3 years
Class B: Yielding 8.50%	To be fully paid off in	6 years
Class C: Yielding 9.00%	To be fully paid off in	12 years
Class D: Yielding 9.50%	To be fully paid off in	20 years
Class E: Yielding 10.00%	To be fully paid off in	30 years

These CMOs pay "interest only" every six months like a traditional bond. There are no monthly payments of principal—making the accounting easier than the accounting for PCs.

Instead, all of the principal (both the regular principal that is paid as part of the mortgages' amortization and any principal repayments) is first used to pay off the Class A bonds. After the Class A bonds are fully retired, the principal is then applied to retiring the Class B bonds, and so on.

Although the different classes have so-called "maximum maturities," most, if not all, of the bonds in a given class are usually retired prior to their maximum maturity date. The maximum maturity date is calculated by assuming that there are no prepayments of principal and that the only source of principal for retiring bonds is the normal amortization of the mortgages.

Investing in a class of CMO bonds has two advantages over investing in a PC. First, the accounting is simpler. Second, investors have greater control over the maturity of their investment.

In exchange for this simplicity and control, investors who purchase the bonds in the shorter-term CMO classes accept a lower yield than they would receive from investing in a PC.

The Major Intermediaries. The major intermediaries that package individual mortgages and resell them as PCs and CMOs are as follows:

The Government National Mortgage Association (GNMA) buys pools of VA-guaranteed and FHA-insured mortgage loans. Both the principal and interest of GNMA securities are backed by the full faith and credit of the U.S. government. The securities offered by the GNMA are commonly referred to as "Ginnie Maes." The Government National Mortgage Association is part of the federal system that encourages and supports home ownership.

The Federal Home Loan Mortgage Corporation (FHLMC) buys conventional mortgages that are not guaranteed by the VA or FHA. The FHLMC itself guarantees the timely payment of interest and the ultimate payment of principal. The securities issued by the FHLMC are commonly referred to as "Freddie Macs." The Federal Home Loan Mortgage Corporation is also part of the federal system that encourages and supports home ownership.

The Federal National Mortgage Association (FNMA) buys a variety of mortgages from lenders and reoffers them to investors. FNMA used to be a government agency but was sold to the public. Now it is one of the largest publicly traded corporations listed on the New

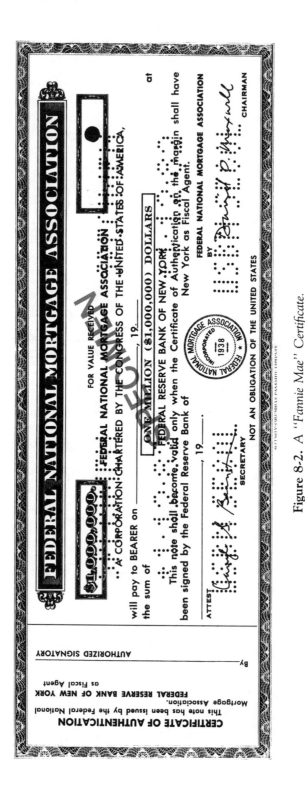

Figure 8-2. A "Fannie Mae" Certificate.

124

York Stock Exchange. Securities offered by the FNMA are commonly referred to as "Fannie Maes."

In addition, many of the larger mortgage companies and investment banking firms sell mortgage securities under their own name with private insurance backing.

Zero Coupon Bonds

A *zero coupon bond* (ZCB) is a bond that is originally sold at a discount to (that is, less than) its face value. The difference between the price at which investors acquire the bond and the price at which they dispose of it represents the entire return. A zero coupon bond makes no periodic interest payments.

Example: A five-year zero coupon bond with a $1,000 face value, yielding 6%, would be priced at $747.26. The difference between the $747.26 purchase price and the $1,000 maturity value ($252.74) represents the investor's return. (See Table 9-1.)

As a ZCB approaches maturity, it increases in value, but its value does not increase in equal annual jumps. Instead, the value is "accreted" over the life of the bond. That is, the market value is computed as if the bond paid interest and the interest was compounded, even though no interest is actually paid or compounded.

The same factors that affect the market value of a coupon bond influence the market value of ZCBs, namely changes in market interest rates, in the credit quality of the bond, in the tax treatment of the bond, and in the "popularity" of the vehicle relative to other investment vehicles.

Table 9-1. *Annual Value of a Zero Coupon Bond as It Approaches Maturity.*

Value of Bond at End of Each Year	Year	Interest Rate	Value of Bond at Start of Each Year
$1,000.00	5	6%	$943.40
$ 943.40	4	6%	$890.00
$ 890.00	3	6%	$839.62
$ 839.62	2	6%	$792.09
$ 792.09	1	6%	$747.26

Why Issue Zero Coupon Debt? Corporate issuers, municipal issuers, as well as the U.S. government and its agencies, have all issued zero coupon instruments. Some examples of such instruments are Treasury bills, Series EE U.S. savings bonds, and the whole collection of "strip securities."

When does financing with zeros make sense?

First, ZCBs offer a way for issuers to borrow money for a fixed term without having to make periodic interest payments to bond holders. If the borrower wants to use the bond proceeds for building a new plant or some other activity that will not generate positive cash flow for a number of years, then financing with zeros makes sense. The new plant will not generate positive cash flow for a number of years, and the debt used to finance construction will not require servicing for a number of years—a convenient match.

Second, an issuer might be able to borrow money at a lower cost by issuing ZCBs instead of some other kind of debt. The reason is that investors might be willing to accept a lower yield in exchange for the convenience that ZCBs offer.

Why Investors Buy Zero Coupon Bonds. Investors buy zero coupon bonds for a number of reasons including:

• Convenience.
• Elimination of reinvestment risk.

Zero coupon bonds are tough to beat for convenience. You invest a number of dollars today and receive a greater number of dollars at a fixed day in the future. Zero coupon bonds provide a simple way to fund a specified and determinable future liability.

Example: Suppose an investor needs $10,000 a year for four consecutive years starting ten years from today to fund a child's college education. That investor can buy 40 zero coupon bonds today with maturities that coincide with the future liabilities: specifically, ten bonds maturing per year, for four consecutive years, starting in ten years.

So for a fixed cost today you can conveniently fund a future liability, *assuming you know what that future liability will be.* This is a very important point because if, in ten years, college costs more than $10,000 a year, then investing in these 40 ZCBs will obviously not fund this liability.

In exchange for this "simplicity," the investor must accept a lower return. The yield of a U.S. government ZCB is usually the lowest yielding of any security with a comparable maturity.

Also, for small investments, zeros offer a practical way to earn a competitive return on the small investments.

Example: If an investor purchases (for her IRA) two coupon bonds at par, yielding 8% a year, then every six months she receives $80 of interest. How does she reinvest such a small sum as $80 for a competitive return? Even money market funds often have a $500 or $1,000 minimum.

Zeros solve the problem of reinvesting small sums by automatically compounding the "coupons" internally. In so doing they eliminate the reinvestment risk and provide investors with great leverage.

Buying and Selling Zeros. Because these bonds sell at a discount— and often at a large discount—the price you pay for such a security is extremely important. Some firms have a policy of charging a point ($10) commission on each bond sold. For a regular coupon bond selling for about $1,000 this commission is only 1% of the purchase price. For a ZCB, however, this same $10 can represent a much higher percentage of the purchase price. Therefore it's essential to check a number of dealers for prices before buying or selling a zero coupon bond.

9

Mutual Funds

Three of the most important rules for a successful investment program are:

1. Never put all your eggs in one basket.
2. Don't invest in anything unless you fully understand it.
3. Don't invest in anything that you will not be able to monitor on an ongoing basis.

DIVERSIFICATION—USING MORE THAN ONE BASKET

No matter how careful you are when you research an investment opportunity, something unforeseen can always go wrong. If you buy a stock, the company's management may turn out to be crooks. If you buy a bond, one of the rating agencies may suddenly downgrade its credit rating. If you buy real estate, the property taxes may suddenly and unexpectedly increase.

Because there is always the chance of the unforeseen disaster befalling any investment, it's prudent to not risk all of your money in any one investment. So if you believe the stock market offers attractive investment opportunities, invest in a number of stocks, not just one. If you feel that way about the bond market, then invest in a number of different bonds. If you like the investment potential of real estate, buy property in a number of different locations.

This investment tactic of putting your money into different "baskets" is called *diversification*.

UNDERSTANDING THE INVESTMENT

You cannot decide whether a given investment is suitable for you unless you first fully understand it. If you don't really understand the intricacies of an investment, you can't make a valid judgment about whether it is inexpensive, fairly priced, or expensive. If you decide to make the investment in spite of your lack of expertise, you will be competing against other, far more knowledgeable, investors. When an expert competes against a novice, the expert almost always wins. So if you don't fully understand an investment—how it works, how you can profit from it, how you can lose money in it, and so on—you shouldn't risk any of your hard-earned money on it.

Monitoring the Investment

Markets are constantly moving and changing. News items and other events affecting the value of your investment occur 24 hours a day, 365 days a year. When something happens that influences the value of your investment, you have to respond quickly or risk suffering the adverse consequences of being the last to act. For example, suppose you own a stock and the company's management announces that, despite its earlier rosy projections, the company's earnings for the year are going to be sharply lower than expected. The market value of the stock will most likely drop—and drop quickly. If you are monitoring the news at the minute the announcement is made and react quickly, you might be able to sell the stock before its price falls too far. If you are not monitoring the news and thus do not react quickly, the stock might be down ten points before you even know what happened.

WHY MUTUAL FUNDS?

Unfortunately, many investors who want to invest in the stock, bond, real estate, or other markets *lack* one or more of the following:

1. the *resources* necessary to build a properly diversified portfolio. (It can take between $50,000 and $1,000,000 or more to build a properly diversified portfolio, depending on the market you are considering.)

2. the *expertise* required to differentiate the attractive investment choices from the unattractive ones. Many intelligent people within the securities industry, who spend their working lives studying the investment markets, have difficulty discerning attractive investment opportunities from unattractive ones with any degree of certainty. If you can donate only a few hours a month to studying the market, you will be at a severe disadvantage in this very competitive environment.

3. the *time and/or facilities* needed to monitor their investments. Because the markets move so fast, often just checking the values of your investments in the daily newspaper is not enough. Many news items that could have an impact on the value of your investment never make it to the evening news or into the newspapers. You not only need access to a continuous stream of information, you also need the capabilities to analyze, interpret, and act on it quickly before the next guy.

Of course, the last two problems can be solved by hiring a professional money manager to handle your investments and make your day-to-day investment decisions for you. You thereby free up time to do whatever you do for a living without having to worry about following the markets. Many wealthy individuals and pension plan fiduciaries do just that—hire money managers and, in effect, manage the managers.

While this approach may be attractive, good money managers do not come cheap. Top money managers demand and get salaries and bonuses well into the hundreds of thousands (or even millions) of dollars per year. Most of them also have a minimum account size ($100,000 and up) and/or a minimum annual fee ($5,000 per year per account and up). Because of these high minimums, most investors aren't in the position to hire personal money managers.

They can, however, obtain many of the same benefits of hiring a money manager by investing in a mutual fund. A mutual fund is, in simplest terms, little more than a collection of investors who pool their money and then *collectively* hire a money manager.

131

Example: If you and four of your friends were each to put $20,000 into an account and then hire a money manager to run the account as a single account, then you would collectively have the $100,000 that the money manager requires. From the money manager's point of view the account is handled as one account even though it is shared by five owners. All of the gains, losses, fees, and expenses are shared equally by the five participants since each investor has a 20% interest in the account.

If one of the participants wants to "cash out," the money manager is instructed to liquidate 20% of the portfolio and the individual who wants to cash out receives the sales proceeds. If the value of the original portfolio has risen between the time the account is started and when 20% of it is sold, the 20% is worth more than $20,000 and the investor has a profit.

Example: The value of the total account rises to $150,000. When 20% of the account is liquidated, the investor receives 20% of $150,000, or $30,000, which is equal to a $10,000, or 50% profit. If the value of the total account goes down, the investor receives 20% of the current value for a net loss on the original investment.

This "pooled account" approach is simple and straightforward for a few friends to use. But it becomes incredibly complicated for thousands or even tens of thousands of investors to share the same pooled account and to be constantly buying and selling interests in the pool. For this reason, when large numbers of investors pool their money for investment securities, it makes more sense to structure the pool as a mutual fund.

STRUCTURE OF A MUTUAL FUND

In a mutual fund, investors own *not* interests in the pool of securities but, rather, shares in the fund, which in turn owns the securities.

Example: Five investors own the pool of securities. If instead the fund issues 10,000 shares and sells them to the investors for $10 each, the manager has the same $100,000. Each share represents a 1/10,000th interest in the entire pool.

If the value of the pool goes up to, say, $150,000, then the value of each share rises to $15. If the value of the pool goes down, so does the value of the shares.

New investors can buy shares and current investors can sell shares at the current value.

ADVANTAGES OF A MUTUAL FUND

By investing in a mutual fund, investors benefit in a number of ways:

1. *Diversification:* They can buy an interest in a well-diversified portfolio with a small investment. Most mutual funds require a minimum investment of only $500 to $1,000. With just this small investment the investor buys a *proportional* interest in a portfolio that may contain thousands of different securities and have a total market value in excess of a billion dollars.

2. *Professional Management:* Even small investors have a manager to decide which investments to make and when to make them. They also have someone to monitor their investments on an ongoing basis.

THE MANAGEMENT FEE

Because the money manager's fee is usually based on a percentage of the total market value of the entire fund, the fee for each investor is very small. For example, management fees generally run between 0.25% and 3.00% of the fund's total asset value, with .50% or so being the most common management fee. (For an investor who invests $20,000 in a fund, the annual management fee is typically about $200, well below the minimum most managers charge for handling individual accounts.)

The size of the management fee (expressed as a percentage) is based on a variety of factors, including:

1. The size of the fund.
2. The type of investment vehicle in which the fund invests.

3. The fund's investment objectives.
4. The manager's prior track record.

Size of the Fund

Generally, the larger the fund, the less the percentage the manager charges because it is almost as easy to run a $200,000 account as it is to run a $100,000 account. (You just buy and sell twice as much of whatever it is you're going to buy and sell.) Additionally, as the fund gets larger, certain economies of scale can be obtained with regard to office space, telecommunications, and other operational expenses.

Type of Investment Vehicle

Certain investments are easier to manage than others. For example, real estate takes a lot of management (collecting rents, arranging for maintenance, dealing with tenants, and so on), and so the management fees for a fund that buys real estate exclusively are generally higher than those for a fund that invests exclusively in corporate bonds.

The Fund's Investment Objectives

If an investment objective is "to significantly outperform the market," then the manager has to spend more time trying to squeeze every single extra penny of profit out of the fund's portfolio by constantly trying to buy low and sell high. However, if the fund's investment objective is "to mirror the performance of the market," then all the manager has to do is buy a weighted average of stocks, bonds, and other vehicles and hold them with very little turnover. Presumably, this "basket" of investments will do as well or as poorly as the market. Since the first strategy is more active, a higher fee is justified.

Prior Track Record

If a portfolio manager has a proven record of above-average performance in both good markets and bad, he or she may be entitled to more compensation than an unproven newcomer.

FINDING THE "RIGHT" MUTUAL FUND

Trying to sift through the universe of available mutual funds to find the one that best suits your investment needs has become an almost overwhelming task. It was not always this way. Prior to the 1980s, mutual funds were not a particularly popular investment. Part of the reason for their lack of popularity was that most funds were very diversified and somewhat boring. These funds generally fell into one of a few categories:

1. Income funds.
2. Growth stock funds.
3. Income with growth.
4. Government bond funds.
5. Corporate bond funds.
6. Balanced funds (combination stock and bond funds).
7. Diversified international funds.

Now, however, a whole host of specialty funds is available, including funds that invest only in:

- Gold stocks
- Canadian mining companies
- The OEX option
- Mexican companies
- Japanese companies
- Long-term bonds of European companies
- Oil companies
- Mortgage-backed securities hedged with financial futures
- Debt denominated in Australian dollars
- Health care companies
- High-tech companies
- Telecommunication companies
- Floating rate notes
- Money market preferreds

Reading Mutual Fund Quotations

	Offer NAV NAV Price Chg.

MUTUAL FUNDS

Thursday, April 10, 1986

Price ranges for investment companies, as quoted by the National Association of Securities Dealers. NAV stands for net asset value per share; the offering includes net asset value plus maximum sales charge, if any.

Fund	NAV	Offer	Chg.	Fund	NAV	Offer	Chg.	Fund	NAV	Offer	Chg.
AARP Invest Program:				44 Wall St	4.04	N.L.+	.03	Val Tr	30.47	N.L.+	.27
Cap Grw	22.29	N.L.+	.23	44 WS Eqt	5.80	5.86+	.11	**Lehman Group:**		....	
Gen Bnd	16.20	N.L.	...	**Founders Group Funds:**				Captl	(z)	(z)	...
Ginnie M	16.16	N.L.	...	Growth	9.74	N.L.+	.09	Invst	(z)	(z)	...
Gro Inc	21.55	N.L.+	.10	Income	15.39	N.L.+	.08	Opprt	(z)	(z)	...
TxFr Bd	16.22	N.L.+	.04	Mutual	11.12	N.L.+	.13	Leverage	8.63	N.L.+	.07
TxF Shrt	15.50	N.L.	...	Special	32.12	N.L.+	.40	**Lexington Group:**			
ABT Midwest Funds:		.....		**FPA Funds:**				CpLdr fr	14.89	15.95+	.06
Emrg Gr	18.48	20.20+	.30	Capital	13.28	14.43+	.22	Gold Fd	3.68	N.L.-	.01
Growth I	13.42	14.67+	.13	New Inc	9.62	10.13+	.01	Gnma	8.11	N.L.+	.01
Int Govt	10.82	N.L.+	.01	Paramt	13.90	15.19+	.05	Growth	11.30	N.L.+	.08
LG Govt	10.92	11.38+	.01	Perennl	18.83	20.58+	.06	Resrch	18.91	N.L.+	.14
Sec Inc	11.01	12.03+	.02	**Franklin Group:**				**Liberty Family Fds:**		......	
Util Inc	15.15	16.57+	.05	AGE Fd	3.79	3.95+	.02	Am Lead	13.58	N.L.+	.12
Acorn Fnd	40.34	N.L.+	.29	Cal TxFr	6.99	7.28	...	Tax Free	10.47	N.L.-	.01
Adtek Fd	12.10	N.L.+	.16	Corp Csh	9.38	N.L.	...	US Gvt S	8.81	N.L.+	.01
Advest Advantage:		....		D N T C	11.44	12.33+	.14	Ltd Term	12.75	13.11-	.01
Govt	10.11	N.L.	...	Equity	6.76	7.29+	.08	Lndner Dv	24.53	N.L.+	.06
Growth	10.66	N.L.+	.08	Fed TxF	11.67	12.16-	.01	Lindner Fd	20.62	N.L.+	.06
Income	10.42	N.L.+	.03	Gold Fnd	7.88	8.50-	.09	LMH Fund	28.18	N.L.+	.11
Specl	10.34	N.L.+	.04	Growth	15.19	16.38+	.11	**Loomis Sayles Funds:**			
Afuture Fd	14.92	N.L.+	.15	Income	2.26	2.44	...	Cap Dev	24.14	N.L.+	.51
AIM Funds:				Ins TxFr	11.67	12.16-	.01	Mutual	23.61	N.L.+	.28
Conv Yld	13.33	14.26+	.03	MN Ins	11.70	12.19-	.01	**Lord Abbett:**			
Grnway	10.53	11.26+	.09	N Y Tax	11.54	12.02-	.05	Affilatd	11.20	12.08+	.13
HiYld Sc	10.08	10.78+	.01	OHIn TF	11.38	11.85-	.01	Bnd Deb	10.96	11.98+	.04
Summit	7.12	(z)+	.09	Optn Fd	6.28	6.77+	.04	Devl Gro	8.77	9.58+	.12
Alliance Capital:				Mich TF	11.35	11.82-	.01	Govt S	3.36	3.60+	.01
Alli Gov	9.44	9.99-	.02	US GvSc	7.51	7.82	...	TxF Natl	10.82	11.36	...
Alli HiY	10.38	10.98+	.01	Utilities	7.90	8.52+	.02	TxFr NY	10.99	11.54	
Alli Intl	20.78	22.71+	.24								
Alli Mtge	9.86	10.43	...								
Alli Tech	23.24	25.40+	.58								
Chem Fd	9.17	10.02+	.11								
Surveyr	(z)	(z)	...								
Alpha Fd	23.03	25.17+	.24								

Monday through Friday *The Wall Street Journal* and other financial publications list mutual funds' net asset values, offering prices, and net asset value changes from the market closings of the previous day. (A "Z" means that no quotation is available.)

Net Asset Value (NAV). Net asset value (NAV) is the intrinsic, or actual, value of a mutual fund's common stock that is based on stock prices at the close of trading. The NAV is computed once a day. The closing price of each stock in the fund's portfolio is multiplied by the number of shares held by the fund. Then the dollar value of each security in the portfolio is totaled, and the fund's debts and liabilities are subtracted. The net sum is divided by the number of shares outstanding. The result is the net asset value of the fund per share.

Example: In the quotations shown, the "Growth" fund under "Founders Group Funds" has a net asset value of 9.74 (that is, $9.74 per share). (The four funds listed under "Founders Group Funds" make up a family, with Founders as the sponsor.)

The net asset value per share now becomes the bid price of a mutual fund's share of stock, and it will change daily as the assets (i.e., the securities owned by the fund) change in value.

For a no-load fund, the NAV is both the bid and the offer—that is, the purchase and redemption price of the fund. For a fund that employs a load (a sales charge), the purchase price is the NAV plus the load. At redemption, it is only the NAV.

NAV Change. Any change in mutual funds quotations is measured from close to close.

Example: In the Founders Group Growth Fund, the change in net asset value from the previous day was +0.09 (that is, up nine cents). (Notice that the NAV is quoted in dollars and cents, not in eighths.)

Offering Price. The offering price is the net asset value plus the sales charge (if any). To figure the amount of the sales charge, simply subtract the net asset value from the offering price. For a no-load fund, the net asset value and offering price are the same.

Figure 9-2. *Mutual Fund Listings.*

- Biotechnology companies

- etc . . .

No matter which sector of the market appeals to you, a mutual fund probably invests exclusively in it. If you like the oil sector, you can invest in a fund rather than trying to pick your own oil stocks.

SALES AND DISTRIBUTION OF MUTUAL FUNDS

Mutual funds are distributed primarily two ways: directly to the public or through sales representatives.

No-Load Funds

First, the fund can sell shares to the public directly, usually by advertising itself in business newspapers and/or journals or direct mail. These types of funds are called *no-load funds* because the investors pay no sales commissions. When investors buy shares in a no-load fund, they pay exactly the current proportional interest in the pool.

Example: If each share represents 1/10,000th of the pool and the total pool is worth $123,400, then investors buying shares pay $12.34 per share ($123,400 ÷ 10,000). This $12.34 is called the *net asset value (NAV)*.

However, all the costs associated with the advertising of the fund—including the cost of developing and placing the ads, the cost of developing and printing sales literature, and the costs associated with the prospectuses—are paid by the investors themselves as part of the annual management fee.

Load Funds

Alternatively, the fund can hire stockbrokers and other licensed professionals to sell fund shares to the investing public. Of course, in that case, the fund has to pay the brokers sales commissions for their efforts. Like all costs of doing business, these costs are passed on to the ultimate consumers, that is, the investors. These charges can be structured in a number of ways.

First, and most commonly, the investor can pay a *front-end sales charge.* In this arrangement, up to 8½% of the money invested is subtracted by the fund before purchasing shares for the investor.

Example: If someone invests $1,000, only $915 would go to purchase shares at the current price ($1,000 less 8½%, or $85). Most of the $85 sales charge is remitted to the brokerage firm making the sale; the rest goes to partially cover the fund's overhead.

Because of the competition posed by no-load funds, many funds have reduced their front-end sales charges, with 4% being common. For larger sales, the fund often drops its percentage sales charge even more.

Example: A fund might have a front-end sales charge schedule like the one below:

Amount Invested	Percentage Sales Charge
$ 1,000–$ 10,000	4.0%
$ 10,001–$ 25,000	3.5%
$ 25,001–$ 50,000	3.0%
$ 50,001–$100,000	2.5%
$100,001 and over	2.0%

The dollar levels at which a lower sales charge is activated are called the *breakpoints.*

Many times an investor can devote a total amount that exceeds a breakpoint but is not able to invest the entire sum all at once. In this case, the investor signs a *letter of intent.* This letter states that the signer will invest a sum that exceeds a breakpoint over a period of time (not to exceed 13 months). In return, the investor receives the reduced sales charge, starting with the first dollar invested.

Example: If an investor wants to invest $1,000 a month for a year, the total investment is over $10,001 within a 13-month period. So the investor is entitled to receive a break on the sales charge from

4.0% down to 3.5%. If the investor does not buy over $10,000 worth of shares within the 13 months, he or she then has to pay the additional ½% sales charge.

Signing a letter of intent in no way obligates an investor to buy additional shares.

The other popular method for assessing sales charges is by means of a *back-end sales charge,* which is a charge paid when the investor sells shares. By assessing the sales charges on the back-end instead of the front end, all of the investor's funds can initially be used to purchase shares and thus to buy *more* shares. Often, if the investor holds the shares for a sufficient amount of time, the back-end sales charges are waived because the fund makes enough from its management fees to cover the costs of paying the broker. Thus a typical schedule for a back-end sales charge might be:

Years Shares Owned	Back End Sales Charge
1	4%
2	3%
3	2%
4 or more	1%

OPEN-END VS. CLOSED-END FUNDS

Funds also differ in how their shares are retired.

Open-end mutual funds stand ready to repurchase their shares at the current net asset value any time the investor wishes to sell. To obtain funds to pay the investor, the fund liquidates some of the securities in the pool. (In practice most funds keep a small portion of their funds in cash equivalents so that they do not have to liquidate securities at an inopportune time.) Thus investors in open-end funds can always sell their shares at the current net asset value.

Closed-end funds do not repurchase their shares for a predetermined number of years after they are first offered. If closed-end fund shareholders want to "cash in" their shares, they may sell them either on one of the exchanges or in the over-the-counter market. Because these shares trade freely their price is based solely on the relative supply of and demand for the shares. Although the market value of the shares can be above or below the fund's net asset value, historically closed-end funds have often sold at a discount. So, unless shareholders are willing to accept a price lower than NAV, they must wait until the fund is redeeming its shares at NAV.

For this reason closed-end funds are not very popular. In fact, for most investors, the term "mutual fund" has come to be synonymous with an open-end fund or no-load fund. This despite the fact that several other investment structures are also considered to be mutual fund investments under the law.

REGULATION OF MUTUAL FUNDS

The principal legislation regulating the creation and sale of mutual fund shares is the Investment Company Act of 1940. This act groups companies that pool investors' funds into three categories:

1. *Management companies*—companies that manage the open- and closed-end mutual funds already described.

2. *Unit investment trust companies*—companies that sell proportional interests in a pool of securities but do not actively trade the portfolio. Usually these companies buy portfolios of bonds that they do not trade and then let investors buy proportional interests in the entire pool. Because they do not trade the portfolio, the management fee charged by the fund is generally very low.

3. *Face amount certificate companies*—companies that collect installment payments from investors and then pay the investors a predetermined sum on a set future date. The difference between the amount the investor pays the fund and the amount returned to the investor represents the interest earned for the use of the funds.

SERVICES THAT MUTUAL FUNDS PROVIDE

Because the mutual fund business has become so competitive, many mutual funds offer a number of special services designed to make the fund more attractive than its competitors to investors. These services include:

- *Free switching within a family of funds:* Many management companies offer a number of mutual funds, with different investment objectives, that invest in a number of different investment vehicles. For example, Fidelity Management in Boston offers over 100 different funds. By allowing investors to switch their investment from one fund to another as market expectations or investment objectives change, these "families of funds" provide a very convenient way for investors to completely swap their portfolios with just one simple phone call.

- Many mutual funds automatically withdraw the monthly installment from the investor's bank account without the investor having to remember to write a check.

- Many mutual funds automatically mail to investors a predetermined sum of money each month. This feature is particularly attractive to retirees and others who are living on their investments.

- Almost all open-end mutual funds allow investors to automatically compound dividends and capital gains into additional shares of the fund.

- Mutual fund shares can be assigned as collateral for a loan.

- Mutual funds have highly visible and readily determinable track records so that potential investors can determine a management company's past performance. All open-end mutual funds are required to provide potential purchasers with prospectuses and semi-annual reports. In addition most major business publications (such as *Barrons, Forbes, Fortune, Financial World, Money Magazine*), as well as a number of handbooks, track the performance of the many, many mutual funds.

- *Free switching within a family of funds:* Many management companies offer a number of mutual funds, with different investment objectives, that invest in a number of different investment vehicles. For example, Fidelity Management in Boston offers over 100 different funds. By allowing investors to switch their investment from one fund to another as market expectations or investment objectives change, these "families of funds" provide a very convenient way for investors to completely swap their portfolios with just one simple phone call.

- Many mutual funds automatically withdraw the monthly installment from the investor's bank account without the investor having to remember to write a check.

- Many mutual funds automatically mail to investors a predetermined sum of money each month. This feature is particularly attractive to retirees and others who are living on their investments.

- Almost all open-end mutual funds allow investors to automatically compound dividends and capital gains into additional shares of the fund.

- Mutual fund shares can be assigned as collateral for a loan.

- Mutual funds have highly visible and readily determinable track records so that potential investors can determine a management company's past performance. All open-end mutual funds are required to provide potential purchasers with prospectuses, quarterly reports, and annual reports. In addition most major business publications (such as *Barrons, Forbes, Fortune, Financial World, Money Magazine*), as well as a number of handbooks, track the performance of the many, many mutual funds.

10

Margin Accounts

Clients do not always have to fully pay for the securities they purchase. Instead, they can pay part of the purchase price at the time of purchase and borrow the balance from their brokerage firm. The money that the client puts up is called the *margin,* and the borrowed funds are called the client's *debit balance.* Before borrowing money to buy securities, the client must sign a *margin agreement,* which provides the details regarding the firm's margin policy and opening a *margin account.*

The securities purchased with the borrowed funds serve as the collateral for the loan. Because the securities are not fully paid for, the firm making the loan holds them in its own name. Any time clients wish to have the securities delivered to them, all they have to do is pay off the loan. In this way, a margin account is like other loans: In a car loan, the bank holds the "pink slip" (the car's title) until the loan is paid off, or in a mortgage the bank holds the house's title until the mortgage is paid off. Like any other loan, the borrower (the client) pays interest on the loan.

LEVERAGE

Why would anyone want to borrow money (and pay interest) to buy securities? The answer is that the purchasers expect the value of the securities to rise at a greater rate than the interest expense incurred. That is, they hope to have a *positive* yield spread over the margin interest cost. If the spread turns out to be positive, purchasers leverage their return on investment (expressed as a percentage).

Example: You have been studying XYZ, Inc. and feel that its common stock, which is currently priced at $25 per share, will appreciate to $50 per share within a year. You can afford to invest about $2,500. You could, of course, simply buy 100 shares of the stock for $2,500, hold it for a year, sell it for $5,000, and make a $2,500 profit. This works out to be a 100% return on the investment. The formula for the return on an investment (ROI), expressed as a percentage per year, is:

$$ROI = (\text{Profit or loss per year/Original investment}) \times 100$$
$$= (\$2,500/\$2,500) \times 100 = 100\%$$

You can also margin your purchase by putting up 50% of the securities' purchase price yourself and borrowing the other 50% from your broker. In this case, you can invest a total of $5,000 and can buy 200 shares. Assuming your projections are right and the market value of the stock rises to $50 per share within a year, you will be able to sell your shares for $10,000.

Of course, from this $10,000 you have to pay back the $2,500 you borrowed and the interest incurred for the use of the borrowed money for the year. If we assume a 10% annual interest rate on the borrowed money, then the interest charge would be:

$$\$2,500 \times 0.10 = \$250$$

After you repay the loan and the interest, you still have $7,250 ($10,000 − $2,500 − $250), representing a profit of $4,750 ($7,250 − $2,500, the original investment). Expressed as a return on investment, this is:

$$ROI = (\$4,750/\$2,500) \times 100 = 190\%$$

This is a significantly higher rate of return.

If you can earn a higher rate of return by margining your portfolio, why not *always* use margin? There are several reasons.

First, *margin is a two-edged sword.* While the rate of return is enhanced if the stock appreciates sharply, your losses are also leveraged if the stock's value declines.

Example: You buy 2,000 shares of XYZ for $25 per share on 50% margin, and the value of the stock drops to the $20 level at the end of a year. You have a substantial loss. The sale proceeds are $4,000 (200 × $20). From the sale proceeds, you need to repay the loan and the interest, a total of $2,750, for a net of only $1,250. Thus a 20% decline in the value of the stock costs you 50% of your initial investment.

Second, *if the price of the stock stays flat, you lose.* Because you are incurring interest charges all the time your securities are margined, the price of the stock has to rise just for you to break even.

Example: In the preceding example, you incur $250 of interest expense over the cost of the year. Since you own 200 shares, the price of each share has to rise by $1.25 ($250/200) to $26.25 for you just to break even.

Third, *not all securities are marginable.* The securities that generally can be margined include:

- Securities listed on a major exchange.
- Certain over-the-counter stocks (generally the larger and more widely traded ones).
- U.S. government and agency securities.

So if a security is not attractive enough to warrant borrowing money to buy it, investors probably shouldn't risk their hard-earned cash on it either.

REGULATION T

Despite these drawbacks, many investors hold the belief that "if it's worth buying, it's worth margining." To some, it might even seem as though the less money they put up, the more attractive the investment will be. If you put up half the money and borrow the other half, the rate of return is enhanced if the price rises. If you put up 25% of the purchase price and borrowed the other 75% and, again, the market value of the stock rises sharply, your rate of return is even higher. In fact, the more money you borrow, the higher your return on investment, because lower margin means higher leverage.

Example: You buy 200 shares of XYZ, Inc. for $25 per share. But you put up only 10% of the purchase price in cash ($500) and borrow the other 90% from your broker ($4,500). If the value of the stock rises to $50 per share in a year, the sale proceeds are, again, $10,000. From this amount, you have to subtract the debit balance ($4,500) and the interest charge ($450), leaving you with a profit of $4,550 ($10,000 − $4,500 − $450 − $500 original investment). The return on investment is:

$$ROI = (\$4,550/\$500) \times 100 = 910\%$$

If you can get such returns by using 10% margin, then why not do it? The answer is that, as of this writing, you cannot legally put up less than 50% of the purchase price of a stock. The rule that regulates the amount of margin you have to deposit to buy stock is part of *Regulation T* (Reg T), as adopted by the Federal Reserve Board.

This regulation, as well as the very creation of the Federal Reserve Board itself, stems from past margin excesses. Prior to the early 1930s, there was no minimum restriction on the amount of margin that a client had to post. Many banks willingly lent clients 90% to 95% of the value of their stocks. Thus an investor could buy a dollar's worth of stock with just a nickel. If the value of the stock rose by just 5%, the investor could use the increase in value as collateral for another dollar's worth of stock. This "pyramiding" meant that even people with average incomes built tremendous portfolios—and assumed equally tremendous amounts of debt.

Of course, if the value of the stock fell by just 5%, the investor's entire deposit was wiped out. The market crash of 1929 was blamed to a large degree on the over-extension of credit fostered by such low margin requirements. When the market started to drop, many investors were forced to sell because they did not have any additional cash to put into the market. This selling pushed prices down, which caused more people to have to sell and so on. The result was a full-blown selling panic that triggered the Great Depression.

INITIAL MARGIN REQUIREMENT

The 50% requirement is called the *initial margin requirement* since it is the amount of money that Reg T requires clients to deposit initially when they buy a stock. (Other types of securities have different margin requirements.)

Example: You buy 200 shares of stock at $25 per share and put up the minimum amount of margin. Your account looks like this after the purchase:

Value of securities	$5,000
Margin	$2,500
Debit balance	$2,500

What happens if the market value of the stock declines? If the value of the stock drops by $5 per share over the next month, then at the end of the month the account looks like this:

Value of securities	$4,000
Margin	$1,500
Debit balance	$2,500

As you can see, as the market value of your stock drops, so does margin. The debt, of course, is still there. Debt plus margin equals the value of the securities. At this point you no longer have 50% of the security's market value on deposit and your debit balance exceeds your margin.

Does this mean that you immediately have to deposit more margin into the account so that:

• The amount of margin again equals the debit balance (which would require a deposit of $1,000), or

• The amount of margin again equals 50% of the stock's market value (which would require the deposit of an additional $500)?

147

MAINTENANCE MARGIN

The answer is no. While the law requires an initial deposit of 50% margin, it does not require that you always maintain 50% margin. Instead, the law, recognizing that the market value of stocks can vary over time, is more flexible after the initial 50% margin has been deposited. For the client to have to deposit additional margin into the account, the margin balance has to drop to less than 25% of the market value of the securities in the account. This 25% is set by the self-regulatory organizations (SROs), such as the NYSE or NASD, and can be changed as the SROs deem it to be necessary to avoid the over- or under-extension of credit for stock purchases.

Example: The value of the stock drops by $5 a share and the client's account looks like this:

Value of securities	$4,000
Margin	$1,500
Debit balance	$2,500

The client's margin balance is still above the 25% threshold: ($1,500/$4,000) × 100 = 37.5%.

In fact, the value of the securities has to drop all the way to about $3,333 (approximately 16⅝ per share) before the client is below the 25% minimum.

Once the margin balance in the client's account drops below this 25% minimum, the firm issues the client a *maintenance call,* usually by telegram. After this call is issued, the account owner has 10 business days to deposit enough funds to make the margin level in the account equal to 25% of the security's market value.

EXTENSIONS AND SELLOUTS

If the funds are not received on time, the firm can either sell enough of the client's securities to reestablish the 25% minimum margin level *or* apply to the exchange or NASD for a two-business-day extension. If the firm applies for an extension on its client's behalf and the extention is granted, and yet the required funds are still not in the account two business days later, the firm has no choice but to liquidate a portion of the client's holdings.

Example: The value of the stock continues to decline until it is worth just $3,000. The client's account looks like this:

Value of securities	$3,000
Margin	$ 500
Debit balance	$2,500

Since $500 is less than 25% of $3,000, a maintenance call is issued for $250, which would bring the margin level up to $750— 25% of $3,000. (Don't forget—once this call is issued, it must be met, even if the value of the stock rises to $100 per share the next day.) If the client does not or cannot come up with an additional $250 dollars, the firm has to sell enough of the client's stock so that the 25% minimum is reestablished. If the firm sells $1,000 worth of the client's stock and uses that sales proceeds to pay off a portion of the client's margin loan, the account looks like this:

Value of securities	$3,000 − $1,000 = $2,000
Margin	$ 500 − 0 = $ 500
Debit balance	$2,500 − $1,000 = $1,500

The 25% minimum would be restored.

House Calls

Nothing prevents a firm from requiring a higher margin level than the minimum. In practice, almost all brokerage firms require that their clients maintain minimum margin levels of 30–35%. Firms raise the minimum margin requirements to make sure of two things: that clients are not overextending themselves and that their loans to their clients always remain fully collateralized.

If the client's margin level drops below the firm's margin minimum, the firm issues a *house call* (so called because the brokerage "house" is calling for additional margin to be deposited to meet its own requirements. The only difference between the two types of calls is that a sharply rising market can save a client from having to meet a house call. If the market value of the stock rises to the point where the margin balance meets the firm's minimum requirement, the house call is cancelled.

SHORT SALES

Short sales have to be done in a margin account.

Let's quickly review how a short sale works. A client sells a security that he or she does not own but instead has borrowed from the brokerage firm. If the value of the security declines, the short seller can then repurchase the security at the lower price, return it to the firm from whom it was borrowed, and keep the difference as profit.

Example: XYZ is now trading at $50 per share. A new president takes over the company, and you believe he is making some poor decisions. As a result of those decisions, you expect the value of the company's stock to decline to $30. To profit from this stock's decline, you:

• Borrow 100 shares from your broker.
• Sell them at the current price of $50 a share.
• Wait for the price to drop to $30 per share.
• Buy 100 shares at $30.
• Return them to your broker.
• And net a profit for yourself.

The risk in a short sale is that the market value of the stock will rise and thus force the investor to buy the security back for a higher price than the sale price.

Initial Requirement

For short sales the initial margin requirement is the same: 50% of the security's market value. However, the sale proceeds are also deposited in the client's account. These proceeds generally cannot be reinvested by the client because they have to be used at some point to repurchase the security. (The firm itself generally invests these funds in a money market fund to offset the costs and overhead it incurs in obtaining the securities for the client to borrow.)

Example: If a customer sells short 100 shares at 50, he or she must deposit all of the proceeds of the short sale plus another amount equal to 50% of the short sale proceeds. In this case, the proceeds are $5,000 (100 shares × $50 per share) plus $2,500 (50% of the $5,000). The account looks like this:

−$5,000	Short market value
+$7,500	Credit balance ($5,000 proceeds plus $2,500)
+$2,500	Equity (margin)

The *equity* ($2,500) is equal to the market value (−$5,000) and the credit balance (+$7,500).

If the stock falls to 40, the account looks like this:

−$4,000	Short market value
+$7,500	Credit balance
+$3,500	Equity (margin)

The margin now required for this account is 50% of the new market value (50% of $4,000) or $2,000. The actual equity is $3,500. The difference ($1,500) is an SMA (excess equity) of $1,500, which may be withdrawn. If the customer withdraws the SMA, the account looks like this:

−$4,000	Short market value
+$6,000	Credit balance
+$2,000	Equity (margin)

If, instead of going down to 40, the stock rises to 70 per share, the account would look like this:

−$7,000	Short market value
+$7,500	Credit balance
+$ 500	Equity (margin)

The credit balance rises because the client is short and the market value of the stock has risen.

MAINTENANCE REQUIREMENTS

The maintenance requirement for short positions selling at 16¾ and higher is 30%. (Some firms establish even more stringent requirements, up to 35% or 40%.) Look at the preceding three examples. The maintenance requirement (figured at 30%) for each is:

$1,500 (30% × $5,000)
$1,200 (30% × $4,000)
$2,100 (30% × $7,000)

In the first two examples, the equity exceeds the requirement. The equity in the third example is $500—beneath the requirement; so this account is on maintenance call for $1,600.

SPECIAL MEMORANDUM ACCOUNT

The *special memorandum account* (SMA) is used by brokerage firms to preserve a client's "buying power." If the trades in a margin account are profitable, the client will have excess margin or equity in the account—that is, more than the 50% required by Reg T.

Example: Long 500 shares of XYZ, Inc., purchased at $60 per share. This purchase ($30,000) requires a minimum of $15,000. After the customer makes the purchase, and meets the initial requirement, the account looks like this:

Long market value	$30,000 (+)
Debit balance	15,000 (−)
Equity	$15,000

Let us assume that XYZ then rises to $80 per share. The account now shows:

Long market value	$40,000 (+)
Debit balance	15,000 (−)
Equity	$25,000

(This customer now owns stock worth $40,000 but still owes the broker only $15,000).

The initial requirement for a $40,000 account is an equity of $20,000 (50% of $40,000). Note that the account now has an equity of $25,000. This is $5,000 greater than the requirement. This "extra" or excess equity is known as SMA (special memorandum account).

With several exceptions, this SMA can be sent to the customer, thereby increasing the debit used to buy additional securities without putting up additional cash. The SMA can be used to purchase *twice* its amount in additional securities. Let's explore both uses—

If we send the customer the $5,000 SMA the account will then look like this:

Long market value	$40,000 (+)
Debit balance	20,000 (−)
Equity	$20,000

Since we sent the customer cash, this naturally *increases* the customer's debit balance, and *decreases* her equity. We have now "used" the SMA and there no longer is any excess equity. Note that the equity is now 50% of the market value.

If, instead of sending the customer cash, we use the SMA's buying power (twice the amount of the SMA), the customer can purchase an additional $10,000 worth of securities without putting up additional cash. After this purchase the account will look like this:

Long market value	$50,000 (+)
Debit balance	25,000 (−)
Equity	$25,000

The customer has purchased $10,000 of additional securities and has not deposited any additional cash. This transaction increases both the long market value, *and the debit,* by $10,000 each. Note that the equity is now 50% of the market value and, again, the SMA has been exhausted.

11

Options

The buyer of an option acquires the *right* to:

- Either *buy* or *sell* a certain *quantity* of a stock, stock index, bond, bond index, commodity, currency, or futures contract (the *underlying security* or *instrument*).
- At a certain *price* (the *strike price*).
- Up to a specified point in time (the *expiration date*).

Options that give the investor the right to *buy* the underlying instrument are called *call* options; the investor has the option of "calling" it away from the seller of the call option. Options that give the investor the right to *sell* the underlying instrument are called *put* options; the investor has the right to "put" the instrument to the seller of the put.

LEVERAGE

Options provide investors with a superlative way to *leverage* their investment dollars, that is, obtain the greatest percentage of return on an investment.

Example: XYZ, Inc. common stock is currently trading at $42 a share, and you expect that its price will rise to $50 a share within the next six months. What is the best way to profit from the expected increase in XYZ's market value?

There are several ways to do so. First, you can simply buy 100 shares of XYZ, Inc. in your cash account. If you buy 100 shares this way, your cost is $4,200. Your profit, if you eventually sell the shares at $50 each (that is, for $5,000), is $800 over the six-month holding period: 19% ($800/$4,200) × 100.

You can also buy the stock on margin (if the stock is marginable). If you buy 100 shares on margin, you spend $2,100 (50% of the purchase price), and you borrow the other $2,100 from the broker. After selling the 100 shares for $5,000, your profit is the same $800, minus six months of margin interest. Assuming a margin interest rate of 8%, then the interest cost is $84 ($2,100 borrowed × 0.08 annual interest rate × 0.5 year), leaving a net profit of $716. However, since you invested only $2,100, the return on your investment is much higher, working out to be 34% over the six-month holding period ($716/$2,100 × 100). The return on investment is higher because you leveraged it by using margin. Of course, if the market value of the stock drops, you also leverage your losses.

There is, however, a third way to profit by XYZ's increase in value. If XYZ, Inc. is one of the many companies on which listed options trade, there is a way to achieve even greater leverage. Assuming that listed options do indeed trade on XYZ, you can buy an "XYZ 40 call" option. This option gives you the right *to buy 100 shares of XYZ, Inc. any time during the next six months at a price of $40 per share ($4,000 for the 100 shares)*. Let's also assume that the price of this option is $400. Since you have acquired the right to *buy* the underlying security, the option is a call option.

The seller (or *writer*) of this option receives the $400, in exchange for standing ready to sell you 100 shares of XYZ, Inc. for $4,000 any time you choose to buy it until the option expires. Since this is a six-month option, you can notify the seller that you intend to force him to deliver the underlying security (the 100 shares of XYZ, Inc.) in exchange for the $4,000 any time during the next six months. Forcing the seller to honor the terms of the option contract is called *exercising* the option.

Assume you buy the option and the price of XYZ rises to $50 a share within the next six months. You may exercise the option (that is, force the seller to deliver to you 100 shares of XYZ at $40 a share) and then sell the same shares in the open market for $50 a share ($5,000).

Thus you make a substantial profit. You pay $400 for the option, but you make $1,000 by purchasing and then immediately selling the 100 shares of XYZ. Effectively, you receive a $600 profit on a $400 investment resulting in a 150% profit over six months.

Let's consider another example. Instead of buying a call that gives you the right to buy 100 shares of XYZ, Inc. at $40 per share, you buy an option that entitles you to buy 100 shares at $45 per share. Instead of $400, the option costs $50.

If again the price of the stock rises to $50 a share, you can:

• Exercise the option.
• Buy the 100 shares from the option seller for $4,500.
• And immediately sell the shares for the current market price of $5,000.

You make a net profit of $450 ($500 profit minus the $50 cost of the option). That represents a return on the original investment of 900%. That's leverage!

ARBITRAGE WITH OPTIONS

You do not, however, have to exercise an option to profit from it.

Example: If the price of the stock rises to $50 per share, then an option to buy 100 shares at $40 per share is worth at least $1,000. If an option is selling for less than $1,000, a sharp investor can make an immediate and guaranteed profit. In this case, let's say that the option is selling for $800. You can buy the option, immediately exercise it (that is, buy the stock for $4,000), immediately sell the stock for $5,000, and realize a $200 profit ($1,000 profit on stock − $800 price of option).

This transaction is a form of arbitrage. Professional arbitageurs are always looking for this kind of opportunity and quickly bid up

---

Understanding Options Quotations

On the facing page is an excerpt from the options section of the financial news. Let's look at the elements.

Underlying Stock. The first column lists the underlying stocks in alphabetical order. Below the name of each company is the day's closing price on the exchange on which the stock is traded. The closing price is repeated for each option series traded on the stock.

Strike Price. The second column lists the strike prices. Notice how they occur in multiples of 5—and, in some cases, in multiples of 2½. Notice also how the strike prices approximate the closing price of the underlying stock. (For underlying stock whose price is over $200, option strike prices occur in multiples of $10.)

Calls and Puts. The next six columns reflect the current expiration cycles for calls and puts. The figures under these column headings are the premiums as of the close of business for the day. In most cases, they reflect a dollar value that has to be multiplied by 100 (shares) to arrive at the dollar cost of the option.

Example: The Alcoa Jul 25 call closed at 4¼, or $4.25. To get the dollar total of the premium, multiply by 100: $4.25 times 100 shares equals $425 for the total cost of the call. The letter symbols in the price columns are explained at the bottom of the newspaper page:

- "r" means "not traded."

- "s" means "no option offered."

- "o" means "old."

Example: Look at a few of the entries in quotations.

- The Alcoa Apr 40 call has an intrinsic value of 2⅞ (stock price of 42⅞ less the strike price of 40). Yet its last trade was at 3⅝. The ¾ point is time value.

- The AT&T Jul 22½ put is ⅛-point in the money (strike price of 22½ less stock price of 22⅜). Its premium of 1¼-point is almost pure time value. The AT&T Jul 30 put is not traded (r), and the October is not even offered (s).

Volume and Open Interest. At the bottom of all the listings for each exchange are tabulations of volume and open interest for puts and calls.

- *Volume* represents the total number of contracts, puts or calls, trading on the exchange for the day.

- *Open interest* is the total number of open positions at the close of trading, which have not been closed either by exercise or covering purchases.

Figure 11-1. *Understanding Options Quotations.*

MOST ACTIVE OPTIONS

Chicago

	Sales	Last	Chg.	N.Y. Close
CALLS				
SP100 Mar220	73012	1⅝	+ 1-16	214.79
SP100 Mar215	60377	3⅝	+ ⅜	214.79
SP100 Mar210	26724	6⅞	+ ⅝	214.79
SP100 Mar225	20760	½	— 1-16	214.79
SP100 Apr220	17243	4	+ ⅛	214.79
PUTS				
SP100 Mar210	59105	1 1-16	— ¼	214.79
SP100 Mar215	47491	2 15-16	— 7-16	214.79
SP100 Mar205	25188	5-16	— 1-16	214.79
SP100 Mar200	13863	⅛	....	214.79
SP100 Mar220	10011	5⅞	— ⅞	214.79

American

	Sales	Last	Chg.	N.Y. Close
CALLS				
MMIdx Mar320	13066	1¼	— 1-16	7.72
MMIdx Mar315	10414	2⅝	+ ⅛	7.72
MMIdx Mar305	7012	7¾	+ ⅜	7.72
MMIdx Mar310	6401	4¾	+ ⅜	7.72
Texaco Apr30	4280	1 1-16	+ 1-16	29⅛
PUTS				
MMIdx Mar305	5443	2⅜	— ⅞	7.72
MMIdx Mar310	4825	4⅛	— 1⅛	7.72
MMIdx Mar300	3494	1 1-16	—11-16	7.72
MMIdx Mar295	2675	½	— 3-16	7.72
MMIdx Apr270	1236	1-16	....	7.72

Philadelph

	Sales	Last
CALLS		
AnheusB Mar45	2748	2⅛
AldSig Jun50	2518	2¾
VL Idx Mar230	1759	2½
McDln May17½	1757	1⅛
AnheusB Jun45	1629	4
PUTS		
F N M Jun30	1449	1¾
VL Idx Mar225	1203	5-16
Waste May40	892	⅞
McDln May15	813	⅞
PhibroS Apr40	740	1-16

Option & NY Close	Strike Price	Calls-Last Mar	Calls-Last Jun	Calls-Last Sep	Puts-Last Mar	Puts-Last Jun	Puts-Last Sep
RalPur	45	10	r	r	r	r	r
55¼	50	5⅝	r	7½	1/16	r	r
55¼	55	1	3¼	4¾	1	2⅜	r
55¼	60	r	1¼	2¾	r	r	r
Sears	35	9¼	10	r	r	r	r
44⅜	40	4⅜	5⅜	5¾	1/16	11/16	1¼
44⅜	45	13/16	2¼	3¼	1¼	2½	3
44⅜	50	s	15/16	1⅝	s	r	5½
SwAir	20	2½	r	r	⅛	r	r
22¾	22½	⅞	2⅜	r	r	1⅜	r
22¾	25	⅛	1¼	2	2⅝	3⅜	r
Syntex	30	20¾	r	s	r	r	s
51½	37½	r	16	s	r	r	s
51½	42½	9	r	s	1/16	r	s
51½	45	6⅜	8⅜	8½	1/16	¾	2
51½	50	2½	4⅞	6½	¾	1¾	r
51½	55	5/16	2½	3½	3½	4¾	r
Tektrn	45	15½	r	s	r	r	s
60¾	50	r	12	r	r	r	r
60¾	55	6½	r	r	r	r	r
60¾	60	1½	r	r	¾	r	r
60¾	65	r	2½	r	r	r	r
Toys	30	r	r	r	1/16	r	r
37⅞	35	3	4½	6	⅛	1⅛	1⅝
37⅞	40	⅜	1⅞	r	2¼	3⅝	r
37⅞	45	r	⅝	s	r	r	s
Viacom	50	7¼	r	r	r	r	r
57⅜	55	3	5¼	r	½	2½	r
57⅜	60	⅞	3⅜	5	r	r	r
57⅜	65	3/16	r	s	r	r	s
57⅜	70	⅛	r	s	r	r	s
WalMrt	25	10¼	r	11¾	r	r	r
36⅛	27½	7⅛	r	s	r	r	s
36⅛	30	6	6⅞	6⅞	1/16	½	⅞
36⅛	35	1 9/16	3⅛	4	11/16	1⅝	2

Option & NY Close	Strike Price	Calls-Last Apr	Calls-Last Jul	Calls-Last Oct	Puts-Last Apr	Puts-Last Jul	Puts-Last Oct
→ Alcoa	35	r	r	r	1/16	r	r
42⅞	40	3⅝	4¼	r	7/16	r	r
42⅞	45	1	1⅞	3	r	r	r
42⅞	50	r	⅞	r	r	r	r
AmGenl	40	1½	2¾	r	r	r	r
AGreet	35	1¾	r	r	r	r	r
→ AT&T	20	2⅜	2¾	3⅛	⅛	⅜	r
22⅜	22½	¾	1¼	1¾	⅞	1¼	1⅝
22⅜	25	3/16	9/16	¾	2¾	3⅛	3¼
22⅜	30	r	⅛	s	r	r	s
Apple	25	1½	2½	r	r	r	r
Avon	20	11	s	s	r	s	s
31	25	6	r	r	r	r	½
31	30	2	2 9/16	2⅞	½	r	r
31	35	¼	¾	1½	r	r	r
Beth S	15	r	5½	r	r	r	r
19¾	17½	r	3½	4	r	½	r
19¾	20	15/16	1 13/16	2⅜	⅞	1⅜	r
19¾	22½	⅜	⅞	1⅜	r	r	r
Burl N	70	7¼	9¼	r	⅜	r	r
77¼	75	3¾	6	r	r	r	r
77¼	80	1⅜	3	r	r	r	r
C N W	20	9¼	9½	s	r	r	s
29⅝	22½	7	r	r	r	r	r
29⅝	25	4⅝	5¾	r	¼	r	r
29⅝	30	1⅛	2½	3¾	1⅞	r	r
CIGNA	50	18	s	s	r	s	s
68¼	60	7⅝	9⅛	10	r	1¼	r
68¼	65	3⅞	6¼	r	1¼	r	r
68¼	70	1½	3¼	4¾	4	r	r

Option & NY Close	Strike Price	Calls-Last May	Calls-Last Aug	Calls-Last Nov	Puts-Last May	Puts-Last Aug	Puts-Last Nov
67¼	60	8	9¾	s	⅝	r	s
67¼	65	5¼	7¼	r	2	3	3¾
67¼	70	2⅝	r	r	r	r	r
67¼	75	1⅜	2¾	3½	r	r	r
Diebld	35	r	7	s	r	⅞	s
41¾	40	2⅞	r	r	1⅛	2⅜	r
41¾	45	1⅛	r	r	r	r	r
Edwrds	35	8	r	r	⅜	r	r
42⅝	40	4	5⅛	r	1	r	r
42⅝	45	2	2⅝	r	r	r	r
FptMc	15	r	1¾	r	⅝	1	r
15½	17½	⅜	¾	r	r	r	r
15½	20	1/16	¼	s	r	r	s
Gn Dyn	65	r	r	s	r	13/16	s
78¼	70	r	12	r	r	r	r
78¼	75	6	8¼	r	2	r	r
78¼	80	3¼	r	7	r	r	r
78¼	85	2	s	s	r	s	s
Harris	25	5¼	r	r	¼	r	r
29¾	30	1⅞	2⅝	r	2	r	2⅜
29¾	35	7/16	15/16	1¾	r	r	r
Hewlet	35	7	8	s	¼	1	s
41¼	40	3⅛	4⅜	6	1 7/16	2¼	3
41¼	45	1⅛	2⅜	3⅝	4⅝	4¾	r
41¼	50	5/16	1¼	1⅞	½	r	r
H Inns	50	14	r	s	r	r	s
64¼	60	5½	7	r	⅞	r	2¼
64¼	65	2¾	5	5	2¾	r	r
64¼	70	1¼	2½	r	r	r	r
Honwll	60	r	r	s	1/16	r	s
73⅞	65	10¼	r	s	½	r	s
73⅞	70	6¾	9½	s	1½	3	s
73⅞	75	3¾	6½	8½	3½	r	r
73⅞	80	2	3½	5½	6⅝	r	8
73⅞	85	1	r	r	r	r	r
73⅞	90	½	1⅞	s	r	r	s
Humana	25	r	7	s	3/16	r	s
31½	30	2½	r	r	1	1⅝	r
31½	35	9/16	15/16	2 1/16	4⅛	4¼	r
In Flv	35	r	4¾	r	r	r	r
38¼	40	13/16	1⅝	r	r	r	r
Limitd	20	15⅜	s	s	r	s	s
35¾	22½	13¼	s	s	r	s	s
35¾	25	r	r	s	3/16	r	s
35¾	30	5⅞	6⅞	7⅝	5/16	r	r
35¾	35	2¼	4	r	1¼	2¼	r
35¾	40	1⅛	2⅜	r	r	5¼	r
Medtrn	50	7¼	r	r	r	1¾	r
56¼	55	4⅛	6	r	2½	r	r
56¼	60	r	3½	5½	r	r	r
Mobil	25	3⅞	4⅛	4½	5/16	⅝	⅞
28½	30	⅝	1¼	1½	2¼	2¾	3
28½	35	⅛	5/16	½	r	r	r
N B I	10	r	r	r	r	9/16	r
N Semi	12½	1¾	2⅛	2⅞	5/16	11/16	15/16
13½	15	11/16	1 1/16	1⅝	2	r	r
13½	17½	¼	½	r	r	r	r
Nthrop	40	8½	9½	r	⅜	¾	r
47¾	45	4½	5¾	r	1¼	2¼	3¼
47¾	50	2 1/16	3⅝	r	r	r	r
47¾	55	⅞	s	s	r	s	s
Occi	22½	3	r	r	¼	⅝	¾
25⅛	25	1⅜	2	2¾	15/16	1½	1 13/16
25⅛	30	¼	9/16	1⅛	4⅞	5	5¼
25⅛	35	1/16	¼	s	9⅝	r	s
25⅛	40	1/16	r	s	r	r	s
Ow Ill	60	5⅛	6	r	r	r	r
64	65	3	4⅛	r	4	r	r
64	70	1	2	r	r	r	r

the price of the option until there is no profit left in the transaction, that is, until the price of the option is at least $1,000.

THE COMPONENTS OF AN OPTION'S PRICE

The premium of an option is expressed on a per-share basis. To arrive at the dollar amount you have to pay to own a stock option, multiply the quoted price by 100 shares of stock, which is the amount that the option entitles you to buy or sell.

Example: If an XYZ 30 put is selling 3, the buyer of this option has to pay $300—$3 times 100 shares of XYZ.

The premium of an in-the-money option has two components: intrinsic value and time value.

Intrinsic Value

The price at which the option owner is allowed to either buy or sell the underlying instrument is called the *strike price*. In the preceding examples the strike prices were $40 and $45, respectively. If the strike price of a call option is *below* the current market price of the underlying security, the option is said to be *in the money* since the option holder, by exercising the option, can buy the underlying security below its current market value. A call option that has the same strike price as the current market value of the underlying security is said to be *at the money*. A call option that has a strike price above the underlying security's current market price is said to be *out of the money*.

Example: With the underlying stock at $42.50, the call option with the $40 strike price is "in the money." The option with the $45 strike price is "out of the money."

For put options, the reverse is true. When the underlying stock's market price is below the put option's strike price, the put is in the money. When the stock and strike prices are the same, the put is at the money. If the stock's price rises above the strike price, the option is out of the money.

Example: An XYZ 40 put is in the money when XYZ stock is trading at 38. The option holder can buy the stock for 38 in the market and sell it to the put writer for 40. If XYZ is at 42, the put is out of the money. The holder would lose money by buying XYZ in the market and exercising the put.

The value that an option holder would receive by exercising the option—the in-the-money amount—is known as the *intrinsic value*. If the option is out of the money, the intrinsic value is zero. The market value of an option is always at least equal to the intrinsic value; otherwise, there would be arbitrage possibilities.

Time Value

Intrinsic value, however, is only one component of option pricing. The other is *time value*, which is equal to any part of an option's price in excess of the intrinsic value.

Example: If an option has a price of $5, they say the option's "premium" is $5, even if $2 of the price is intrinsic value.

Although not technically correct, this practice is so widespread that newcomers to the market should be aware of it.

How intrinsic value is determined is clear. Not so clear is how the market "adds" a premium value to the price of an option. To illustrate the concepts of premium and intrinsic value, let's consider two examples.

Example 1: The price of an XYZ 40 call option is 4 ($400), with XYZ trading at 42. The owner of this option can immediately recoup $200 of the option's price by:

• Exercising the option, that is, buying the stock at $4,000.
• And then immediately selling the stock in the open market for $4,200.

The option therefore has $200 of intrinsic value.

The premium is equal to the option's price less the intrinsic value, and it is also $200 ($400 − $200).

Example 2: An XYZ 50 put is selling for $2 when XYZ stock is trading at 52. Since the put is out of the money (the stock's price is higher than the strike price), the option has zero intrinsic value. So the $2 price of the put is pure premium.

Buyers of options are willing to pay premiums for options for several reasons. They get:

1. A potentially higher return on the dollars invested.
2. A limited amount of risk.
3. The ability to speculate with fewer dollars.

Higher Return. Options offer the possibility of making a very large return on an investment, compared to the profit that they can make by buying the underlying security.

Limited Risk. The most an option buyer can lose is 100% of the investment.

Example: The most the option buyers in our prior examples can lose is $400 and $500, respectively. In contrast, investors who buy 100 shares of the stock can lose thousands of dollars if the company goes bankrupt.

Speculation at Reduced Cost. It takes fewer dollars to speculate on the future market value of an underlying security.

Example: Many investors who would like to speculate that the market value of XYZ will rise may not have the $4,200 necessary to buy 100 shares in their cash accounts. However, these same investors may have $400 available to risk on an in-the-money XYZ call option.

Option Pricing

The premium therefore reflects the needs and expectations of market participants, that is, supply and demand. What the total price of an option "should be" is the result of a couple of influences:

1. Volatility of the underlying security.

2. Time remaining to expiration.

Volatility of the Underlying Stock. If the market price of the under-lying stock is capable of large and/or sudden swings, it is said to be *volatile*. In such cases, the likelihood that a price swing will bring the option into the money is regarded as better than on a less volatile stock. So the premium for an option on a volatile stock is also higher.

Example: Consider options on two stocks: Wizz Bang Computers and Fuddy Duddy Utilities. The market value of Wizz Bang's common stock swings wildly, depending on the company's latest successes or failures, while the market value of Fuddy Duddy Utilities remains relatively constant. If both stocks are currently selling for $33 a share and both have six-month call options available for a $1, the Wizz Bang options are a better buy because they have a better chance of providing a higher profit. Thus you should expect to pay a *higher premium* to buy the options of a *more volatile* underlying security.

Time Remaining to Expiration. The more time left to expiration, the more time there is for the price of the underlying stock to move so that the option is in the money and profitable. The part of an option's premium attributable to time remaining is known as *time value*.

Example: For two options, the prices of the underlying stock are $1 away from the strike prices. One option expires in a week, and the other in two months. All other things being equal, the second option (with the longer time to expiration) is the better investment.

Thus the longer the time remaining until the option expires, the higher the option's premium will be, because on expiration day no one will pay any premium to buy an option. Consequently, the amount of premium naturally decreases over time, and you need to take time into account when deciding what to pay for, or what to ask for, an option.

By some estimates as many as 90% of all options are unexercised. Time is therefore the natural enemy of option buyers and always on the side of the seller, or writer. Option buyers have to be right not only about the direction in which the price of the underlying security will move, but also when it will move. This timing factor stacks the deck against option buyers.

For this reason option buyers should have the financial resources and temperament to withstand many complete, albeit small, losses while seeking to achieve a few large gains. Option writers, on the other hand, by virtue of having time on their side, should be able to make many small gains while only occasionally suffering a large loss.

BREAKEVEN

The presence of intrinsic value in an option's price does not guarantee a profit. The total price of the option has to be considered when the contract is going to be exercised. For a call option, the price of the underlying stock must exceed the strike price at least by the amount of the option price. For a put, the opposite is true: The strike price must exceed the stock's price by the amount of the option's price.

Example 1 (*cont.*): The stock has to rise to $44 for the call option holder to break even: $40 strike price + $4 option price = $44 per share.

Example 2 (*cont.*): The stock has to fall to $48 for the put holder to break even: $50 strike price − $2 option price = $48 per share.

Of course, any time an option is in the money—that is, has any intrinsic value—at the expiration date, it is exercised. This is so even if the option holder does not profit from exercising the contract.

Example 1 (*cont.*): If the stock's price stays at $42 until the option's expiration date, exercising the contract gives the holder at least $200 back on the investment of $400 (the option's price): $4,000 purchase price through exercising deducted from $4,200 proceeds from selling the stock at the market price. The $200 is better than nothing.

Finally, any time the price of the stock is below the strike price at expiration, the option expires worthless. After all, the right to buy a stock at $40 isn't worth much if the stock is trading in the $20 range.

SELLING OPTIONS

So far we have looked at call options from the buyer's point of view. Let's now consider the seller's, or writer's, point of view.

Sellers can write *covered* or *uncovered* (that is, *naked*) call options. If the seller is long the corresponding amount of underlying stock, then the option is "covered." If the seller does not own the underlying stock, the option is "naked."

Example: With XYZ trading at 44, the owner of 100 shares of XYZ sells a six-month XYZ 44 call for $4. This is a covered call. (If the writer did not own the stock, the call would be naked.) The buyer of this option is betting that the price of the stock will rise more than 4 points ($400) over the next six months.

The seller benefits in two ways: a partial hedge against price decline and additional income.

Example: If the market value of XYZ declines to $40, the seller is protected against the loss by the $400 income received for the option. If XYZ continues to decline, of course, the seller is exposed to loss. Thus the $400 revenue from the sale of the option provides partial downside protection.

If, over the next six months, XYZ's price remains the same, the option is not likely to be exercised. So the $400 "premium" revenue represents incremental return on the investment—the option expires worthless.

In exchange for these benefits, the call writer has to be ready to sell the buyer 100 shares of XYZ at $44 any time during the next six months. If XYZ's price increases the option is likely to be exercised.

When is an option a "better deal" for the buyer, and when is it a "better deal" for the seller? The answer depends on the investment objectives of each party to the contract and on the future market value of the underlying security.

No one would write a call option for a stock that is expected to rise sharply over the option period. Sellers write call options only if they expect that the market price of the underlying stock has a high probability of either staying flat or going down.

Example: If the writer of the XYZ 44 call thought the stock was going to rise to $50 a share, he wouldn't sell the option—or at least he wouldn't sell it at 4. Thus the net effect of the covered call write is as follows:

The Buyer	*The Seller*
• Buys the option.	• Sells the option.
• Pays the premium.	• Gets the premium.
• Receives no income	• Receives income.
• Acquires the right to buy the underlying stock.	• Incurs a potential obligation to sell the underlying stock.
• Expects the price of the underlying security to rise.	• Expects the price of the underlying security to fall or to remain constant.
• Receives no hedge.	• Receives a hedge if owns the underlying security.

PUTS

Let's look at another example using a put option.

Example: You own 100 shares of MNO, Inc., which is currently trading at 23. You are concerned that the market value of MNO's stock will decline, want to take some steps to protect yourself against the possible decline, but do not want to sell the stock outright.

You can write a call against this position, but this strategy provides only a partial hedge against a price decline. Also, if you sell a call, you limit your upside potential; if the market value of MNO stock rises, you have to sell your stock to the owner of the call at the option's strike price.

As an alternative strategy, you can buy a put.

Example: A put gives you the right to sell 100 shares of MNO at the strike price until the option's expiration date. A three-month MNO 20 put is selling for $0.50, and a three-month MNO 25 put is selling for $3.75. Given these two choices, which better suits your objectives? You can either pay $50 and have the right to sell your stock at $20 per share, or pay $375 and have the right to sell your stock at $25 per share. If the price of the stock drops to $10 per share, the net effect for each of these options is:

	MNO 20 Put	MNO 25 Put
Initial stock value	$2,300	$2,300
Cost of option	$ 50	$ 375
Price of stock put	$2,000	$2,500
Net gain or (loss)	($ 350)	($ 175)

If, however, the price of the stock drops to $22 per share:

	MNO 20 Put	MNO 25 Put
Initial stock value	$2,300	$2,300
Cost of option	$ 50	$ 375
Sale price of stock	$2,200	$2,500
Net gain or (loss)	($ 150)	($ 175)

If, however, the price of the stock rose to $35 per share:

	MNO 20 Put	MNO 25 Put
Initial stock value	$2,300	$2,300
Cost of option	$ 50	$ 375
Sale price of stock	$3,500	$3,500
Net gain or (loss)	$1,150	$ 825

Thus you can see that buying the put option with the $20 strike price is a better buy if the market value of the stock rises despite your concerns. The put option with the $25 strike price is a better buy if the market value of the stock declines. The option with the $25 strike price is already $200 in the money since the market value of the stock is currently $200 *less* than the strike price.

The sellers of these put options receive the premium and must stand ready to *buy* 100 shares of stock at the strike price any time prior to the options' expiration. The sellers can be either speculators or investors who want to partially hedge a short position in the underlying security (analogous to covered call writing).

TRADING OPTIONS

Options are traded on many of the major securities exchanges (listed options), as well as in the over-the-counter market.

Listed Options

Most individual stock options, stock index options, and futures options trade on one of the major exchanges, such as the Chicago Options Exchange, the New York Futures Exchange, the Philadelphia Stock Exchange, the American Stock Exchange, and so on.

Listed options are traded in a way similar to how listed stocks are traded.

1. Each option has a bid price and an asked price, which are determined by the same factors that determine the bid and asked prices of any securities—supply and demand.

2. The trading takes place at a trading post, and each option has a specialist assigned to provide liquidity and to maintain an orderly market.

3. The premiums have minimum price moves.

Example: For individual stock options, the minimum premium move is usually $12.50 (⅛-point).

Other types of options have other minimum price moves. The minimum price move for each type of option is usually shown in the major business newspapers.

4. Listed options come only with standardized strike prices:

• Strike prices are set at 2½-point increments if the price of the stock is less than $25.

Example: If the price of the underlying stock is currently $15, the option strike prices are $10.00, $12.50, $15.00, $17.50, $20.00, and so on.

- Strike prices are set at 5-point increments if the price of the underlying stock is between $25 and $200 per share.
- Strike prices are set at 10-point increments if the price of the underlying stock is currently over $200 per share.

For other types of option contracts, strike prices are set at even intervals. They can be obtained from the exchange where the security is listed or from any major business newspaper.

5. Expiration date and distance between strike prices are also standardized. Most options run in quarterly cycles, meaning that they expire in cycles as follows:

- January/April/July/October.
- February/May/August/November.
- March/June/September/December.

Example: If a stock has an option that expires in January, it also has options that expire in April, July, and October.

By convention, options need to be exercised before the third Saturday of the month in which the option expires, no matter what date the third Saturday turns out to be.

6. All trades are settled through the listed Options Clearing Corporation (OCC). By acting as an intermediary between buyers and sellers, the OCC in effect guarantees to each party that the options will be honored and that obligations incurred by all parties to options transactions will be met. In other words, when buyers exercise their options, the ultimate responsibility for delivering the underlying securities falls to the OCC.

It is also up to the OCC to collect the underlying security from the other party in the transaction, through the other party's broker; this is not the responsibility of the option's owner. Therefore buyers need not concern themselves with the creditworthiness or character of the other party to their option transactions.

The OCC also handles the *assignment* of option exercise notices. In other words, if you bought a call option and want to exercise your option—that is, actually buy the security at the option price—it falls to the OCC to decide which brokerage firm has to deliver the underlying security. The firm selected is usually the one with the oldest outstanding short position.

The firm receiving the delivery notice then selects the actual client to receive the exercise notice, usually at random. It's up to the firm to make sure that the client delivers the underlying security. If for any reason the client doesn't deliver the security, then the firm itself has to make delivery. In the event the firm doesn't, then the OCC must deliver. Again, as far as the buyers and sellers of the options are concerned, the responsibility starts and stops with the OCC.

The bid and asked prices of various options can be found daily in the financial section of any major newspaper.

OVER-THE-COUNTER (OTC) OPTIONS

Over-the-counter options trade primarily on currencies and on individual bonds.

Each of these options contracts is the direct result of negotiations between the buyer and the seller. They can agree on any strike price, any expiration date, and any premium that is mutually agreeable. Hence the advantage of OTC options is that the contract can be customized to meet the individual needs of the option's buyer and seller.

The disadvantages of the over-the-counter option market are threefold:

1. Getting accurate price information is very difficult, and thus the possibility exists for either the buyer to overpay for the option or for the seller to undersell it. For this reason, the over-the-counter market is the arena of sophisticated investors with independent means (usually sophisticated computer-based pricing systems) of determining an option's mathematically correct value.

2. The options, once purchased, are very hard to resell because no ready market exists. While listed options are generally very liquid, OTC options are not.

3. There is no clearing house to guarantee OTC option transactions, and thus credit risk can become a problem in this market.

SPECIAL OPTION CONTRACTS

Over the last decade the types of listed option contracts have exploded. Not only has the number of listed contracts on equities increased, but also the number of contracts on foreign currencies, stock indexes, and options on futures contracts. Figure 11-2 shows a partial list of the options that were trading as of the beginning of 1987.

Figure 11-2. *Types of Listed Option Contracts.*

```
Options on Stock Indexes
    New York Stock Exchange Composite Exchange
    Standard & Poors 100 Index
    Standard & Poors 500 Index
    Major Market Index
    Computer Technology Index
    Oil Index
    Institutional Index
    National OTC Index
    Value Line Index

Options on Currency Indexes
    Australian Dollar
    British Pound
    Canadian Dollar
    German Mark
    Japanese Yen
    Swiss Franc

Bond Options
    Treasury Notes—6⅝ of 1992
    Treasury Bonds—12 of 2013
    Treasury Bonds—7¼ of 2016
```

Stock Index Options

Stock index options are based on an underlying stock index. A stock index is a mathematical expression of the value of a collection of stocks. For example, the New York Stock Exchange Index is an index that reflects the change in market value of all the stocks traded on the exchange. "Buying the index" is effectively the same as buying a portfolio composed of all the common stocks that trade on the New York Stock Exchange.

The value of the index, like the values of both stocks and bonds, is quoted in points, but each point equals $500.

Example: If the value of the index is 150.00, the dollar value of the index is $75,000 (150 × $500). If the value of the index rises to 150.15, the dollar value is: $75,075 (150.15 × $500).

The NYSE Index options allow you to buy and sell both calls and puts on the value of this index.

Example: The current value of the index is 150. Yet you feel that the market price of the average stock on the NYSE is going to rise by 10% over the next six months (and that therefore the value of the index is going to rise by 10%). How do you profit from this move? You could either:

1. Buy a small quantity of every common stock listed on the exchange.
2. Or buy a call option on the index.

Of course, buying a small quantity of every stock on the exchange would require over 1,700 separate transactions and transaction costs of more than $40,000. As an alternative, buying a call option takes one transaction and costs perhaps $50.

Assume that the six-month call option with a strike price of 152 is 2¼. Then, if the value of the index rises by 10% from its 150 starting price to 165, the net effect of the transaction is:

Cost of option	2.25 × $500 = $ 1,125
Exercise option at the strike price	152.00 × $500 = $76,000
Sell option at the then current market price	165.00 × $500 = $82,500

Net profit = $82,500 − ($76,000 + $1,125)
Net profit = $5,375

Return on investment = $5,375/$1,125 = 477.78%

To facilitate settlement, the option (like all stock index options) uses *cash settlement*. It's impossible to actually deliver a portfolio composed of all the stocks traded on the New York Exchange. So the losers pay the winners the amount of cash that the winners would have received had they actually exercised the option, received the stocks, and then sold them.

Example: If you are the call option buyer in the preceding example, you do not actually have to come up with $76,000 to exercise your option. Instead you simply pay the difference between the index's current market value and the strike price. In this case: 165 − 152 = 13 points × $500 per point = $6,500. After subtracting your initial cost of $1,125, you end with the same profit: $5,375.

Thus stock index options can be used to speculate on the price movement of a diversified portfolio.

They can also be used to hedge a large diversified portfolio.

Example: If you are managing a $75,000,000 portfolio that was composed primarily of NYSE-listed securities and are worried about a market decline, you can hedge the portfolio by buying NYSE index puts. By buying 1,000 NYSE index puts with a strike price of 150, you have a very good hedge: 1,000 contracts × 150 × $500 = $75,000,000. (Determining the optimal number of options to buy to hedge a portfolio is actually a rather complex process that is beyond the scope of this text.)

Other stock index options are based on different portfolios but the theory remains the same. By buying or selling the options, the investor can buy or sell the equivalent of the underlying portfolio or hedge an entire portfolio. If the portfolio to be hedged is made up primarily of OTC stocks, the portfolio manager would use the NASDAQ Index Option. The investor who wants to speculate on the future of the computer industry can buy calls on the computer index. And so on.

TREASURY BOND OPTIONS

A bond option gives you the right to buy or sell 100 of the underlying bonds at the strike price. Of the many Treasury bonds in the marketplace, only a few have listed options available at any one time. For this reason most bond options are still traded OTC, primarily between the primary government bond dealers and their institutional clients.

12

Forwards and Futures

In simplest terms, a *forward* or *futures contract* is simply an agreement in which a buyer and a seller agree to consummate a transaction at a predetermined time in the future at a price agreed upon today.

THE FORWARD CONTRACT

Consider the case of the corn farmer who's about to plant a summer corn crop. The farmer estimates that it will cost $1.50 per bushel to grow the corn and also that the crop will be 100,000 bushels during the summer. The farmer can enter into a contract with a food processor (the buyer) to sell the anticipated 100,000 bushels of corn at a price that represents a profit *before the crop is even planted.*

Example: The farmer and the food processor agree that the farmer will sell 100,000 bushels to the food processor for $2.00 a bushel on September 1 (five months later), regardless of the price of corn at that time in the cash market. The *cash market* (also known as the *spot market*) is the price at which corn is being sold on that day for immediate delivery.

If the farmer actually does grow 100,000 bushels and if the cost of growing the corn actually turns out to be $1.50 a bushel, then the farmer will have a profit for the year of 100,000 bushels × $0.50, or $50,000.

By agreeing today on the price of the corn, both the farmer and the food processor can benefit. The farmer is assured of a ready buyer for the crop five months from now, at a price that he considers to be fair. The food processing company knows what it will be paying for corn well in advance of when it actually purchases the corn and can use this information to help it in its ongoing corporate planning. For example, let's say that the food processor is Kellogg and the company is going to use the farmer's corn to make corn flakes. By knowing the cost of its raw material (corn), Kellogg is better able to determine what it has to charge for its product, how much advertising it can afford to do, how many food coupons it can afford to distribute, and so on.

Of course, in farming, where Mother Nature is both a major and an unpredictable factor, anything can happen.

Example: The summer corn crop turns out to be a poor one and, because of supply and demand pressures on the market, the price of corn on the open market rises to $2.25 in five months. The farmer misses out on additional profit potential. Having entered into the forward contract with Kellogg, the farmer is obligated to deliver the crop to Kellogg at $2.00 a bushel—despite the fact that, if he had waited until harvest time to sell the crop, he could have sold it at $2.25 a bushel. Thus he receives $200,000 for the crop when he could have received $225,000 had he waited to sell.

By the same token, suppose the summer corn was a bumper crop and the price in the cash market on September fell to $1.75 a bushel. Then the food processing company would effectively be over-paying the farmer by $0.25 a bushel (or $25,000 for the 100,000 bushels), and the farmer would have a $25,000 windfall.

So by agreeing to enter into this type of contract, *both parties limit both their potential risk and their potential reward.*

The type of contract in which a *specific* seller agrees to deliver a "crop" to a *specific* buyer at a fixed future price and on a specific date in the future is called a *forward contract.* This contract was (and in some cases still is) prevalent in agriculture and ranching.

However, there are some problems associated with forward contracts. Since only two parties are involved in the transaction, each is dependent exclusively on the other for performance of the contract. Suppose the farmer presold the crop to a food processor but the food processor went broke prior to taking delivery of the corn—or worse, *after* taking delivery but *before* paying for the corn. The farmer would then be faced with the very problem he was trying to avoid by originally entering into the contract. Likewise, if the farmer went bust, the food processing company would have to scramble to find alternative, and possibly higher-priced, sources of corn for its corn flakes.

Another potential problem with forward contracts is that the farmer may have either underestimated or overestimated the size of the crop or the expenses in raising it.

Example: If the farmer is able to grow only 80,000 bushels of corn, he would have to go out and buy 20,000 bushels of corn in the cash market at higher prices in order to honor his 100,000-bushel forward contract. Thus the farmer might have to buy 20,000 bushels of corn at $2.25 per bushel for the sole purpose of selling those same bushels for $2.00 to the food processor for a net loss of ($0.25 × 20,000 bushels), or $5,000.

Similarly, if expenses should rise suddenly during the growing season, the farmer may find that it costs more to grow a bushel than originally estimated. Many a farmer has realized halfway through a growing season that it was going to cost $2.10 per bushel to grow a crop already sold for $2.00 per bushel, guaranteeing a loss for the year.

By the same token, of course, surplus crops and cost containment can enhance the farmer's bottom line.

Unfortunately a forward contract, by its very design, is an inflexible document. Even if the farmer or the food processor realizes that a mistake was made after entering into the contract, little can be done to correct the mistake. Thus both parties to forward contracts often try to find other, more flexible ways to hedge their business risks.

THE FUTURES CONTRACT

A futures contract, by virtue of its flexibility, solves some of the problems associated with forward contracts and, as such, is usually considered to be a better way to hedge a business risk. A futures contract, while similar to a forward contract, has some very important differences.

1. Exchange Listing. A futures transaction is generally handled on an exchange and not out in the field between farmers and food processing company representatives. Since an exchange brings a large number of buyers and sellers together in one location (either directly or indirectly via the use of brokers), there is a better determination about what a fair future price is for a given commodity. In a forward contract, a food processor in one part of a state might be paying less than a second food processor in another part of the state for an identical forward contract. Because each of two people in different parts of the state may be unaware of what the other is doing, either party—farmer or food processor—can be exploited. Using a futures contract as the principal hedging tool, however, all the farmers and food processors can compete directly in one location on the basis of the same information about prices, supply, and demand. Thus a market creates a future price that more accurately reflects total supply and total demand for a given economy and allows for faster and more accurate dissemination of price information.

2. Elimination of Credit Risk. By using an exchange-listed futures contract, instead of a forward contract, both parties all but eliminate the credit risk inherent in futures contracts. In exchange-listed futures transactions, both the buyers and the sellers never know who is on the "other side of their transactions." The clearing corporation (see chapter on operations) serves as an intermediary in all the transactions. Sellers sell to the clearing corporation and buyers buy from the clearing corporation. So if a food processor goes broke, the farmer still gets paid and vice versa.

The performance of all futures contracts is guaranteed by the full faith and credit of the owners of the exchanges and the clearing houses. These owners include the largest brokerage firms in the world. As we shall see, these brokerage firms take steps to protect themselves from credit risk as well.

Figure 12-1. *A Commodity Trading Floor (notice the steps leading down into the pit).*

3. Standardization. Unlike forward contracts, futures contracts are standardized. Forward contracts can be drawn up for any commodity, in any amount, in any quality, for delivery at any time that is mutually agreeable to both the buyer and the seller. Exchange-listed futures contracts, however, require the delivery of a specific quantity of a specific commodity that meets minimum quality standards at predetermined dates.

4. Marking to the Market. The losses or gains of forward contracts are not paid until the contract comes due.

Example: The farmer presells the corn crop to Kellogg, via a forward contract, at $2.00 a bushel, and the cash price of corn rises to $2.25

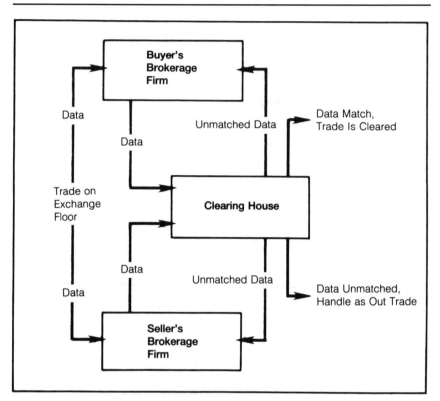

Figure 12-2. *The Relationship of the Clearing House to the Buying and Selling Brokerage Firms.*

by harvest time. The only "loss" the farmer takes is on the day that he fulfills the contract and receives $2.00 a barrel instead of $2.25. If the farmer, instead of honoring the forward contract, sells the corn to a third party at $2.25 a bushel, Kellogg has to start expensive and time-consuming legal actions to recoup its losses.

With a futures contract, however, any gains are received every day. Specifically, if the price of the underlying commodity moves away from its agreed-upon price in the contract (the exercise price), the party losing as a result of that price move must pay the one benefiting by it. Such payment, called *marking to the market,* is made every trading day.

Figure 12-3. Representative Futures Contracts.

Underlying	Trading Months	Contract Size	Minimum Price Fluctuation	Exchange
Wheat (hard red winter)	Mar/May/July Sept/Dec	5,000 bushels	$0.0025 per bu. ($12.50)	Kansas City Board of Trade
Cattle, Live	Feb/Apr/Jun Aug/Oct/Dec	20,000 pounds	$0.0025 per lb. ($5)	Mid-American Commodity
U.S. Treasury Bonds	Mar/June Sept/Dec	$100,000 face value 8% coupon	1/32 point ($31.25)	Chicago Board of Trade
Standard & Poor's 500 Stock Index	Mar/June Sept/Dec	500 × S&P stock index value	5 points ($25)	Chicago Mercantile Exchange/and Option Division
U.S. Dollar	Mar/June Sept/Dec	$100,000 U.S. dollars	$0.0001 ($10)	Toronto Futures Exchange
No. 2 Heating Oil (New York)	All months	42,000 gallons	$0.0001 per gal. ($4.20)	New York Mercantile Exchange
Japanese Yen	Jan/Mar/Apr Jun/July/Sep Oct/Dec, and spot month	12,500,000 Japanese yen	$0.000001 per Japanese yen	Singapore International Monetary Exchange

FUTURES PRICES

Thursday, April 10, 1986.

Open Interest Reflects Previous Trading Day.

GRAINS AND OILSEEDS–

CORN (CBT) 5,000 bu.; cents per bu.

	Open	High	Low	Settle	Change	Lifetime High	Lifetime Low	Open Interest
May	228½	229½	227	228	– ¼	291¼	222½	33,049
July	220¼	221¾	218½	219¼	– 1½	286	218½	30,339
Sept	204¼	205¼	202¾	203	– 1¾	270	202¾	8,086
Dec	200½	201¼	199	199¼	– 2	235½	199	37,218
Mar87	209½	210¼	207¾	207¾	– 2	242½	207¾	5,283
May	213½	213¾	212	212¼	– 1½	242	212	1,423
July	215	215	212¾	212¾	– 1¾	222	212¾	175

Est vol 49,000; vol Wed 46,044; open int 115,573, +4115.

SOYBEANS (CBT) 5,000 bu.; cents per bu.

	Open	High	Low	Settle	Change	Lifetime High	Lifetime Low	Open Interest
May	525	529¼	521½	524¾	+ 1¾	657	489	23,833
July	521½	527¼	518½	522¾	+ 2¾	658	497	27,993
Aug	519½	526	517½	521¼	+ 2	609	498½	3,898
Sept	510½	514	508½	510	....	555½	496	3,265
Nov	509	511¾	504½	507¾	– 1	556½	498	19,093
Jan87	516¼	521	514	516¾	– ½	565	509	1,512
Mar	524½	529	522½	526	– ½	576	519½	1,367
May	531	533¼	527½	530½	– 1½	556	527½	142

Est vol 29,500; vol Wed 28,643; open int 81,115, +1,330.

SOYBEAN MEAL (CBT) 100 tons; $ per ton.

	Open	High	Low	Settle	Change	Lifetime High	Lifetime Low	Open Interest
May	154.40	156.00	153.50	154.90	+ 1.00	163.90	134.00	15,674
July	153.90	155.40	152.80	154.40	+ 1.00	167.00	134.00	13,588
Aug	153.20	154.80	152.30	154.10	+ 1.20	163.50	135.50	4,603
Sept	151.00	152.60	149.50	151.10	+ .60	159.30	137.50	3,306
Oct	148.10	149.00	146.50	148.50	+ .50	156.00	136.00	4,017
Dec	149.20	150.50	147.50	149.60	+ .40	157.00	136.00	6,910
Jan87	....	....	....	150.70	+ .50	157.50	136.00	820
Mar	....	....	....	151.00	....	159.00	149.00	275

Est vol 12,000; vol Wed 11,530; open int 49,193, –30.

SOYBEAN OIL (CBT) 60,000 lbs.; cents per lb.

	Open	High	Low	Settle	Change	Lifetime High	Lifetime Low	Open Interest
May	17.50	17.64	17.41	17.43	+ .02	27.45	16.76	16,734
July	17.77	17.97	17.72	17.75	+ .04	25.25	17.05	16,469
Aug	17.85	18.05	17.80	17.88	+ .06	25.15	17.16	5,659
Sept	17.95	18.07	17.95	17.95	....	24.05	17.10	2,959
Oct	18.05	18.15	17.95	17.97	....	22.80	17.25	3,666
Dec	18.45	18.55	18.35	18.40	....	22.50	17.51	7,714
Jan87	18.60	18.65	18.50	18.50	– .05	22.35	17.70	1,127
Mar	19.00	19.05	18.85	18.90	....	20.25	18.20	398

Est vol 12,000; vol Wed 20,055; open int 54,762, +170.

WHEAT (CBT) 5,000 bu.; cents per bu.

	Open	High	Low	Settle	Change	Lifetime High	Lifetime Low	Open Interest
May	[illegible]	298	285	286¾	– 9¼	350	274	5,224
July	250½	251	246	246¼	– 4½	310	246	16,154
Sept	252	253	248½	249	– 3½	299	248½	6,627
Dec	260¾	260¾	256	256	– 4½	308¼	256	5,442
Mar87	261½	261¾	257	257	– 4¾	287	257	614

Est vol 11,000; vol Wed 8,921; open int 34,105, –269.

WHEAT (KC) 5,000 bu.; cents per bu.

	Open	High	Low	Settle	Change	Lifetime High	Lifetime Low	Open Interest
May	280	281	272	273¼	– 8½	301	263½	3,898
July	242	242¾	239½	239½	– 2½	298½	239½	8,425
Sept	245½	245¾	243½	243½	– 2	281½	243½	1,633
Dec	253½	253½	253	252½	– 2	283	253	799
Mar87	....	....	....	256	– ½	259¾	256½	52

Est vol 2,962; vol Wed 3,115; open int 14,807, +143.

WHEAT (MPLS) 5,000 bu.; cents per bu.

	Open	High	Low	Settle	Change	Lifetime High	Lifetime Low	Open Interest
May	338½	340	336¾	336¾	– 3¼	363	318¾	3,368
July	300½	301¾	299½	300	– 2½	247½	294	1,454
Sept	276	276	273¾	274	– 2¼	350	273¾	1,221
Dec	282½	282½	281	281	– 2¼	302	281	335

Est vol 1,448; vol Wed 1,036; open int 6,378, –3.

BARLEY (WPG) 20 metric tons; Can. $ per ton

	Open	High	Low	Settle	Change	Lifetime High	Lifetime Low	Open Interest
May	90.00	90.90	89.60	89.60	– 2.30	130.00	89.60	2,585
July	89.50	90.30	89.50	89.50	– 2.70	119.17	89.50	2,513
Oct	86.50	87.10	86.40	86.40	– 2.30	106.00	86.40	2,759
Dec	87.00	87.80	86.90	86.90	– 2.50	99.50	86.90	1,749

Est vol 2,420; vol Wed 566; open int 9,606, –68.

FLAXSEED (WPG) 20 metric tons; Can. $ per ton

	Open	High	Low	Settle	Change	Lifetime High	Lifetime Low	Open Interest
May	281.80	281.80	279.70	279.70	– 2.10	352.50	279.60	2,739
July	289.20	289.20	287.30	287.50	– 1.70	326.20	287.30	1,426
Oct	293.00	293.10	291.20	291.70	– 1.80	333.80	291.20	1,144

	Open	High	Low	Settle	Change	Lifetime High	Lifetime Low	Open Interest
May	1,835	1,840	1,818	1,828	+ 13	2,422	1,792	5,480
July	1,880	1,889	1,865	1,878	+ 17	2,429	1,844	7,833
Sept	1,930	1,935	1,915	1,925	+ 17	2,430	1,891	3,373
Dec	1,972	1,974	1,960	1,965	+ 15	2,425	1,934	4,720
Mar87	2,004	2,014	2,000	2,003	+ 18	2,385	1,978	1,320

Est vol 3,064; vol Wed 2,547; open int 22,824, –49.

COFFEE (CSCE)–37,500 lbs.; cents per lb.

	Open	High	Low	Settle	Change	Lifetime High	Lifetime Low	Open Interest
May	224.50	231.75	233.25	227.96	+ 3.74	272.62	131.00	5,031
July	229.25	237.00	228.25	232.49	+ 3.77	278.38	135.50	5,451
Sept	234.50	239.28	233.00	238.76	+ 5.48	282.78	137.50	3,233
Dec	239.50	244.75	237.00	243.58	+ 4.83	287.10	138.00	1,600
Mar87	243.00	247.00	241.00	246.00	+ 4.10	290.33	156.75	700
May	251.00	251.00	251.00	249.50	+ 4.50	291.83	188.00	206

Est vol 2,987; vol Wed 2,139; open int 16,242, +182.

COTTON (CTN)–50,000 lbs.; cents per lb.

	Open	High	Low	Settle	Change	Lifetime High	Lifetime Low	Open Interest
May	62.05	62.35	61.60	61.65	– .90	70.00	58.80	2,647
July	62.90	63.10	62.57	62.65	– .48	70.05	56.05	5,787
Oct	39.05	39.20	38.80	38.85	– .30	65.50	38.50	1,705
Dec	38.95	39.15	38.80	38.81	– .35	59.25	38.45	9,459
Mar87	40.00	40.10	39.85	39.85	– .35	49.50	39.50	692

Est vol 3,000; vol Wed 4,119; open int 20,426, –297.

ORANGE JUICE (CTN)–15,000 lbs.; cents per lb.

	Open	High	Low	Settle	Change	Lifetime High	Lifetime Low	Open Interest
May	94.55	95.00	94.20	94.50	– .95	162.50	82.60	1,706
July	94.40	94.80	93.70	93.70	– 1.00	157.50	83.50	1,823
Sept	93.70	93.90	92.60	92.60	– 1.40	127.25	82.00	1,020
Nov	93.60	93.60	92.50	92.50	– 1.35	125.00	82.50	467
Jan87	93.00	93.00	92.10	92.10	– 1.00	113.00	83.75	270
Mar	93.25	93.25	92.90	92.85	– .80	122.00	83.90	948
May	94.00	94.00	94.00	93.20	– 1.20	94.75	84.50	665
July	....	....	....	93.70	– 1.10	95.00	84.75	306

Est vol 650; vol Wed 743; open int 7,205, –122.

SUGAR–WORLD (CSCE)–112,000 lbs.; cents per lb.

	Open	High	Low	Settle	Change	Lifetime High	Lifetime Low	Open Interest
May	9.45	9.45	8.85	8.91	– .46	9.58	3.58	31,072
July	9.45	9.45	8.65	8.74	– .61	9.50	3.79	27,053
Sept	9.39	9.42	8.83	8.83	– .50	9.42	4.05	357
Oct	9.38	9.40	8.80	8.80	– .50	9.40	4.02	42,446
Jan87	9.50	9.50	9.50	8.80	– .50	9.50	5.65	169
Mar	9.61	9.64	9.06	9.10	– .45	9.64	6.03	14,198
May	9.80	9.82	9.25	9.27	– .41	9.82	6.75	3,520
July	9.85	9.90	9.32	9.34	– .44	9.92	7.77	1,500

Est vol 28,688; vol Wed 23,784; open int 120,315, +314.

SUGAR–DOMESTIC (CSCE)–112,000 lbs.; cents per lb.

	Open	High	Low	Settle	Change	Lifetime High	Lifetime Low	Open Interest
July	20.65	20.70	20.62	20.68	....	21.60	19.35	1,295
Sept	20.65	20.70	20.65	20.70	– .03	21.45	19.35	588
Nov	....	....	....	20.62	– .03	21.29	19.65	282

Est vol 100; vol Wed 183; open int 2,165, –113.

–METALS & PETROLEUM–

COPPER (CMX)–25,000 lbs.; cents per lb.

	Open	High	Low	Settle	Change	Lifetime High	Lifetime Low	Open Interest
Apr	....	....	....	64.30	+ .40	65.25	63.00	0
May	64.00	64.75	64.00	64.55	+ .40	74.00	60.00	34,680
July	64.75	65.40	64.70	65.25	+ .40	72.55	60.35	26,994
Sept	65.35	65.85	65.35	65.80	+ .40	70.90	60.90	8,197
Dec	65.90	66.60	65.90	66.45	+ .40	70.30	61.60	6,976
Mar87	67.15	67.15	67.15	67.10	+ .40	70.00	62.55	1,558
May	....	....	....	67.45	+ .40	70.00	62.90	437
July	....	....	....	67.85	+ .40	69.95	63.25	197

Est vol 7,700; vol Wed 13,440; open int 79,141, +929.

GOLD (CMX)–100 troy oz.; $ per troy oz.

	Open	High	Low	Settle	Change	Lifetime High	Lifetime Low	Open Interest
Apr	337.50	339.50	337.50	338.90	– .40	496.80	314.70	1,721
June	339.80	342.80	339.00	341.70	– .50	433.50	320.50	60,368
Aug	343.00	346.00	343.00	345.10	– .50	427.50	328.00	17,586
Oct	347.00	348.60	346.30	348.30	– .50	395.70	331.50	7,271
Dec	349.00	353.00	349.00	351.70	– .50	392.00	336.50	13,538
Feb87	354.50	355.00	354.40	355.20	– .50	397.50	337.30	11,716
Apr	357.00	357.00	357.00	358.30	– .50	405.00	346.30	8,147
June	360.00	360.70	360.00	361.60	– .50	409.00	350.50	7,368
Aug	....	....	....	365.10	– .50	408.50	356.00	6,472
Oct	368.70	366.70	366.70	368.70	– .50	420.00	361.00	4,973
Dec	372.00	372.00	372.00	372.60	– .50	399.40	367.00	1,666
Feb88	....	....	....	376.70	– .50	....	....	230

Est vol 27,000; vol 33,678; open int 141,056, +3,142.

PLATINUM (NYM)–50 troy oz.; $ per troy oz.

	Open	High	Low	Settle	Change	Lifetime High	Lifetime Low	Open Interest
Apr	428.70	430.50	425.00	427.90	– .80	444.50	264.50	544
July	428.00	435.50	425.50	431.10	+ .10	448.00	273.00	14,448
Oct	430.50	438.30	430.00	434.30	+ .50	450.00	303.50	2,374
Jan87	435.00	440.50	434.00	437.50	+ 1.00	450.00	347.00	835
Apr	437.50	442.50	436.00	440.70	+ 1.60	448.50	361.00	494

Est vol 4,985; vol Wed 5,703; open int 18,695, +743.

PALLADIUM (NYM) 100 troy oz.; $ per troy oz.

	Open	High	Low	Settle	Change	Lifetime High	Lifetime Low	Open Interest
Apr	....	....	....	105.75	– .30	114.00	106.00	2
June	106.25	107.80	106.25	106.75	– .30	119.30	91.50	4,238
Sept	108.25	109.00	108.25	108.15	– .30	119.00	91.70	1,139
Dec	110.00	110.00	109.75	109.55	– .30	120.00	94.25	576
Mar87	111.75	111.75	111.75	110.95	– .30	127.50	90.00	145

Est vol 303; vol Wed 295; open int 6,100, –85.

ACC–Amex Commodities Corp.; CBT–Chicago Board of Trade; CME–Chicago Mercantile Exchange; CMX–Commodity Exchange, New York; CRCE–Chicago Rice & Cotton Exchange; CSCE–Coffee, Sugar & Cocoa Exchange, New York; CTN–New York Cotton Exchange; IPEL–International Petroleum Exchange of London; IMM–International Monetary Market at CME, Chicago; KC–Kansas City Board of Trade; LIFFE–London International Financial Futures Exchange; MCE–MidAmerica Commodity Exchange; MPLS–Minneapolis Grain Exchange; NYFE–New York Futures Exchange, unit of New York Stock Exchange. NYM–New York Mercantile Exchange; PBOT–Philadelphia Board of Trade; WPG–Winnipeg Commodity Exchange.

Figure 12-4. *Understanding the Futures Quotations.*

Understanding Futures Quotations

Futures contract quotations are typically listed alphabetically by commodity, with the expiration dates grouped below each commodity. Notice also that these commodities all fall under the heading of "Grains and Oilseeds." Other categories are "Livestock and Meat," "Metals and Petroleums," "Wood," and "Financial," among others. When a commodity is traded on more than one exchange, it is repeated with the abbreviation for the exchange in parentheses after the commodity name. Wheat, for instance, is listed three times because it trades on the Chicago Board of Trade (CBT), the Kansas City Board of Trade (KC), and the Minneapolis Grain Exchange (MPLS). These abbreviations are explained in a key at the bottom of the quotation section. Next to the commodity names are the standard contract size, such as 5,000 bushels of corn, and the unit of quotation, such as cents per bushel.

- "Open": The price at which each contract opened.
- "High/Low": The high and low prices of the day.
- "Settle": The price at which the contract closed.
- "Change": The difference between the closing prices of this day and the previous day.
- "Lifetime High/Low": The highest and lowest prices at which the contract has traded in its lifetime to date.
- "Open Interest": The total number of futures contracts (purchases or sales) that have not been offset by an opposite transaction or fulfilled by delivery.

Note that open interest is not the same as volume, which is the number of contracts *traded* during the course of the day. Think of the two this way: Every time a futures contract is traded, volume increases; it *cannot* go down during the course of the day—it can only go up or remain the same. Open interest, on the other hand, is the number of contracts left open (not offset) at the close of trading. During the day, open interest can go up (if a transaction opens a position), go down (if a transaction offsets a position), or remain the same (if there is no trading or if opening and closing transactions exactly equal each other).

Example: The size of a corn contract on the CBT is 5,000 bushels, and the price quotes represent cents per bushel. Five yearly corn contracts settle on the same months: May, July, September, December, and March. As soon as a March contract for one year expires, a new contract begins trading for July of the next year on the CBT.

The May contract opened at 228½ ($2.285) per bushel. During the trading day, the highest price was 229½ ($2.295), and the lowest was 227 ($2.270). It closed at 228 ($2.28), which represents a ¼-point change from the previous day's close. Since the contract began trading, the highest price has been 291¼ ($2.9125) and the lowest, 222½ ($2.225). There are 33,049 positions (buys and sells) in the May contract that have not been offset by opposite transactions or by delivery.

The value of a futures contract depends on the market price of the underlying commodity in the *spot*, or *cash,* market. To determine the value of a contract, multiply the spot market price by the size of the contract.

Example: If gold is quoted at $305 per ounce on COMEX, one contract of gold is worth $30,500 ($305 per ounce × 100 ounces per contract). A minimum price movement of $0.10 in the price of gold is therefore equal to a $10 change in the price of the contract ($0.10 per ounce × 100 ounces in a contract).

Expiration months tend to be standardized even from one exchange to another.

Figure 12-4. (cont).

Example: The farmer and Kellogg enter into a futures contract with the same terms as the forward contract: start date of February 1, 100,000 bushels of corn at $2.00 a bushel, for delivery on September 1. Every time the price of the "September corn" contract moves up or down in the futures market, either the farmer or the processor must "mark to the market." If, on the day after entering into the contract, the price of corn to be delivered on September rises in the futures market to $2.01 per bushel, the farmer has to pay the food processor the sum of 100,000 bushels times .01 cents per bushel, or $1,000 dollars. The move in the price of the corn made the contract more valuable to the processor by one cent per bushel.

If, on the next day, the price of September corn falls by 3 cents, from $2.01 to $1.98 per bushel, then the food processor has to pay the farmer $3,000 (100,000 bushel × 0.03). The contract has become more valuable to the farmer, who has a locked-in price of $2.00 a bushel when a bushel is selling for $1.98.

So each day the "winner" gets paid by the "loser." In actuality, since neither party knows who is on the other side of the transaction, the losers pay the clearing house and the clearing house pays the winners.

This process of transferring daily gains and losses on futures contracts from the accounts of the losers to those of the winners—that is, marking to the market—serves several purposes.

First, each of both parties in a futures transaction is assured that the other will honor their responsibilities. This assurance is secured by the "good faith" deposits of the participants in the futures market. Each participant in a futures contract is required to open a futures account for depositing margin. The size of the initial deposit (called the *initial margin*) is regulated by the exchange but it is usually just a few percentage points of the face value of the contract. This deposit can be made in either cash or in U.S. government securities (such as T-bills).

Be aware that margin in futures accounts does not represent partial payment of the security as it does in stock transactions. No loan is involved. Margin in futures contracts simply represents a good faith deposit against performance.

Each day the money is taken out of the loser's accounts and added to the winner's accounts by the clearing house. If the balance in a participant's futures account drops below a minimum level, which is also determined by the exchange and is called the *maintenance margin,* the account holder must either immediately deposit additional funds or face liquidation of the futures positions. In this way the members of the exchange protect themselves from large defaults by losers in the futures market.

Second, by forcing the daily transfer of losses and gains, all of the losses are "prefunded." Since all losses are prepaid, delivery can take place at the then current cash price of $2.25 a bushel.

Example: Having entered into a contract to sell the food processor $100,000 bushels at $2.00 a bushel, the farmer sees the cash price rise to $2.25 a bushel by harvest time (September 1). Over the term of the contract the farmer has transferred $25,000 ($0.25 × 100,000 bushels) from his futures account to that of the food processor, indirectly via the clearing corporation. When the farmer makes delivery, he is paid $2.25 a bushel, the going cash price.

Why should the farmer have to pay the processor the lost profit potential of $25,000? Paying that amount takes away the financial motivation for *not* making delivery. Seeing that he could make an additional $25,000 by selling the corn elsewhere, the farmer might be tempted to ignore the contract—leaving Kellogg without the corn needed for September's batch of corn flakes. If for any reason the farmer chose to sell the corn elsewhere, the best he can do is the original $2.00 agreed to in the first place; the added profit of $0.25 a bushel has already been "lost" to Kellogg's account. As for the other side of the account, the food processor can add the farmer's $25,000 to $200,000 of its own and buy corn in the cash market for $225,000 at no loss. Thus the farmer's performance is assured.

The farmer delivers the corn and gets paid $2.25 per bushel, or $225,000, and the food processor accepts delivery at $2.25 per bushel, paying $225,000. Because the farmer has already paid the food processor $25,000, the net transaction price is $200,000 or $2.00 a bushel to both buyer and seller. The farmer receives $225,000 and pays back the $25,000 already paid the food company over the life of the contract, for a net price of $200,000 or $2.00 per bushel. The food company pays $225,000 but it also *receives* $25,000, making its net cost also $200,000 or $2.00 per bushel.

Thus even though delivery takes place on September 1 at the cash price of $2.25 a bushel, both buyer and seller have a net price of $2.00 per bushel—the same price they originally agreed to back on February 1—because gains/losses were transferred on a daily basis.

Marking to the market has another effect. Because, upon expiration of a futures contract, the price at which the commodity is delivered is the same as the cash price, there is no reason for the commodity producer to actually deliver on the contract. Instead it is often easier for the producer just to offset the open futures position and sell the commodity in the cash market. Correspondingly, the processor offsets the contract in the futures market and buys the commodity in the cash market.

Example: Instead of delivering the corn to Kellogg, both the farmer and the processor close out their futures positions at the then current price and buy or sell the corn in the cash market. Here's the resulting situation for the producer: The farmer grows $100,000 bushels of corn at a cost of $1.50 a bushel, for a cash outflow of $150,000. He sells the crop in the cash market on September 1 for $2.25 per bushel ($225,000 for the crop) for a net cash profit of $75,000. In February the farmer sells one 100,000-bushel future contract at $2.00 a bushel in the futures market. On September 1, the farmer buys the contract back at its then current price of $2.25 for a net loss on the contract of $0.25 × 100,000, or $25,000. The net result of taking both the future position and a cash position is that the farmer makes $50,000 on the crop ($75,000 sales proceeds in the cash market less the $25,000 loss on the contract).

Thus it makes no difference whether the farmer delivers the crop to Kellogg or simply closes out the futures position and sells the crop in the cash market.

Because closing out the contract on the futures exchange is often much simpler than actually delivering the underlying commodity, most futures contracts end up in being offset, not delivered. To offset a contract, you take a long position if you are short (that is, buy a contract if you've sold one), or take a short position if you are long (that is, sell if you've bought a contract). Most futures contracts are closed out this way. In fact, fewer than 3% of all commodities contracts are closed by actual delivery; the balance are offset prior to expiration. In some situations, depending on the cost of transporting the commodity and other costs, there may actually be a small profit incentive to either deliver against an open position or to close the position out in the market itself.

FUTURES CONTRACTS AS HEDGING TOOLS

Because futures contracts:

- are marked to the market,
- are for standardized quantities and qualities of the underlying commodities,
- trade on a central exchange, and
- can be easily offset,

they have evolved into risk-management tools that are both liquid and flexible. This liquidity, one of the principal benefits of futures contracts over forward contracts, stems from the superior design of a futures contract and its relative advantages over an equivalent forward contract.

Example: If our farmer realizes that it is going to cost more than $1.50 a bushel to grow the corn, he might be able to offset his short futures position and reduce his losses. If the farmer realizes that the crop is going to be larger or smaller than the 100,000-bushel projection, he could sell or buy additional futures contracts.

Since corn futures trade in 5,000-bushel pieces, the farmer originally sold 20 contracts to cover the anticipated 100,000-bushel crop. If later the crop appears to be only 80,000 bushels, the farmer can offset four of those contracts, thus keeping the futures position in line with the expected crop size or cash position. This type of flexibility is not available with one 100,000-bushel forward contract.

SPECULATING IN THE FUTURES MARKET

In the farmer-producer example, both parties to the contract were involved in the food industry. Both were hedging what they perceived to be the risks inherent in the corn market. However, you do not have to be employed in an industry to benefit from that industry's futures market. Instead you can speculate on the future value of the related commodity.

Example: You might believe that corn prices are going up because you expect the Russians to buy huge quantities of corn over the next few months, because you expect locusts to descend from the heavens, because supply and demand will be temporarily imbalanced, because you've done a technical study on the history of corn prices, or because your astrologer told you corn prices were going up.

Whatever your reasons, you want to find a way to profit from this expected price move. You could, of course, go out and buy a silo full of corn, wait for the price to rise, and then sell the corn at a profit—an approach that is both very expensive and time-consuming. Even if you bought 100,000 bushels at $2.00 a bushel and the price rose to $2.25 a bushel, you would make a profit of only 12.5% on your money, less whatever it cost you to rent the silo space, to borrow the initial $200,000, to pay sales commissions, to insure the corn, and so on. Since a nickel per bushel is considered a big price move over a short period, buying physical corn doesn't seem like a very efficient or successful investment approach.

Instead you could open a futures account, deposit $5,000 in margin into the account, buy a contract for 100,000 bushels at $2.00, and sell it when the price reached $2.25. You would make the same $25,000, but on an initial investment of only $5,000 for a 500% return on your investment.

Thus the futures market provides you with a highly leveraged way to speculate on the future price of a commodity or other underlying interest. In addition there are no storage fees, no insurance charges, no financing costs, and only minimal commissions, making this method of speculating not only more leveraged but also more efficient and less time-consuming.

Like any leveraged investment, however, remember that leverage is a two-edged sword. If the price of corn drops to just $1.95 at any time during the holding period, your entire investment would be lost. Also, if the price of corn drops by more than just a few cents, you would have to put up more margin or risk liquidation of your position.

Speculative investors generally have a positive effect on a futures market. They expand the daily trading volume and thus enhance liquidity for the hedgers. They also accept the risk that the hedgers are unwilling to accept in exchange for the chance of making a profit that the hedgers are willing to forgo.

Speculators can bet that the market value of the commodity is going to rise by *going long* (that is, by buying) a futures contract. They can also bet that the market value is going down by *going short* (or selling) a futures contract. Whether the initial transaction is to go long or short, it is called the *opening transaction.* When the investor executes the offsetting transaction, it is called the *closing transaction.*

CONTRACT SPECIFICATIONS

Before you attempt to do any commodity speculation or hedging, make sure you become completely familiar with the specifications of the contracts you plan to trade. They all have their own peculiarities and nuances. Some of the factors you need to consider about a given contract are:

1. *The exchanges on which the contract is traded:* Some commodities trade on several exchanges whereas others trade on only one.

2. *The hours of the day that the contract is traded:* Some contracts trade for only a short period each day, whereas others have long trading hours.

3. *The amount of the underlying commodity that each contract represents.*

4. *How liquid the market is or how many future contracts trade per day:* The more liquid the market, the more contracts you can buy or sell without disturbing the market.

5. *The grade or quality of the underlying commodity that can be delivered to satisfy the futures obligation:* In other words, what quality repre-

sents *good delivery?* To satisfy an orange juice future contract, you have to deliver juice that has a certain sugar content; to satisfy a gold contract you have to deliver gold of a certain purity. Some futures contracts even specify that only the profit or loss be delivered in cash. No actual commodity is involved in the delivery.

6. *The available delivery months:* Some futures have contracts that expire every month for the next year, others have contracts that expire every three months, and others have more irregular schedules.

7. *The days of the month on which delivery can be made:* Some contracts allow delivery any time during the delivery month, while others allow delivery only on a certain day during the month. Still others give you the choice of a few days during the month. When the short (seller) decides to deliver the underlying commodity, the clearing corporation selects who has to accept delivery. This decision is usually made either on the basis of who has the oldest long position or by random selection depending on the contract involved.

8. *Which day during the month the contract expires:* The expiration date is the last day in which the contract can be traded, although there is frequently a period after the expiration day when delivery can still occur.

9. *The minimum price fluctuation for each contract:* A single price fluctuation (often called a *tick*) for a futures contract often means a price move of $25 or more.

10. *The maximum daily price move:* Some contracts have no limit as to how far the price can move in a day, and others have clearly defined limits.

11. *The maximum position limits:* To prevent large investors from taking such large positions in one delivery month that they end up controlling the market, the exchanges limit the number of contracts that can be owned or shorted by any one investor.

12. *The reportable position requirements:* Once investors have acquired a certain number of contracts in one delivery month (usually 25), they must report their positions to the exchange of the Commodities Futures Trading Commission.

THE VARIETY OF FUTURES CONTRACTS

Forward and futures changes were first traded on agricultural products and livestock. Lately, however, new contracts have proliferated on a wide variety of commodities and even on noncommodity products like bonds and stock indexes. New contracts are being proposed and adopted all the time. Some of the many commodities futures contracts are grouped by category in Figure 12-5.

Figure 12-5. *Categories of Futures Contracts.*

Grains
  Wheat
  Corn
  Oats
  Soybeans
  Soybean oil
  Soybean meal

Meats
  Cattle
  Feeder cattle
  Hogs
  Pork bellies

Bonds
  Treasury bonds
  Treasury notes
  Ginnie Maes
  Municipal bonds

Money Markets
  Treasury bills
  Eurodollars
  Certificates of deposit

Metals
  Silver
  Gold
  Copper
  Aluminum
  Platinum
  Palladium

Oils
  Crude oil
  Heating oil
  Unleaded gasoline

Currencies
  European currency units (ECUs)
  British pounds
  Canadian dollars
  French francs
  German marks
  Japanese yen
  Mexican pesos
  Swiss francs
  U.S. dollars

Stock Indexes
  Standard & Poor's 500 Index
  New York Stock Exchange Composite Index
  Commodity Research Bureau Index
  Value Line Index
  Major Market Index

Other Contracts
  Cotton
  Orange juice
  Potatoes
  Sugar
  Coffee
  Cocoa
  Lumber

PRICING OF FUTURES CONTRACTS

The price of a futures contract is determined by a variety of factors, the most important of which are (1) the cost of carry and (2) the collective price expectations of investors.

Cost of Carry. This involves the cost of financing a cash inventory.

Example: You are a jewelry manufacturer, and you need to acquire 100 ounces of gold. You want to know your future cost and to fix your purchase price today. However, you won't be using the gold for three months; so you don't need to take delivery for three months. Therefore you have the following choice:

1. Buy the gold now.
2. Or go long one three-month gold future contract and take delivery in three months.

If you buy the gold now, it will sit for three months. The money that you have tied up in the gold could be invested in T-bills or in another money market instrument that could be earning interest. Since you lose the ability to earn this interest by buying physical gold, it costs you money to acquire the gold today.

Example: Assume T-bills are yielding 6% per year. If you own gold outright for three months (a quarter of a year), then the "cost" of outright ownership is 1.5% of the cost. The 1.5% is three months', or a quarter-year's, worth of the 6% interest you would have earned if you'd bought a T-bill instead of the gold. If gold is presently $400 an ounce, then the "cost" of owning 100 ounces for three months is:

$$100 \text{ ounces} \times \$400 \text{ per ounce} \times 0.015 = \$600$$

This $600 is called the *cost of carry.*

What is the significance of the cost of carry? Refer again to Figure 12-4, specifically the settle prices for copper. Notice that the prices for the near months are lower than the months farther out.

The market for copper is said to be a *normal*, or *carrying cost*, market—that is, the distant months sell at a premium over near months. The premium is attributed to the carrying cost (or carrying charge), which is added to the value of the contract and which represents not only the "lost" return opportunity, but also the costs of insurance and warehousing. The more distant months cost more because they entail greater carrying costs.

In a normal market, the most that a distant month can sell over a near month is the total of the carrying charges. If a price includes more than these charges, professional traders would engage in *arbitrage*. That is, they would sell the distant month short and take delivery with the nearer, cheaper month, thus locking in a profit whether or not the more distant month's price rises or falls.

An *inverted market* is the opposite of a normal market; that is,

Figure 12-6. *Specifications of a Standard Gold Contract.*

Specification	Example
Commodity name	Gold
Exchange name	Commodity Exchange, New York (COMEX)
Size of contract	100 troy ounces
Grade	
Delivery months	Current calendar month, the next two months, and Feb/Apr/June, Aug/Oct/Dec $0.10 per ounce ($10)
First delivery date	First Friday of the delivery month; this is the first day on which delivery may be made.
First notice date	Two business days before the first delivery date; this is the first day on which a seller may issue notice of intention to deliver.
Expiration date	Second Friday before delivery of the futures contract; this is the last day on which an option may be exercised.
Minimum price fluctuation (basis points)	$0.10/per ounce; this is the smallest change allowable, in the price movement of a contract.

the distant months sell at lower prices than near months. In Figure 12-4, the market for corn is inverted, with May contracts trading at a higher price than all others. The implication of an inverted market is that the commodity is in short supply. Buyers are bidding up the price of the near months to the extent that these months' prices more than offset the carrying charges included in the prices of contracts for the distant months.

In an inverted (or *discount*) market, each contract that is further out in time trades at a lower price than one closer in. Whereas in a normal market the prices of the further-out contracts are limited by the carrying charges, *there is no limit to the amount that a near contract can trade over a more distant contract* in an inverted market. Inverted markets usually occur during spurts of extreme bullishness.

Collective Expectations of Investors in the Market. If investors expect the price of gold to rise, they will bid up both the price of physical gold and the price of the future value of gold. However, the arbitrage possibilities will keep the relationship between the two prices approximately $600 apart so long as the financing cost remains at 1.5% per quarter.

FLOOR TRADING

One visitor to the floor of a commodities exchange remarked that the wild trading activity reminded him of an "organized riot." That is an apt description. The trading of futures contracts takes place in *trading pits,* usually octagon shaped depressions with a series of progressively lower stairs around the circumference. In order to execute a transaction, a trader has to be "in the pit." Once in the pit, all trading takes place by *open outcry.* This means that all the traders trying to buy contracts yell their bids, while all the traders trying to sell are simultaneously shouting their offers.

To do business, one trader catches another's eye and, by means of a very sophisticated set of hand signals, executes a transaction. Both parties then write on a trading slip the number of contracts they traded, with whom they traded them, and at what price they traded. Every half-hour, the trading slips are taken to a back room to be matched up. Mistakes are common.

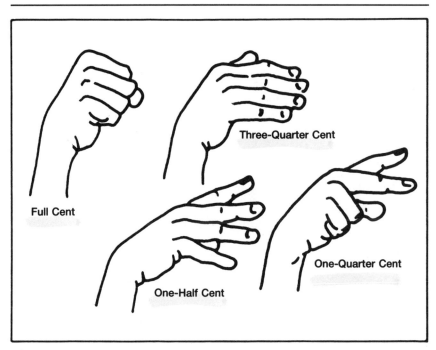

Figure 12-7. *A Few of the Many, Complicated Hand Signals Used in Trading Futures in the Pit.*

The justification for this frenzied trading approach is that it is the only way to bring all the buyers and all the sellers together in one place. In theory each trader has the same potential of doing business with every other trader, although in practice the loudest screamers have a definite advantage in the pits. After all, in the futures pits, you can't do business if you can't be heard.

OTHER TYPES OF FUTURES CONTRACTS

Traditional commodities, such as soybeans or gold, form only a part of the futures marketplace. Like options, futures contracts are now traded on financial instruments, stock indexes, and even the inflation rate!

Financial Futures

Trading in financial futures started in this country on May 16, 1972, when the International Monetary Market (IMM) of the Chicago Mercantile Exchange started trading futures on the pound, deutschmark, yen, and peso. In 1975 the Chicago Board of Trade began trading GNMA futures, and one year later the rival Chicago Mercantile Exchange began trading T-bill futures. In a time of currency fluctuations and huge budget deficits, trading in agricultural and precious metals futures has declined, while trading in financial futures has just as consistently grown.

Financial futures fall into two categories, both traded by speculators and hedgers: currencies and interest rate futures. Hedging is conducted primarily by *commercial* traders, that is, large businesses and financial institutions seeking to protect themselves against radical swings in currency or interest rates.

Such institutions used to—and to some extent still do—hedge their currency needs by trading forward contracts in the foreign currency, or *forex*, market. Like its agricultural counterpart, the financial forward contract is tailor-made to the hedger's needs. It is not standardized, nor is there trading in a secondary market. Futures trading in foreign currencies represents a more standardized and liquid market than does forward contracting.

Stock Index Futures

The first stock index future was the Value Line Stock Index futures contract, which is based on the unweighted average of the Value Line 1600 and which began trading on the Kansas City Board of Trade in February 1982. Having proved successful, it was followed in the same year by several others, such as the Standard & Poor's 500, which began trading on the Chicago Mercantile Exchange Index and Option Market Division. Since 1982, other indexes have followed.

The stock index futures contract allows investors or speculators to play practically the whole market, through a single investment instrument, with great leverage.

Although similar, these contracts should not be confused with their near relatives, the stock index options. Both stock index futures and options contracts use the same or similar indexes and have been in use only since 1982. The stock index futures contract, however, far outdistances the stock market index option in leverage. For this reason, experienced individual professional traders, investment banks, and the more sophisticated funds tend to trade the stock index futures contract (usually the Standard & Poor's 500 stock index futures contract) in preference to the index option. Retail clients are more attracted to the index option because, in buying an option, they can limit their risk to the amount of investment. Owners of futures contracts, on the other hand, are required to put up more margin if the index goes into a substantial decline. Similarly, investors who are short an index futures contract are required to put up more margin as the index rises. Thus, although index futures offer greater leverage, the possible losses are also greater than with the index option.

Unlike traditional commodity futures contracts, there is no underlying commodity in deliverable form. Instead, the underlying "commodity" is a cash amount that is based on the value of the index. For most index futures contracts, there is a daily cash settlement.

Example: The S&P 500 stock index futures contract is computed on the S&P 500 index. The *minimum fluctuation* (or *tick size*) is 0.05 point. Because the value of a contract is 500 times the value of the S&P 500 index, a change of 0.05 represents a $25 tick ($500 × 0.05). The S&P 500 futures contracts usually trade either at a premium above or below the actual, or cash, index. Because the daily trading limit is 3 points, a move from 210 to 215 would be the daily maximum, representing a change of only $1,500 per contract ($500 × 3). Positions are revalued, or marked to the market, every night. So if you owned the S&P contract during such a move, you would have $1,500 more in your account. If you were short the contract, your brokerage house would give you a margin call, probably for that amount.

CONCLUSIONS

Is the futures contract a security? If it is a security in the eyes of the law, investors who feel they have been defrauded can literally "make a federal case out of it" under either the Securities Act of 1933 or the Securities Exchange Act of 1934. If it is not a security, then investors must seek legal relief under state and local laws.

Generally, futures contracts are not recognized as securities, chiefly because their value is not determined by a party other than the buyer or seller. By contrast, a stock goes up in price because of anticipated earnings, and those earnings depend ultimately on the success of the company's management. When you buy a share of IBM or Exxon, you may buy it from another shareholder rather than from the company. Yet the stock's value depends neither on your own efforts nor on those of the previous shareholder but, rather, on the competence of a third party—the corporation's management.

Not so with futures contracts. Supply and demand, not managerial ability, ultimately determine the contract's price. If you buy stock in a gold mining company, you buy a security, because the company's earnings spring from management's abilities. If you buy either gold or a futures contract on gold, no management is involved.

13

Underwriting: Raising Capital

"It takes money to make money." Consequently, one of Wall Street's primary economic functions is to raise capital for both the private and the public sectors of our economy.

RAISING CAPITAL FOR INDUSTRY (THE PRIVATE SECTOR)

In the private sector, corporations raise capital to start new ventures, to expand existing facilities, to make acquisitions (buy other companies), or to meet other needs. There are two major types of corporate securities—common stocks and bonds.

Common Stock

When a corporation sells shares of its "common stock" to the public, it sells ownership or *equity* interests in the corporation. For example, if a company has a total of 100 shares of common stock and you own one of them, you own 1/100th of the company.

As a partial owner you share in the perils and rewards of business ownership. If the business thrives, the value of your ownership interests may rise substantially from the price at which you purchased it.

If the business fails, then your investment in it is lost, as it is for the owner of any failed business. Thus common stock offers a high potential return but no guarantees. For this reason, capital raised through the sale of common stock is often called *risk capital.*

The common shares are sold by the company to the *initial shareholders,* and the money they pay for their shares goes into the corporate coffers. After the shares are issued, however, the initial shareholders (as well as any subsequent shareholders) generally cannot sell the shares back to the company. Instead, owners can sell their shares only to other investors, at whatever price they are willing to pay. The company receives none of this money, however, because all the sale proceeds go from the buyer of the shares to the seller of the shares.

As the company's prospects change, so does the market value of ownership interest (that is, the share) in the company.

Bonds, unlike stock, represent a loan, from the investor to the company, which the corporation must eventually pay back after a specified number of years. The dollar amount of a bond, or its *face value* (the figure printed on the bond certificate), is the principal of the loan. Interest on the face value is paid periodically (usually twice a year) by the company to the owners of the bonds (called *bondholders*). Thus bondholders are not owners but rather creditors of the company.

Most corporations prefer to issue stock rather than bonds when they *first raise money* from the public. New companies generally do not have the stable cash flow necessary to make the periodic interest payments on bonds. (Making the periodic interest payments is often called *servicing the bonds.*) However, financially mature companies such as AT&T and Coca-Cola are more inclined to raise new capital by issuing bonds (called a *debt offering*).

RAISING CAPITAL FOR GOVERNMENTS (THE PUBLIC SECTOR)

In the public sector, governmental entities require capital for such projects as national defense systems, highways, airports, sewage systems, schools, hospitals, and the like. Because states, cities, counties, other municipalities, and the federal government are not privately owned, they may not issue stock. (Contrary to the U.S. savings bonds ads, you cannot buy "stock" in America.) Instead, they must raise the capital for projects by issuing bonds, which are purchased by banks, insurance companies, mutual funds, pension plans, individuals, and other types of investors.

Government bonds have tax advantages associated with them. The interest that an investor earns on a U.S. government bond is exempt from state and city taxes. The interest that an investor earns on a municipal bond (issued by a state or political subdivision of a state) is *generally* exempt from federal tax (see the chapter on municipal bonds).

THE PRIMARY MARKET

The term *primary market* refers to the initial sale of new issues of stocks and bonds. For this reason, the securities offered in this market are referred to as *primary issues*. However, before a company or government makes the decision to issue stocks or bonds, it first considers its other potential sources of funds, particularly whether simply borrowing from a commercial bank will meet its capital needs. After all, why bother with issuing securities if a simple bank loan will suffice?

Unfortunately, banks loans often prove to be inadequate for four main reasons:

1. Banks are often unable to lend potential borrowers the amount of money that they need to borrow. For example, Uncle Sam has borrowed over $2 *trillion,* and not even a consortium of the largest banks could make a loan of this size.

2. Banks are often unable to provide the terms that a borrower wants. For example, a company might want to borrow money at a fixed rate for 20 years, whereas most banks will not make fixed-rate commercial loans with terms longer than seven years.

3. Banks are often unable to lend to companies or governmental bodies with low credit ratings. New companies often do not have enough collateral to secure bank financing. Because banks have a duty to their depositors not to take excessive risks with their deposits, there is some truth to the adage that "the only way to get a bank loan is to have so much money that you don't need one." Individual

investors, on the other hand, are often willing to invest in risky situations if they feel the potential reward justifies the risk.

4. Banks often charge borrowers higher interest rates than credit-worthy companies and governments have to pay if they raise capital directly from investors.

THE INVESTMENT BANKER

Companies and governments that cannot be adequately served by the commercial banks often turn to an "investment banker" for help in raising capital. *Investment banking firms* serve as intermediaries between potential investors and the companies and governments wishing to raise capital. Because such firms, through their brokers, are in contact with thousands of investors, they can match issuers of securities with investors for whom the securities are appropriate.

For example, if a small growth company needs to sell stock to raise the money, it needs to continue its promising research and development program. The investment banking firm matches the company with investors who are seeking high-risk/high-reward investments. On the other hand, if the issuer is the U.S. government, the investment banking firm matches it with investors who do not want any credit risk. The term *underwriter* is used to describe the investment banker's role in this procedure.

Once the distribution is completed (that is, the securities are sold), the investment banker's formal primary market relationship with the issuer ceases.

FULL DISCLOSURE

Because investors are at risk when purchasing any security, the underwriting process is subject to tight regulation, particularly under the requirements of the Securities Act of 1933. Before this law went into effect, almost anyone could sell stocks or bonds issued by any type of issuer. Although many firms sold valid, worthwhile securities in companies of substance, others fraudulently sold worthless certificates to naive investors. Issuers did not have to disclose any information to the investors to assist them in making valid investment decisions. Consequently, the successful distribution of securities was based more on skillful selling ability than on the sound, informed judgment of the investors.

Amid the aftershocks of the 1929 stock market "crash," Congress passed the Securities Act of 1933. To enforce the requirements of the 1933 Act, The Securities Exchange Act of 1934 created the *Securities and Exchange Commission* (SEC), whose function with respect to underwriting is to supervise the registration of new securities and to make sure that the important information about an investment is disclosed to the public. Various other federal and state laws also protect the investing public from being given false, inaccurate, or misleading information, or being otherwise defrauded. Offenders are subject to stiff fines and imprisonment.

When a corporate issuer sets out to offer its securities to the public, it must first file a *registration statement* with the Securities and Exchange Commission. Some of the information that must be included in this document is listed in Figure 13-1.

The SEC examines the statement and, if it is accepted, the statement becomes effective after 20 days. (This 20-day period is often called the *cooling-off period.*) In its review, the SEC neither approves nor disapproves of the securities, nor does it pass judgment on the investment merit of the proposed offering. The SEC merely "accepts" or "rejects" the registration statement on the basis of whether it includes all of the information that the SEC feels potential investors require when considering the purchase of the securities. By accepting a registration, the SEC is saying *only* that all the legally required information is adequately disclosed and that the necessary supporting documents have been included. Nevertheless, acceptance is crucial to an underwriting, because the securities cannot be sold to the public until the SEC accepts the registration statement, which is then said to be *effective.*

While the SEC is reviewing the registration statement, a flurry of preparatory activity takes place as the officers of the corporation and the investment banking firm make final arrangements to implement the public offering.

CONTACTING CUSTOMERS

No securities may be sold before an offering becomes effective (that is, before the registration is approved). However, customers may be

1. The name of the issuer.
2. The name of the state or sovereign power under which the issuer is organized.
3. The location of the issuer's principal office.
4. The names and addresses of the directors and other senior officials.
5. The names and addresses of the underwriters (if any).
6. The names and addresses of persons owning 10% or more of any class of the issuer's stock.
7. The quantities of securities owned by the directors, senior officials, underwriters, and 10% or greater holders.
8. The general character of the issuer's business.
9. A statement of the issuer's capitalization.
10. A statement of securities reserved for options outstanding, with names and addresses of persons allotted 10% or more of these options.
11. The amount of capital stock of each class included in this offer.
12. The issuer's funded debt.
13. The purposes to which the proceeds of this offering will be applied.
14. Remuneration payable to the issuers directly, naming them specifically when annual payments exceed $25,000.
15. The estimated net proceeds to be derived from the offering.
16. The price at which the public offering will be attempted.
17. Commissions, fees, and so on, to be paid to the underwriters.
18. An itemized detail of expenses incurred by the issuer in connection with this offering.
19. The net proceeds derived from any securities sold by the issuer in the preceding two years and pertinent details of those sales.
20. Any consideration paid to a promoter in the preceding two years.
21. The names and addresses of any vendors of property or goodwill to be acquired with the proceeds of this offering.
22. Full particulars of any dealings between the issuer and its officers, directors, and holders of 10% or more of its stock that transpired in the preceding two years.
23. The names and addresses of counsel passing upon the legality of the issue.
24. The dates and details of material contracts created outside the issuer's ordinary course of business within the preceding two years.
27. Certified financial statements of any issuer or business to be acquired with proceeds of this offering.
28. A copy of the underwriting contract or agreement.
29. A copy of the law firm's written opinion attesting to the legality of the issue.
30. A copy of all material contracts referred to in item 24.
31. A copy of the issuer's charter, bylaws, trust agreement, partnership agreement, and so forth, as the case may be.
32. A copy of the underlying agreement or indenture affecting any security offered or to be offered by the issuer.

Figure 13-1. *Information Included in the Registration Statement.*

informed in general about the proposed offering and its expected offering price (or interest rate for a bond issue) to see if they are interested in investing in it. By lining up investors who are interested in the offering in advance of the actual offering, the investment banker helps to ensure that, when the offering becomes effective, the securities are sold out very quickly. (One of the hallmarks of a successful offering is that the securities are placed with investors very quickly, usually in less than one business day after the offering becomes effective.)

If investors want to read something about the proposed offering (many investors do), the firm sends them a *red herring*. This document is a summary of the information contained in the registration statement filed with the SEC. Red herrings got their name because of the warning to investors on the cover in red ink that the information contained in the summary may be incomplete (see Figure 13-2). After all, the SEC, upon reviewing the registration statement, may find that there is "insufficient disclosure." If the registration statement does not contain enough information, the summary of that document is probably also incomplete.

While the firm's brokers are busy lining up potential investors, the firm's investment banking group is busy building a *syndicate*. Most firms do not attempt to sell an entire new offering by themselves (unless the offering is a small one). Instead, they solicit the help of other firms. All of the firms involved in selling a new offering, acting as a group, are referred to as the syndicate. The firm that puts the deal together is called the *lead manager* of the syndicate.

Figure 13-2. *The Statement Printed in Red on the Registration Statement Filed with the SEC.*

A registration statement relating to these securities has been filed with the Securities and Exchange Commission, but has not yet become effective. Information contained herein is subject to completion or amendment. These securities may not be sold nor may offers to buy be accepted prior to the time the registration statement becomes effective. This prospectus shall not constitute an offer to sell or the solicitation of an offer to buy nor shall there be any sale of these securities in any State in which such offer, solicitation or sale would be unlawful prior to the registration or qualification under the securities laws of any such State.

At the same time, the firm's legal department is submitting the registration statement and other supporting documents to the state securities regulators in *every state in which the securities will be offered.* This process of obtaining state approval for a securities offering is called *blue skying the issue.*

Assuming no problems with the registration statement, then, sometime after the 20-day cooling-off period, the SEC informs the investment banking firm that the offering has become effective (or approved).

The same day as the receipt of the SEC's approval, the lead manager invites representatives from all of the firms that are going to be selling the securities to a meeting that is called the *due diligence meeting.* There are several purposes for holding this meeting:

1. Any last-minute details are ironed out.
2. Each firm that is going to participate in the offering indicates how many shares or bonds it thinks it can sell (based on the input from its salespeople).
3. The final price at which the security is to be offered is determined. Because there is no market for the security prior to this offering, it has no market-determined value. Instead, the firms selling the security try to make a business estimate of the fair value for it. They consider how strong the company is, how much demand there is for the security, how strong or weak the overall market is, and other considerations.

This price setting is a tightrope walk. The issuing firm, of course, wants to sell the securities for as much as possible. The potential investors want to pay as little as possible. The firms need to determine a price that is fair to both parties. By tradition, a security that's "priced right" rises slightly in value right after it is issued. If the market value of a security drops right after the offering, then it was priced too high (and the investors lose). If the market value soars, it was priced too low (and the issuer loses).

After the final offering price is determined, the lead manager notifies the printing company so that it can immediately start printing final prospectuses for the offering.

THE FINAL PROSPECTUS

The *final prospectus* contains the same information as the red herring, except that now the information (including the price) is complete. By law the prospectus must be sent or given to any subscriber to a registered distribution of securities no later than with the delivery of the confirmation of the purchase.

Now the firms' salespeople can accept orders from customers. The next morning the firms start calling their clients with the final price information. Throughout the offering period the firms participating in the offering keep the lead manager posted on the amount of the securities they have sold. The lead manager keeps track of these sales figures so that it knows at any time approximately how many securities are left to be sold and how many shares or bonds each firm in the syndicate has sold. This is called *keeping the books* for the offering.

If demand for the securities is strong, the underwriter may ask the issuer for permission to sell more securities than were originally planned.

Example: A company may have initially planned to sell 1,000,000 shares of stock at $10 per share, but it may authorize its underwriter to sell up to 1,050,000 shares if the demand is strong. These extra 50,000 shares are called a *green shoe* offering after a company whose offering was so expanded.

Also, the lead underwriter may stabilize the value of the newly issued security in the secondary market. To do so, the lead firm buys any and all shares that are resold by the original investors at a price very near the offering price. This prevents the market value of the security from dropping immediately after the offering. Right after a new offering is one of the few times that a firm can blatantly and legally manipulate the market price of a security. After the market value of the newly issued security becomes stable, the firm ceases any further support activities.

Once the stabilization, if any, is terminated, the offering is completed. At this point the syndicate is disbanded, and the deal is said to have *broken syndicate.* The market value of the security now rises and falls on its own merits.

PROSPECTUS

$75,000,000

DynaFlow Technology, Inc.

7¾% Convertible Subordinated Debentures Due 1998

(Interest Payable February 1 and August 1)

The Debentures are convertible at any time prior to maturity, unless previously redeemed, into shares of Common Stock of the Company at a conversion price of $46.43 per share, subject to adjustment under certain conditions. On January 26, 1983, the last reported sale price of the Company's Common Stock on the American Stock Exchange was $40⅜ per share.

The Debentures are redeemable at any time on not less than thirty days' notice at the option of the Company, in whole or in part, at the redemption prices set forth herein, including interest accrued to the date of redemption, provided that the Debentures may not be redeemed prior to February 1, 1985, unless prior to the mailing of the notice of redemption the price of the Company's Common Stock has been at least 150% of the conversion price for 30 successive trading days. Mandatory sinking fund payments sufficient to retire $7,500,000 principal amount of Debentures annually commencing February 1, 1991 are calculated to retire 70% of the issue prior to maturity. The Company may credit against mandatory sinking fund payments Debentures previously acquired, converted or redeemed other than through the mandatory sinking fund.

The Debentures will be subordinated to all Senior Indebtedness (as defined) of the Company. As of December 31, 1982, after giving effect to the application of the estimated net proceeds from the sale of the Debentures, the Company's Senior Indebtedness would have been approximately $2,193,000. There will be no restrictions in the Indenture upon the creation of Senior Indebtedness.

Application will be made to list the Debentures on the American Stock Exchange.

THESE SECURITIES HAVE NOT BEEN APPROVED OR DISAPPROVED BY THE SECURITIES AND EXCHANGE COMMISSION NOR HAS THE COMMISSION PASSED UPON THE ACCURACY OR ADEQUACY OF THIS PROSPECTUS. ANY REPRESENTATION TO THE CONTRARY IS A CRIMINAL OFFENSE.

	Price to Public (1)	Underwriting Discounts and Commissions (2)	Proceeds to Company (1)(3)
Per Debenture	100%	2.75%	97.25%
Total.......................................	$75,000,000	$2,062,500	$72,937,500

(1) Plus accrued interest, if any, from February 1, 1983 to the date of delivery.
(2) The Company has agreed to indemnify the Underwriters against certain liabilities, including liabilities under the Securities Act of 1933.
(3) Before deducting expenses of the Company estimated at $260,000.

The Debentures are being offered by the several Underwriters named herein, subject to prior sale, and when, as and if delivered to and accepted by the Underwriters, and subject to approval of certain legal matters by counsel. It is expected that delivery of the Debentures will be made against payment therefor on or about February 3, 1983, at the offices of **Stone, Forrest & Rivers**
160 Wall Street
New York, NY 10041

Securities Brokerage
INCORPORATED

Giant, Recker & Crane

Figure 13-3. *A Prospectus.*

208

Issues by a Political Unit

Obligations of (or those guaranteed by) a state, municipality, or the federal government are exempt from the filing requirements of the 1933 Act. Consequently, these entities need not issue a prospectus. However, many political units make what is in effect "full disclosure" by distributing a prospectus-like brochure called an *official statement* or *offering circular*. This publication contains information similar to that found in the prospectus for a new corporate issue.

TYPES OF UNDERWRITINGS

There are two basic types of underwritings—firm and best efforts. They differ primarily in the level of "commitment" to the underwriting by the investment banking firm.

Firm Underwritings

As the name implies, *firm underwritings* represent a very high level of commitment on the part of the investment banking firm. In such an underwriting, the syndicate literally buys the securities from the issuing company using the firms' own capital, and then resells the securities to investors that the syndicate has lined up to purchase them (usually on the same day). The investment banking firms charge the investors a slightly higher price than what they paid the issuer so as to make a profit on the overall transaction. If, after the firms have purchased the securities from the issuer, they are unable to resell them for any reason, then the syndicate firms *own* the securities. The issuing company still gets its sale proceeds.

In building a syndicate for a firm offering, a brokerage firm can play three different roles.

1. If the firm puts the deal together, then it is the lead manager and runs the books.

2. If the firm does not put the deal together but is willing to commit its own capital to buy a portion of the securities for later resale to its clients, the firm is called an underwriter.

3. If it does not commit its capital to buying the securities, but only helps to sell the securities, the firm is considered to be a member of the *selling group*.

The distinctions among roles are important because the commission is split differently depending on the role of the firm in the offering.

Example: XYZ, Inc. wants to sell 1,000,000 shares of stock to the public. Dependable Brokerage agrees to handle the offering on a firm underwriting basis. The firm agrees to pay XYZ, Inc. $9.50 per share for every share issued. It then resells the shares to investors for $10, generating a 5% or $0.50 commission per share for its efforts. Of that $0.50 per share:

• $0.05 per share goes to the lead manager for putting the deal together (that is, to Dependable Brokerage).

• $0.20 per share goes to the firm that underwrites the share sold, to compensate it for risking its capital.

• $0.25 goes to the firm that actually sells the share, to compensate it for lining up the investor.

Thus, if Dependable Brokerage both underwrites and sells a share, it is entitled to keep the entire $0.50 commission for itself.

If another firm both underwrites and sells a share, it will be entitled to $0.45 of the $0.50 commission. The remaining $0.05 goes to Dependable for serving as the lead manager.

If another firm only underwrites a share but does not sell it, it is entitled to only $0.20 of the commission.

If another firm only sells but does not underwrite the share (that is, either a member of the selling group or an underwriter that sells more shares than it underwrote), the firm is entitled to $0.25 of the commission.

Let's assume that Dependable's syndicate for this 1,000,000-share offering looks like this:

Firm	No. Shares Lead	No. Shares Underwritten	No. Shares Sold
Dependable	1,000,000	250,000	200,000
Acme		250,000	200,000
S&F		250,000	200,000
Harting		250,000	200,000
Jones			100,000
Smith			100,000
	1,000,000	1,000,000	1,000,000

Dependable, the lead manager, is underwriting 250,000 shares and is responsible for selling 200,000 shares. In this case the firm earns:

$$(1,000,000 \times 0.05) + (250,000 \times 0.20) + (200,000 \times 0.25)$$
$$= \$150,000$$

The Smith firm, whose only responsibility is to sell 100,000 shares, earns $(100,000 \times 0.25) = \$25,000$.

Negotiated Versus Competitive Underwritings

If XYZ Inc. is a fairly large, financially solid company that offers truly attractive growth prospects, many investment banking firms may be interested in underwriting its securities. In this case the company selects the firm that offers to pay it the most for its securities. This type of underwriting is said to be *competitive*.

If, however, XYZ is a small company, perhaps only one invest-ment banking firm is interested in it. In this case the company's management negotiates directly with the underwriter over the price that the company receives for its securities. If the company cannot get what it thinks is a fair price, it simply does not sell its shares.

If the company were even smaller, *perhaps no investment banking firms would be willing to risk their capital on a firm underwriting of the company's securities.* In this case, the company would have to resort to a *best efforts offering,* in which the firm does not buy the securities from the company and then resell them but rather acts only as the firm's sales agent. It tries to find buyers for the company's securities, earning a commission on each order it generates. The securities them-selves, however, are transferred directly from the issuing company to the investors. The firm agrees to sell as many shares as it can but makes no guarantee that it can sell all the shares the company wants to sell. In other words, the firm uses its "best efforts" to place the stock (hence the name).

HOT ISSUES

A *hot issue* is a new security offering that is very actively sought after by investors. The brokerage firm handling the issue has no trouble finding buyers for all the securities. In fact, its problem is that it doesn't have nearly enough securities to meet the demand.

Because the demand for the securities is so great, it's a good bet that the market price of the security will rise sharply in the secondary market as the investors who were unable to buy the securi-ties from the syndicate seek to buy them from other investors. For this reason, anyone who can buy the stock when it is initially offered is practically guaranteed a large and almost immediate profit. To prevent "Wall Streeters" from keeping these easy profits for them-selves, neither the firms themselves, nor their employees, nor the relatives of their employees are allowed to buy any shares of a "hot issue" during the offering.

One of the most dramatic examples of a hot issue is the demand-versus-supply imbalance that occurred when Apple Computer, Inc. went public (that is, sold stock for the first time). During the first day of trading, the market value of the newly issued stock nearly tripled, netting a very handsome profit for those investors who were fortunate enough to get shares at the offering price.

AFTER THE OFFERING IS COMPLETED

After the offering, the lead manager and several of the underwriters usually start "making a market" in the security unless the security is immediately listed on an exchange (see Chapter 15 on the over-the-counter market).

SHELF DISTRIBUTIONS

To make the underwriting process more efficient, the underwriting procedure for large, prestigious, financially sound companies is different from the process for smaller, riskier companies. The issues of these large firms are well backed and highly salable. The SEC recognizes this difference in *Rule 415*, which permits some companies to register securities that they intend to issue over a period of up to two years, without the usual services of an underwriter. Instead, the issuer distributes the new securities directly into the open market through a broker. Although the issuer pays commissions to the brokers for executing the orders, it saves many times this amount by avoiding the hefty fees charged by investment bankers. Because the company sells its own stock, as if it were coming "off the shelf," this type of distribution is called a *shelf distribution.*

Not all companies are eligible for Rule 415 registration. To be eligible, a corporation must already be established. It must have kept reports to the SEC current, and it must be up-to-date on its financial obligations.

14

Exchange Markets

When most investors think of trading securities, they think first of the New York Stock Exchange located at 11 Wall Street. Indeed, many of the common stocks, preferred stocks, and bonds of America's largest corporations are traded on this exchange. Since the exchange is the oldest, the largest, the most powerful, the most prestigious, and the most visible securities exchange in the United States, it is an appropriate model of the exchange market.

But what exactly is a stock exchange? In simplest terms, a stock exchange is nothing more than a place where buyers and sellers of securities that are *listed* (that is, traded) there can come together to transact business. By being all in one location, buyers and sellers are able to transact business at a fair price determined solely by supply and demand.

To transact business on the floor of the exchange, an individual or a company must buy a membership. Buying this membership is usually called *buying a seat*. Because the number of memberships or seats is limited, to buy one you have to find a current member willing to sell and negotiate a mutually agreeable price. In April, 1987 a seat sold for $1,000,000—the first time the price has ever reached that level.

THE EXCHANGE FLOOR

The first thing new members have to do is learn their way around the trading floor. The floor of the New York Exchange is divided into several large rooms, the largest of which is called the *main room.*

Throughout the trading floor are trading posts. Each trading post is assigned one or more of the securities listed on the exchange, so that every listed security is traded at one and only one trading post. Because all the trading in a given security takes place at a single location on the exchange floor, it is easier for potential buyers and sellers of the security to find each other and get their respective clients' orders executed. After all, over 1,700 stocks alone are traded on the floor of the exchange. Without some form of organization, trying to find a member who wants to sell the security that you want to buy (or buy the security you want to sell) would be pretty much impossible.

On either side of the main room are additions to the original exchange (called the *garage* and the *blue room,* respectively). These additions were built so that the exchange could add additional trading posts and list more securities.

TYPES OF MEMBERS

After new members become familiar with the layout of the exchange floor and learn where all the securities are traded, they are ready to do their first trade. The types of trades that they do, however, depend to a large degree on the capacity or role in which they choose to operate. The exchange recognizes six different roles that members may assume:

- Floor broker.
- Two-dollar broker.
- Specialist.
- Competitive trader.
- Competitive market-maker.
- Bond broker.

Floor Broker

A *floor broker,* also known as a *commission house broker,* is usually an employee of one of the many brokerage firms that own seats on the exchange. The brokerage firm hires the floor broker to execute the transactions sent down to the floor on behalf of the firm's clients. Floor brokers get their instructions to buy or sell from the firms' *floor clerks* who are located in the many phone booths surrounding the trading floor. The floor clerks, in turn, receive their instructions from the firm's order room, which has collected instructions from the firm's retail and institutional salespeople. Thus the order flow goes from customer to sales representative (registered representative) to order room to floor clerk to floor broker. At the conclusion of the transaction, the floor broker notifies the floor clerk of the results. The floor clerk then passes the execution information back up the same pipeline to the customer.

Two-Dollar Broker

Very often, the commission house brokers are unable to handle the volume of orders that their firms receive from customers. Even if the firm receives only two orders, it can sometimes be impossible for one floor trader to execute both transactions in a timely manner. For example, the securities may be traded on opposite sides of the exchange, or one of the orders might be such that it takes a long time to fill it properly.

When the floor brokers are too busy to execute all the firm's orders in a timely manner, to avoid delays in executing client orders, the floor clerks use a two-dollar broker to execute some of those orders. Two-dollar brokers are usually individuals who own their own seats. They execute transactions for any brokerage firm that's too busy to properly execute all its clients' orders. For their services two-dollar brokers charge the brokerage firms a fee based on the number of shares in the order, as well as on how well they executed the order. The name "two-dollar broker" stems from the fact that they used to be paid $2 for every hundred shares they bought or sold on behalf of a brokerage firm's client.

Sometimes, when floor brokers are not busy, they act as two-dollar brokers for other firms.

Specialist

One of the hallmarks of the exchange method of securities trading is that each security is assigned a specialist. *Specialists* are members of the exchange who are ready, willing, and financially able to make sure that the trading in the stock (or stocks) they are assigned remains both liquid and orderly. By "liquid and orderly" we mean that specialists almost always stand ready to both buy and sell the assigned stocks at a fair price. Since the specialist always makes a market, most client orders can be executed immediately—even if no other customer wants to take the other side of the transaction.

Example: A client of Merrill Lynch wants to buy 1,000 shares of a stock that is listed on the New York Exchange. The client gives her broker an order, and the order is quickly communicated to the exchange floor. One of Merrill's floor brokers carries the order to the trading post where the stock is traded. When the floor broker arrives at the trading post, no other brokers there have orders to sell 1,000 shares. To facilitate the completion of the client's order, the specialist sells 1,000 shares to Merrill's broker at the current price. Thus the specialist takes the other side of the client's trade using *his own money to do so.*

Because specialists are required to maintain an orderly and liquid market, they must stay at the stock's trading post all day long. When there is much selling, they must see to it that the price of the stock drops in an orderly manner. Likewise, if there are many buy orders, they must make sure the stock's price rises in an orderly manner.

Specialists raise and lower the market price of the stock by raising or lowering the price they are willing to pay to buy the stock and the price at which they are willing to sell the stock. Specialists post their prices on an electronic screen above the trading post.

Example: A specialist might make a market for a certain stock at 34¼-34½. This means the specialist stands ready to *buy* the stock at a price of 34¼, the *bid price*, or to sell it at a price of 34½, the *offer price*.

The difference between the bid and the offer is called the *spread.* By buying the stock at a slightly lower price than the price at which they sell it, specialists make a profit. This profit compensates them for the services they provide to the exchange and to the public customers.

Ideally, specialists like to buy as many shares as they sell on a daily basis, so that they can go home each night without owning any stock. They attempt to balance their sell orders and buy orders by raising and lowering their bid and asked prices.

Given a lot of buy orders from floor brokers, specialists will have to sell more shares than they buy. In response, they raise their bid price and ask price, usually by an eighth of a point. Because the stock is now slightly more expensive, the number of investors willing to buy the stock should fall, and the number willing to sell should rise, thus bringing the market back into balance. If the buying continues, specialists raise the price again and keep on raising it until the numbers of shares being bought and of shares being sold are in equilibrium. Of course, if inundated with sell orders, specialists lower the price so as it make it less attractive for investors to sell and more attractive to buy.

Specialists usually also indicate the number of shares—that is, *quantities*—they are willing to buy and/or sell at the posted prices. Quantities, along with prices, are available on the overhead screens, and they change constantly throughout the trading day.

Example: A market might be 27½-24⅝ (20 × 30), meaning the specialist stands ready to buy 2,000 shares at 27½ and to sell 3,000 shares at 24⅝. The number of shares is expressed in "round lots" of a 100, thus "20" equals 2,000 shares (20 round lots of 100 each).

A price quote of 28¾-29 (40 × 50) means that the specialist is ready to buy 4,000 shares at 28¾ and to sell 5,000 shares at 29.

Specialists, however, are not the only ones prepared to buy and sell a given stock. Any other member can compete with them by offering the stock at a lower price or bidding at a higher price. If a group of members are all trading a stock at a trading post, they are collectively called the *trading crowd.*

If other members want a better price, either for their own account or for a customer, they are free to try buying or selling at a better price.

Example: If the specialist is making the market at 28¾-29, a floor broker who is trying to buy 1,000 shares for a client can *bid* (that is, try to buy) at 28⅞, which would be an eighth of a point less than the price the specialist would charge. If another broker at the trading post is trying to sell 1,000 shares of the same stock, he would also be better off selling at 28⅞ than at the specialist's bid of 28¾.

Thus, specialists don't always offer the best price, but they always offer a price. If you want to sell or buy and no one wants to take the other side of the transaction, you can always do the trade with the specialist. But that might cost you an eighth of a point. Liquidity has its price.

Bids and Offers. So that everyone at a trading post knows whether you are buying or selling, bids and offers are made differently. To make a *bid,* the broker first states the purchase price and then the number of shares he or she wants to buy.

Example: "54 for 2,000" means, "I'm bidding $54 each for up to 2,000 shares." To sell shares to the broker making this bid, another broker has only to say "sold" and the quantity, such as "Sold to you 1,000." This is called *hitting the bid.* At this point the two brokers have effected a transaction of 1,000 shares at $54. The broker trying to buy 2,000 shares has to buy only 1,000 more shares to fill the client's order.

Sale offers are made by first stating the quantity and then the price.

Example: "1,000 at 24½" means, "I want to sell 1,000 shares at 24½." Another broker can execute the transaction by saying "Take" followed by the quantity. "Take 500" means another broker is buying 500 shares at the first broker's offering price.

The more volume specialists do, the more "spreads" they earn. In this respect, the roles of specialists are similar to that of a grocer:

- Buying stock at wholesale (that is, the bid price).
- Selling stock at retail (the offer price).
- Offering a "sale" when the inventory is too high (lowering the price of the stock).
- Boosting the price of the stock when the demand exceeds the supply.

The specialist is also responsible for handling the special types of orders (explained later in the chapter) that clients sometimes want to use. The ability to handle these orders is one of the advantages that the exchange/specialist system offers.

Protecting Customers' Interests. Specialists are elected to their positions by a committee of other exchange members, and every specialist's performance is periodically reevaluated by the other members of the exchange.

Specialists come under special scrutiny because they are, of course, in a position that entails an inherent conflict of interest. They are responsible for maintaining a fair and orderly market for the public, and yet they are trying to make a profit for themselves from trading the stock. To prevent specialists from profiting unfairly at the expense of the public, they must adhere to strict rules. The most important of these rules is that customer orders always take preference over the specialists buying or selling for their own benefit. Thus if both a client and the specialist want to sell at a certain price, the customer's order must always be executed first.

Another service that the specialist is obliged to provide is *stopping stock*. (This has nothing to do, by the way, with stop orders.) If a floor broker has a customer's order to execute but is trying to get a better price than the one currently available price, he can ask the specialist to "stop the stock." To do this, the specialist guarantees the floor broker the current price but does not immediately execute the order. Because the order is "put on hold," the floor broker has time to try for a better price without worrying that the market will move against him (and the client) in the meantime.

Specialists may grant such a privilege (though they are not obligated to do so) under the following conditions:

1. The buy or sell order must be for a public customer's account, not for a member's account.

2. The floor broker must ask for the stop. The specialist may not solicit requests.

3. The spread between the bid and the ask must be at least a quarter point when the request is made.

4. The specialist must be willing and able to trade as principal if necessary to avoid defaulting on the guarantee.

In summary, the specialist provides a number of services in exchange for the privilege of executing stop and limit orders for clients. Specialists provide a liquid and orderly market by always standing ready to risk their own capital to take the other side of a customer's trade. As we shall see, specialists also service small customers.

Competitive Trader

Competitive traders own their own seats. That is, they are entrepreneurs; they are not on the payroll of employers, who pay for their memberships. Competitive traders can therefore buy or sell any security for their own benefit. They are very similar to other individual investors in that they try to buy low and sell high. However, because they are on the trading floor itself, they have an advantage over the public in that they know which stocks are rising or falling a few seconds before that information is disseminated to the public. Given this advantage, they are also restricted in the types of trades they can do so as to prevent them from taking advantage of the public. Competitive traders also sometimes act as two-dollar brokers.

Competitive Market-Maker

Competitive market-makers buy and/or sell stock in any listed issue at the request of a floor official or other broker holding a customer's order. They have the ability to deal in any stock, which differentiates them from specialists who are limited to their assigned issues. They also differ from competitive traders in that they are required to provide market depth and narrower spreads in order to accommodate the public's orders.

TYPES OF ORDERS

Another advantage of doing business on an exchange is that clients can use a wide variety of types of orders to accomplish their investment objectives.

The three basic types of orders allowed on the exchange floor are:

- Market orders.
- Limit orders.
- Stop orders.

Market Order

A *market order* is an order to buy or sell a specified number of shares of a security immediately at the best available price.

Example: If the last trade in a stock was at $24 a share, and you enter a market order, your order will probably be executed at a price close to $24 a share.

The actual execution price, however, could be higher or lower if the price of the stock changes before the order reaches the trading post. If the brokerage firm has handled the order promptly, the customer has to live with the effects of the price change—whether favorable or not. On the other hand, what happens if a brokerage firm does not execute a market order immediately (because the order is lost or because the floor broker takes too long to get to the trading post), and a price change adversely affects the client? In such a case, the brokerage firm becomes liable to the client for the difference.

To avoid these situations, a client can add a qualification to a market order: "market not held (NH)." By entering a *market not held* order, the client gives the floor broker some discretion with regard to *when* to execute the order.

Example: If the client submits an order to buy 1,000 shares of ABC at the market and marks the order "not held," the floor broker is free to use his or her judgment as to when to execute the order. Perhaps, when the floor broker gets to the trading post where the stock is traded, a number of other brokers are all trying to sell the stock. The floor broker concludes that all these sell orders will push the price of the stock down and that, in a few minutes, there is a good chance the stock's price will be lower. By coming back a little later to execute the buy order, the floor broker can probably get the 1,000 shares of ABC for the client *at a lower price.*

In exchange for giving the floor broker discretion, the client also forfeits the right to compensation if the floor broker guesses wrong. So, while you may get a better price, you may also get a worse price if you elect to use the "not held" option.

Limit Order

A *limit order* is an order to buy or sell a quantity of a security, but only if the client can get a specific price or better.

Example: A client wants to sell 1,000 shares of a certain stock, but only at a price of $24 a share or better. In this case the client enters a "sell limit at 24" order. If, when the floor broker gets to the trading post, another broker (either from another firm or the specialist) is willing to pay 24⅛, the floor broker sells the client's stock at 24⅛. If the best price available is 24 a share, then the floor broker accepts 24. If, however, the highest bid is 23⅞, which is below the client's minimum, the shares are not sold.

If a limit order cannot be executed immediately, the floor broker leaves the order with the specialist. If the price of the stock changes so that the order can be executed at the limit price or better, the specialist executes the trade and notifies the client's floor broker of the transaction. This is another very useful service that specialists provide for clients.

Stop Order

A *stop order* is an order to buy a stock above its current market price or to sell a stock below its current market price. At first glance, entering an order to buy at a higher price or sell at a lower price than the current price might not appear to make much sense. However, stop orders serve a number of useful purposes.

Example: Having bought stock at $10 a share, the value of the stock rises, over time, to $40 a share. You have a very nice profit. Based on your analysis of the stock, you feel that the stock's market value can rise even higher, but you don't want to lose the profit you already have. So you are torn between selling the stock (taking your profit) and holding onto the stock for a little longer and trying to get a higher price.

A stop order can solve your problem.

If you enter a "sell stop order at $38," then *if and only if* the market value of the stock drops to a point where it trades at $38, your sell stop order becomes a market order to sell. Your shares are automatically sold for *about* $38 a share, thus protecting the majority of your profit.

On the other hand, if the price of the stock rises, the order is not executed. If the market value of the stock rises to $45 ($5 higher), you might also want to raise the price of your sell stop order by $5 to protect more of your now larger profit.

Here is another situation in which a stop order becomes useful. Suppose you like a stock but want to wait to buy it until it starts to move up. In other words, you're worried that the value of the stock may decline or stay flat before it starts moving up.

Example: If the value of the stock is $20 a share, you enter a "buy stop order at $21" a share. If the price of the stock reaches $21 (that is, if a trade occurs at $21), then your buy stop becomes a buy market order and you'll own the stock. However, if the price of the stock drops or stays flat, your buy stop order is not executed and so you are not adversely effected. Like orders, stop orders are usually left with the specialist for execution.

Additional Instructions

Limit and stop orders may be qualified by a number of additional instructions that relate to tactics and/or timing.

Day Orders vs. Good till Cancelled (GTC) Orders. Every limit and stop order entered on the exchange is automatically cancelled at the end of the trading day unless it is marked "good till cancelled (GTC)." A GTC order remains good until it is cancelled by the client. So if enter a stop or limit order with the qualifier "GTC" and you don't get an execution one day, you might get it the next.

Some brokerage firms accommodate their customers by accepting orders "good through the week" or "good through the month." Because orders with these specifications may not be entered on the trading floor itself, the firms enter them as GTC orders and then cancel the orders at the end of the week or month if they are not executed by then.

All or None (AON). An *all or none* (AON) qualification means that, unless the floor broker can surely fill the entire order, he shouldn't fill any of it.

Example: A buy limit order for "2,000 shares at $40 a share AON" means that the client will accept the trade if the floor broker can buy the entire 2,000 shares at $40. If there are only 1,000 shares available to be purchased at $40, the floor broker holds off from buying any shares. If an order is not marked AON, the client will accept a partial execution (in this case, the 1,000 shares available).

Fill or Kill (FOK). An FOK order calls for an *immediate and complete* purchase or sale of a specified amount of stock at a specified price. If the entire order cannot be filled immediately at the order price or better, it is cancelled.

Immediate or Cancel (IOC). This qualification is similar to a fill or kill order except that the client will accept a partial "fill." Thus the floor broker immediately fills as much of the order as possible and cancels any remaining balance.

At the Open or At the Close. An order so marked means that the client wants the execution to occur as close to the opening or closing bell as possible. These types of instructions are often used by clients who detect a pattern in the daily price movement of the security.

226

Execution of Different Size Orders

Orders to buy or sell large quantities of stocks are handled differently from smaller orders. While the market is sufficiently liquid to handle smaller orders without any problems, large orders have the potential of severely disturbing the market.

Basically, orders fall into four different size categories:

1. Odd lots.
2. Small orders.
3. Large orders.
4. Very large orders.

Odd Lots. An odd lot order is an order for less than the normal unit of trading. For most stocks the normal unit of trading, usually called a *round lot,* is 100 shares. (For a few infrequently traded stocks, a round lot is considered to be 10 shares.) Only round lot orders or multiples of round lot orders (200, 300, 400, and so on) can be executed on the floor of the exchange.

To allow investors to buy or sell odd lots, the exchange has installed an automatic odd lot order execution system. Clients seeking to buy an odd lot buy it from the specialist, and clients seeking to sell an odd lot order sell it to the specialist. The stock involved in the trade is automatically either subtracted from or added to the specialist's inventory.

Because odd lot orders require a lot of processing for a very small order, specialists are allowed to offset those costs by paying an eighth point less or charging an eighth point more than the price at which a round lot order would be executed. This price adjustment is called the *odd lot differential.* This "eighth" is subtracted from or added to the price at which the next round lot order is executed.

Example: If the specialist receives an order to buy 50 shares at the market at exactly noon, and the next round lot transaction takes place at 12:03 at 24½, the odd lot is executed at 24⅝. While a client can enter an odd lot limit order, clients should keep in mind that the limit price has to include this odd lot differential.

For execution purposes, brokerage firms can bunch odd lot orders from either the same customer or different customers into round lot orders. However, prior to bunching the orders, the firm must obtain the permission of every client whose orders are to be bunched. Most brokerage firms' new account agreement forms include a provision that allows the firm to bunch any of the client's odd lot orders so as to avoid paying the odd lot differential.

Small Orders. Small orders are orders that are for between 100 shares and 5,099 shares. Most people find it hard to think of 900 shares of a $150 stock ($135,000) as a small order, but that is a small order by NYSE standards. These orders can also be executed electronically and automatically via the exchange's computer system called the *Dot (Designated Order Turnaround) System.* By using this system, a brokerage firm's order room can be connected electronically to all the trading posts on the floor, and it can sell or buy at the specialist's bid or offer electronically without actually having to send the order to the floor and without having to have a floor broker execute the order. The stock that is bought or sold again comes from, or is added to, the specialist's inventory.

Large Orders. Large orders are too large to be executed on the Super Dot system (a 1,000 shares or more) but don't require special handling. These orders can be handled by the floor brokers and the specialists, with the occasional help of the competitive market-makers if necessary.

What is the maximum size of a large order? The maximum depends on the stock and specifically on its liquidity. For the most liquid stocks—IBM, GM, AT&T, and the like—an order to buy 25,000 shares or more can easily be absorbed by the market without special handling. However, for many of the smaller companies that trade on the New York Exchange, an order of 10,000 shares may well require extraordinary means in order to get a client a fair order execution. So each stock has its own upper limit depending on its average daily trading volume.

Very Large Orders. Very often, institutional clients want to buy or sell large quantities of a given stock that the market can readily accommodate. In this case the brokerage firm may request approval from the NYSE to use one of the special procedures available for very large orders. These procedures are:

• Exchange distributions or acquisitions.
• Special offerings or bids.
• Secondary distributions.

Exchange Distributions or Acquisitions. The firm handling this type of transaction furnishes the NYSE with a written notice regarding the total number of shares its client expects to buy or sell within the near future. Then, rather than going directly to the floor, the firm asks other firms (generally one or two) to canvass their clients for offsetting orders (buy orders if the initiating firm is selling, sell orders if the initiating firm is buying). Once the initiating firm is convinced that it has enough offsetting interest to allow it to execute its client's order, all the orders are sent to the floor in a coordinated manner and traded at the current market price. The client who initiated the transaction generally pays a special commission both to its firm and to the firms that rounded up the offsetting orders to compensate them for their extra efforts. This trade is then sent across the price ticker preceded by the letters "DIST" so that everyone will know that the trade was prearranged.

Special Offerings or Bids. Sometimes a client wants an order executed that is too large to be handled via a special distribution, because one or two firms cannot generate enough offsetting transactions in a short period to offset it. In this case, the firm handling the large transaction might elect to open the distribution to every firm. In this case the distribution is called a *special offering* or *special bid.* The terms (usually including a waiver of commission charges for the clients taking the other side of the transaction) are announced over the price ticker. As the special offering progresses, periodic announcements are made over the ticker regarding the number of shares still needed to be bought or sold before the special offering or bid is completed.

Secondary Distribution (Offering). Some orders are too large even for a special offering or special bid. While special offerings/bids are open to every firm, they are announced with no warning and may not give the other firms much time to line up enough offsetting transactions. So, if the order is very large, the firm handling the transaction may elect to use a secondary offering or a secondary bid.

A secondary offering/bid is announced on the tape as an offer to buy or sell a large quantity of a stock. The actual transactions take place after the market closes and off the exchange floor. Again the clients who provide the offsetting transactions are not charged commissions. Because the offering takes place after the market is closed, the firms that want to canvass their clients to solicit offsetting orders have more time to do so. Also, the secondary offering or bid can be repeated day after day until the desired number of shares are either sold or bought.

SHORTING STOCK

When most people think of investing in the stock market, they think of buying a stock, waiting for its market value to rise, and then selling the stock for a profit. In other words, "Buy low and sell high." While buying low and selling high is, of course, the way to make money in the market, the order of these two steps is irrelevant. If you sell high and then buy low, the result is the same as if you buy low and then sell high. Your profit is still the difference between the two prices. But how do you sell something you don't own?

The answer is to sell short. In a short sale you borrow shares of stock from someone who owns them and sell them in the open market for the current price. At some point in the future, you repurchase the shares and return them to the person from whom you borrowed them. The aim is to repurchase the shares at a lower price than the price at which you originally sold them—for a net profit. Short selling, then, is basically a bet that the market price of a given stock will decline.

Example: XYZ, Inc. is currently selling for $50 a share. You feel that XYZ is a weak company and that the value of its stock will decline. To profit from this decline, you borrow 1,000 shares of XYZ and sell them at $50 each. Your prediction proves to be correct, and the market price of XYZ stock falls to $20 per share. At this point you repurchase 1,000 shares of XYZ, Inc., which you return to the person from whom you borrowed the stock, securing a profit of $30,000 ($30 × 1,000) for yourself.

Of course, if the value of the stock rises after you sell it short, you are forced to rebuy it at a higher price than the price at which you sold it, which results in a loss.

Example: If you sell short 1,000 shares at $50 per share and then repurchase the shares at $60 per share, you lose $10,000. Since there is no maximum price for stocks (at least theoretically), there is no limit to the loss you can sustain on a short sale.

In the early 1900s it was fairly common for a wealthy investor (or group of investors) to select a company and then to sell short a massive amount of the company's stock. The sheer volume of these sales would depress the market value of the company's stock. Small investors who were long the company's stock would not know why the stock was going down, panic, and sell their shares at the now lower price. The buyers would inevitably be the short sellers themselves, repurchasing the stock to lock in their profits.

To prevent the same type of market manipulation from occurring today, there are rules regarding when you can make a short sale. In particular, short sales can be executed on only either an "uptick" or a "zero uptick." That is, you can execute a short sale only if *the price at which the sale occurs is either:*

1. One eighth point higher than the last transaction (an uptick sale).

2. Or at the same price as the last transaction, providing that the last price change was an uptick (a zero uptick rule).

Example: Thus if transactions in XYZ, Inc. common are done at these prices (assuming the first sale is a downtick):

Transaction	Price
1	40
2	40⅛
3	40¼
4	40¼
5	40¼
6	40⅛
7	40⅛

Here is when short sales may occur:

Transaction	Effect
1	No. The trade is a downtick (given).
2	Yes. The trade is an uptick.
3	Yes. The trade is an uptick.
4	Yes. The trade is a zero uptick.
5	Yes. The trade is a zero uptick.
6	No. The trade is a downtick.
7	No. The trade is a zero downtick.

Because there are rules governing when a short sale can be done, every sale order sent to the floor must be clearly marked as either a *short sale* (selling shares the client does not own) or a *long sale* (selling shares the client does own). Specialists often short an order to fill customers' buy orders.

Borrowing Stock

When investors buy stock, they don't know whether the seller is selling short or selling long—nor do they care. The buyer simply wants the purchased stock to be delivered as promised on the trade's settlement date. So, to sell short, you have to borrow the shares sold for delivery to the buyer as promised. Fortunately, borrowing shares is relatively easy.

For most customers the firm handling the short sale arranges the loan of the stock at no additional charge. The firm can borrow stock from four sources:

1. The firm's other customers.
2. Other firms' customers.
3. Certain institutions.
4. Specialty firms.

First, the firm may borrow other customers' securities that have been bought on margin and that have outstanding loan balances. Before being permitted to buy stock on margin, clients must sign a "margin agreement." One of the clauses in this agreement is that the brokerage firm can lend the client's securities (on which there is an outstanding loan balance) to other firms or to other clients of the same firm so that they can sell the shares short. Clients who are long the shares in their margin accounts can still sell their shares at any time.

Example: If a client of Smith Barney brokerage firm wants to short XYZ, Inc. and none of Smith Barney's other clients are long the stock in their margin accounts, the firm tries to borrow the stock from another firm with a client who owns XYZ in a margin account. Smith Barney might borrow the stock from Kidder Peabody, who will get it from one of its client's margin accounts. The next time Kidder Peabody needs a stock for one of its clients, it will borrow it from Smith Barney. This type of cooperation benefits both the firms and the clients.

If another firm cannot be found to lend the needed shares, the next possible source of stock is one of the many other types of financial institutions, mostly insurance companies. These institutions are the third alternative because they generally charge brokerage firms a small fee for lending the securities. By charging a fee the insurance company enhances the overall return it earns on its stock portfolio.

If no such institution has the stock to lend, the borrowing firm has to retain a specialty firm to hunt down the stock it needs. Because these specialty firms charge large fees, they are the lenders of last resort. Frequently, if many investors all want to short the same stock, borrowing the stock becomes difficult and brokerage houses have to turn to these specialty firms to hunt down borrowable shares.

Margin Requirements

Whenever a client borrows stock, that stock must be returned to the party from whom it is borrowed. To ensure return of the stock at a future date, the party shorting the stock must open a margin account and make an initial margin deposit equal to 50% (according to Reg T) of the value of the shorted stock.

Example: If Bill Smith wants to short 1,000 shares of a $50 stock, he has to open a margin account and deposit $25,000 of initial margin.

When Bill sells the stock, he receives the $50,000 sale proceeds, bringing the total account balance to $75,000. Thus, if the price of the stock should rise (to the detriment of the short seller), the lender of the security is fully protected until the stock's price reaches $75 a share. Of course, before the price of the stock reaches $75, the investor who shorted the stock would have to post additional margin.

Timing

Once a short position is established, it can be closed at any time by simply repurchasing the security and returning it to the party from whom you borrowed it. No prior notification is required. Similarly, the lender of the security can usually recall the security at any time. If the lender wants the security back, the client who shorted the stock has no choice other than to repurchase the shares unless another lender can be found.

If there is no regulatory requirement dictating when a short sale must be closed, how long is a short seller likely to keep the position open? The answer is not long. Because investors can short stock only in a margin account, those who want to short stock always incur some margin interest expense. So timing becomes important in short sales—no one wants to pay margin interest on a position that's just sitting flat. To have a *profitable* short sale, it is very important to pick stocks whose market value will not only drop, but also drop quickly.

OTHER EXCHANGES

In addition to the New York Stock Exchange, a number of other major exchanges (the American Stock Exchange in New York, the Philadelphia Exchange, the Pacific Exchange, and so on) have similar trading policies and operational procedures.

Some companies have their stocks listed on more than one exchange. Naturally, arbitrageurs work to assure that the market value of the same stock on different exchanges remains close.

CONCLUSION

Exchanges offer many advantages: a centralized location for trading, liquid and orderly markets, and supervision of the trading activity. At one time, no doubt, these were *big* advantages. A question is being debated within the industry, however, as to whether these benefits justify the costs associated with exchange-based trading. In an age when interactive, global telecommunications systems allow traders on different continents to transact deals in seconds, the need for a central location is cast in doubt.

15

The Over-the-Counter Securities Market

Any security transaction that does not take place on a security exchange is said to occur in the over-the-counter (OTC) market. Usually traded in the OTC market are:

- U.S. government securities.
- U.S. agency securities.
- Corporate bonds.
- Municipal bonds.
- Stocks of companies with small capitalizations.
- Stocks of most banks and savings & loans.
- Options on bonds.
- Warrants.
- American depository receipts.

A MARKET WITHOUT GEOGRAPHIC BOUNDARIES

Many investors are initially confused by the OTC market because it has no central location, unlike an exchange with its centralized trading floor. Instead the OTC "market" is a telecommunications market.

It consists of firms located throughout the country, any of which can trade with another firm over the phone. Since phone lines reach almost everywhere in the country, the OTC market is said to be a market without geographical or physical boundaries.

Many of the brokerage firms in this country are not members of any exchange, and so they cannot transact business on an exchange. Instead they deal exclusively in securities that are traded OTC. In fact, some firms are so specialized that they deal only with one kind of security, such as U.S. government securities or municipal bonds.

BROKER/DEALERS

In any one transaction, a firm can act as either a broker or a dealer.

When a firm takes an order from a client and then merely executes the order (either in the OTC market or on an exchange), it is said to be acting as the client's *agent*, or as a *broker*. In this type of transaction, the firm never owns the security but merely performs an order execution service for the client.

When a firm buys securities from its clients (using its own money) or sells securities to its clients (out of its own inventory), it is acting as principal, or as a *dealer*. In these transactions, the firm itself is on the other side of the client's trade (the contra party). So the firm itself is one of the two principals (the buyer or the seller) in the transaction.

Most firms act in both capacities at different times. They act as brokers when their clients want to buy securities either that the firms do not have in inventory or that are traded on an exchange. They act as dealers when their clients want to sell securities that the firms want to buy or when their clients want to buy securities that the firm inventories.

Firms that act in both capacities are called *broker/dealers* because they can buy or sell securities either as brokers (agents) or as dealers (principals).

The broker/dealer's compensation depends on its capacity in a transaction. When acting as agent, the brokerage firm charges its clients a *commission* for the services it provides. When acting as *principal*, the firm does not charge commissions, but instead:

- Tries to buy the securities for less than the price at which the firm thinks they can be resold. Or . . .
- Tries to sell the securities for more than the price paid for them.

Sometimes the firms are successful at making a profit on principal trades, and sometimes they are not.

Example: Dependable Brokerage, Inc. gets three orders from its clients in a given morning.

The first order is to sell 2,000 shares of an exchange-listed security. The firm sends the order to the floor of the exchange where it is executed at the best possible price for its client. For its services, the firm charges the client a commission.

The second order is to buy 500 shares of stock that is traded OTC. The firm itself does not have any of this security in its own inventory; so it has to buy the stock, on the client's behalf, from another firm. The firm contacts a number of firms that have the stock in their inventories to see which firm will sell it for the lowest price. After finding the lowest price, the firm buys the 500 shares and bills the client for the purchase price plus a commission. The firm again acted as its client's agent, but this time in the OTC market.

The third order is from a client who wants to buy 3,000 shares of a different OTC security. The firm has this security in its own inventory, and so it becomes the seller and fills its client's buy order. Because the firm acted as a principal in this transaction, it cannot charge the client a commission. If the firm bought these 3,000 shares for less than the price at which it sold them to the client, the firm makes a profit on the transaction. If, however, the firm bought the shares at a higher price than the price at which it sold the shares to the client, the firm incurs a loss on the transaction.

MARKET MAKING

When a firm buys and sells securities for its own account, it is said to be *market making*. Before a firm can "make a market" in a security, it has to meet certain qualifications relating to its net capital, as detailed in the NASD regulations. These regulations are designed to make sure that a firm has enough capital to back up its quotes so that there is no credit risk in the market.

The department that decides which securities to buy and sell and for what prices is called the *trading department*.

Each trader within a firm is assigned certain securities to trade. For example, one trader may be responsible for trading OTC oil stocks, while another may be responsible for trading OTC computer stocks. Every minute of every day that the market is open, these traders decide:

- What prices their firms will pay to buy the securities that they trade.
- The prices at which their firms stand ready to sell the securities that they trade.

The price at which a firm stands ready to buy a security is called its *bid price*. The price at which a firm stands ready to sell a security is called its *offer price*. By offering to both buy and sell a given security, a brokerage firm "makes a market" in the security. As market conditions change during the day, the trader raises or lowers the firm's bid and offer prices. By standing ready to buy or sell securities at their posted prices, these traders play the same role that the specialists and competitive market makers do on the exchange floor.

Example: A trader at Dependable Brokerage, Inc. is responsible for "making the market" in OTC computer stocks. For one of these companies, Wizz Bang Computers, Inc. (WBCI), the trader is currently making the market:

$$29\frac{3}{4} \text{ by } 30$$

In other words, the firm stands ready to buy WBCI stock at $29.75 and to sell it for $30. Note that the price at which the firm stands ready to sell the stock is $0.25 higher than the price at which it will buy it. This $0.25 difference, called the *spread*, is how the firm makes a profit. By buying the stock for $0.25 less than it sells it for, the firm makes a profit of a quarter on every share it buys and then sells.

So if the price stays constant throughout the day and the trader buys 5,000 shares and also sells 5,000 shares, the firm makes a profit of ($0.25 × 5,000) or $1,250.

Unfortunately for the brokerage firms and their traders, trading is not quite this easy. Ideally, traders would like to buy and sell the same number of shares each and every day so that, at day's end, they would not have any inventory to be worried about overnight. If traders are getting "more buyers than sellers" (that is, having more people buy from them than are selling to them), they compensate by raising the bid and asked prices.

Example: The trader was making the market 29¾ by 30. Now, getting "more buyers," she might now make the market:

30 by 30¼

In other words, the trader is now willing to pay $30 per share and to sell for $30.25 a share. By raising the bid price (increasing the price she is willing to pay), the trader hopes to attract more sellers. By raising the offer price (increasing the price at which she is willing to sell), the trader hopes to attract fewer buyers. By attracting more sellers and fewer buyers, the trader hopes to bring the number of buy and sell orders back into balance.

Maintaining balance is important so that the trader does not get caught with a lot of inventory in a bad market.

Example: While making a market in WBCI at 30 by 30¼, the trader receives more sell orders (totaling 10,000 shares) than buy orders (totaling 5,000 shares). By the middle of the trading day, the firm owns 5,000 shares of WBIC. If the market suddenly drops or if a negative news item about WBCI should be announced, the most anyone might be willing to pay for WBCI is, say, $28. In such a case, the market for WBCI falls to 28 by 28¼, and the firm has a loss of $10,000 ($2 per share × 5,000 shares).

The same situation results when the price of the stock moves up sharply after the trader goes short the stock. (Many traders sell stock short to fill buy orders if they do not have any shares in inventory. They then hope to buy the shares at their lower bid price to cover the short position.)

So traders who do not want to speculate with the firm's capital always try to adjust their bid and offer prices so that they are buying and selling approximately the same number of shares at all times.

241

Traders are generally not hurt by a sharply rising or a sharply falling market *unless* they build up a substantial long or short position in the security. If they are willing to settle for a small profit on each transaction, little market risk is involved.

But why settle for a small profit? If the firm profits by buying low and selling high, why not widen the spread? For example, instead of bidding 29¾ for WBCI and offering it at 30, why not bid 28 and offer to sell at 34? The firm would then make $6 on every share it bought and then sold.

Widening the spread for greater profit is not feasible for several reasons.

First, the National Association of Securities Dealers (NASD) has the 5% guideline prohibiting price differentials of more than 5% except under extraordinary circumstances. Only if a firm incurs an extraordinary expense in trying to fill a client's order can it exceed this 5% guideline.

Second, the competition among dealers for each other's business and for clients' business is fierce. Very often a number of firms all make markets in the same securities. Anyone who wants to buy the security—either other firms or clients—of course, buys it from the firm offering it at the lowest price. Likewise, any firm or client wanting to sell a security will sell it to the firm willing to pay the highest price for it. Thus a firm that posts low bids and high offers will just not do any business.

POSTING QUOTES

How do firms make their prices known to other dealers and to clients? The answer depends on the security itself and on the amount of capital that the issuing company has.

The Pink Sheets

If the issuing company is small or the security rarely traded, the security is listed in the *National Quotation Bureau* (NQB) sheets. These daily "sheets" list:

1. The securities currently being offered for sale and the firms (with their phone numbers) trying to sell them.

THE NATIONAL DAILY QUOTATION SERVICE

Published by NATIONAL QUOTATION BUREAU, Inc.

P. O. Box 49, Peck Slip Station,
New York, N. Y. 10038

212-349-1800
LISTING DEPT. 212-349-2213

TWX 710-581-6560

SYMBOLS / Listings received by mail today. All other listings current today.

* Correspondent.

"Other arrangement."

VJ In Bankruptcy or receivership or being reorganized under the Bankruptcy Act, or securities assumed by such companies.

RBA Representative Bid—Asked Quotations supplied through NASDAQ as of 11:A. M.

N Q B OVER – THE – COUNTER INDUSTRIAL STOCK AVERAGE.

35 ISSUES. DIVISOR 2.16 ADJUSTED FOR SPLITS AND STOCK DIVIDENDS.

	OPENED	CLOSED	CHANGED	HIGH	LOW
1975	282.91	375.07	+ 92.16	459.83 JUN 26	282.91 JAN 2
1976	377.64			461.02 FEB 26	377.64 JAN 2
JUN	403.23	407.83	+ 4.60	407.83 JUN 30	389.93 JUN 10
JUL	408.46	409.38	+ 0.92	413.97 JUL 15	406.55 JUL 21
AUG	411.53	398.34	– 13.19	414.47 AUG 4	394.34 AUG 25
SEP	397.93			408.34 SEP 8	397.93 SEP 1
SEP 2	3		7	8	9
404.24 + 6.31	404.06 – 0.18		406.26 + 2.20	408.34 + 2.08	408.23 – 0.11

N Q B INSURANCE STOCK AVERAGE

15 ISSUES. DIVISOR 6.17 ADJUSTED FOR SPLITS AND STOCK DIVIDENDS.

	OPENED	CLOSED	CHANGED	HIGH	LOW
1975	69.55	74.45	+ 4.90	87.15 JUL 18	65.04 JAN 15
1976	74.80			92.95 AUG 18	74.63 JAN 28
JUN	76.21	80.18	+ 3.97	80.18 JUN 30	75.91 JUN 7
JUL	80.75	88.65	+ 7.90	88.65 JUL 30	79.20 JUL 7
AUG	89.73	88.74	– 0.99	92.95 AUG 18	88.27 AUG 27
SEP	89.22			90.74 SEP 8	89.22 SEP 1
SEP 2	3		7	8	9
90.21 + 0.99	90.82 + 0.31		90.40 – 0.12	90.74 + 0.34	90.52 – 0.22

```
A C E PLASTIK PAK CO COM    NCC PRICE AVG    7  5/8
   AMSWISS INTL CORP J CY    800 631 3080
A A I CORP                   NCC PRICE AVG    5  1/4
   PBW STOCK EXCHANGE LISTED 215 563 4700
AAR CORP                     NCC PRICE AVG    9 27/32
   AMSWISS INTL CORP J CY    800 631 3080
A A V COMPANIES              NCC PRICE AVG    5  7/8
A B A INDUSTRIES INC   ABAI
   VOL- N/A HB-  5 1/2 LB-   5 1/4          5 1/4   6
   DPCO*HRZG,JANS,SRCO
A B C INDUSTRIES INC         NCC PRICE AVG       5/8
   TROSTER SINGER & CO NY    212 422 2400
   B S LICHTENSTEIN & CO NY  212 425 4311    1/8
A C C S CORP COM
   E J QUINN & CO INC J CY   212 425 1240
A C F INDUSTRIES INC         NCC PRICE AVG   34
   AMSWISS INTL CORP J CY    800 631 3080
ACS INDUSTRIES INC           NCC PRICE AVG       3/4
   BERNARD L MADOFF NY       800 221 2242
   M RIMSON & CO INC NY      212 964 2634
   AMSWISS INTL CORP J CY    800 631 3080
   SHERWOOD SECS CORP J CY   212 425 0300    1/2    7/8
   CARR SECS CORP NY         212 425 8220    1/2    7/8
A C S INVESTOR INC           NCC PRICE AVG   1 5/8
   CARR SECS CORP NY         212 425 8220
ADA FINANCIAL SVCE CORP      NCC PRICE AVG       1/4
   HERZOG & CO INC J CY      800 631 3095
   NEUBERGER SECS CORP NY    212 732 6030    1/8    1/2
ADM INDUSTRIES INC           NCC PRICE AVG      21/32
AEG TELEFUNKEN ADR           NCC PRICE AVG   32 1/2
   CARL MARKS & CO INC NY    212 437 7100
   MERRILL LYNCH PFS NY      212 766 7820   34      36
AES TECHNOLOGY SYSTEMS       AEST
   VOL- 19 HB-  1 3/8 LB-    1 1/4          1      1 1/2
```

```
A L D INC COM
   COOK INVESTMENT CO CG     800 621 8015
A M F INC 3 90 PR            NCC PRICE AVG   40 1/4
   MCMULLEN & HARD NY        212 349 1080
   LEHMAN BROS NY            212 344 6627
   SWIFT HENKE & CO NY       212 425 0360
   M S WIEN & CO INC J CY    800 631 3088
A M F INC COM                NCC PRICE AVG   19 7/8
   AMSWISS INTL CORP J CY    800 631 3080
   H S KIPNIS & CO CG        800 621 6630
A M I C CORP N C             NCC PRICE AVG   13 3/8
   AMSWISS INTL CORP J CY    800 631 3080
A M I INDUSTRIES INC AMIN
   VOL-  8 HB-  5 3/8 LB-    5 3/8          5 3/4   6 1/4
   BOET*TSCO,ILCO,WBLR
A M I INDUSTRIES INC COM     NCC PRICE AVG   2 5/8
A P F ELECTRONCS INC COM   APFE
A M I INDUSTRIES INC NY      NCC PRICE AVG  10 3/4  11 1/2
   BJCO,GALS,LOEB,NASH,MRKS,MSRO*SHWD,SHDN
   CONLON DIV BAIRD PAT NY   212 425 1130
   MULLER & CO NY            212 952 9444
   GALLANT SECS INC NY       212 593 2320
   CARL MARKS & CO INC -MRKS 212 437 7100
API TRUST SBI             APTS
   VOL-  30 HB-  3 1/2 LB-   3 1/2          3 1/2   4 1/4
   AMIC,LOEB,NASH,SHDN
A P L CORPORATION COM        NCC PRICE AVG  14 7/8
   AMSWISS INTL CORP J CY    800 631 3080
A P L CORP WTS             APLCW
   VOL-  6 HB-  4 1/2 LB-    4 3/8          4 1/2   5
   HRZG,JLSS,NASH,SGMK,WIEN
   HERZOG & CO INC    -HRZG  800 631 3095
A P S INC COM             APSI
   VOL-  6 HB-  7 3/4 LB-    7 1/2          7 1/4   8
   BEST,EMUT,GSCO,KPCO,NASH,RMDU,SGMK,WEDB
```

Figure 15-1. *Part of Page 1 of a Daily "Pink Sheet."*

2. The securities currently being sought and the firms (with their phone numbers) trying to buy them.

The sheets that contain the stock and warrant listings are called the *pink sheets* because they are printed on pink paper. On any given day, the listings contain about 11,000 different OTC stocks and warrants.

The sheets that contain the corporate bond listings are called the *yellow* sheets because they are printed on yellow paper.

Because these sheets are printed only once a day, and the value of the securities can change constantly, a prospective buyer or seller of the securities listed in the sheets must call the firms listed in the sheets and get their current bids or offers.

The NASDAQ System

Quotes for more actively traded securities or for securities issued by larger companies can be found on the *National Association of Securities Dealers Automated Quotation System* (NASDAQ). Founded in 1971, this system is an electronic communication network with hookups for market makers, registered representatives, and regulators. Firms that wish to buy or sell securities can post their bids or offers electronically. Because the system is computerized, firms can change their bids and offers throughout the day as market conditions change.

Because subscribers use this information system for different purposes, not all subscribers need access to the same level of information. For this reason three different levels of service are available, representing various levels of complexity and, of course, of cost.

Level One. This level shows only the highest bid price and lowest offer price for a given security without disclosing the name of the firm making the bid or offer. It is used by registered representatives so as to indicate the current "market" to potential buyers and sellers of a security. Often one firm is making the highest bid while another is making the lowest offer. Neither the broker nor the client really cares which firm they buy from or sell to; they care only about price. The highest bid and the lowest offer are often called the *inside market*.

Level Two. Service at this level shows what every firm is bidding and offering for every NASDAQ listed security. Retail traders use it to know not only the best quotes, but also the firms making the

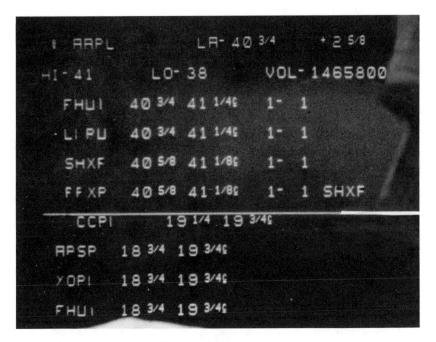

Figure 15-2. A NASDAQ Trading Screen.

quotes. By knowing the firms' names, traders know whom to call to buy or sell the security to fill an order.

Level Three. This service is the same as level two service, except that traders may enter, delete, or update quotations for securities in which they are making a market. Thus the senior traders who decide their firms' bid and offer prices are the only ones who need level three service. Because every firm that lists a quote on this system must stand ready to buy or sell a round lot of the security at the price it quotes, code letters are used to prevent unauthorized parties from changing a firm's quotes.

TYPES OF QUOTATIONS

Securities dealers, particularly those who deal primarily in thinly traded securities can make or obtain several types of quotes: firm, subject, and workout.

Firm Quotes

Firm bids or offers are prices at which the broker/dealer is committed to buy or sell a specified amount of a security. A firm bid or offer is usually good for the moment that the quote is given, but it may also be firm for a longer period. Also, unless otherwise stated, it is good for at least one unit of trading. In other words, the broker/dealer's commitment to buy or sell at the quoted price is limited to 100 shares of stock or 10 bonds at the quoted price. (Bond dealers vary with regard to the size of their firm quotes.) Any quote on the NASDAQ system is considered firm for one round lot. Orders for more than a round lot are subject to negotiations between the buying firm and the selling firm.

Subject Quotes

When a broker/dealer gives a quote and says it's *subject,* then the quote is "subject" to confirmation. The broker/dealer needs more information before making the quote firm. Subject quotes can be expressed in several ways:

Example:

- "It's quoted [that is, I'm not quoting it] 10–10½."
- "Last I saw, it was 10–10½."
- "It is 10–10½ subject."

Workout Quotes

Sometimes there is a very wide spread and the broker follows the quote with the word *workout.* This quote is not firm. It merely provides a range in which the broker/dealer believes a price can be "worked out." These quotes are frequently used for infrequently traded securities.

National Market System (NMS)

National Market System stocks, approximately 4,000 at this writing, meet guidelines set by the National Association of Securities Dealers (discussed later in the chapter).

The National Market System consists of stocks for which more information is available than for other OTC stocks. For most stocks traded over the counter, the newspaper listing shows the name, dividend, volume, bid/asked, and day-to-day price changes. In addition to this information, listings for NMS stocks include high and low prices for the previous 52 weeks, as well as high and low prices for the day. Trades in NMS stocks are reported within 90 seconds of when they occur.

THIRD MARKET TRANSACTIONS

Over-the-counter trades of stocks listed on the New York Stock Exchange (or on any other national stock exchange) are called *third market* transactions. These transactions were very popular prior to 1975 when the NYSE had fixed commission rates. Once the NYSE rates became negotiated (in effect, reduced), the number of third market transactions dropped drastically.

Today, however, third market transactions are again on the upswing. Frequently, a firm that is accumulating shares in a potential takeover target wants first to accumulate a sizable block of its prey's stock in the OTC market before it starts buying large quantities on the exchange floor. The third market offers a way for an acquiring firm to accumulate a large number of shares of a listed security without causing the daily volume figures, as reported by the exchange, to rise sharply.

FOURTH MARKET TRANSACTIONS

Fourth market transactions are over-the-counter trades made directly between large institutional investors, such as insurance companies or pension funds, and bank trust departments. Broker/dealers are not involved in these trades.

Institutional investors interested in buying and selling large blocks of securities do a substantial business in the over-the-counter market for several reasons. For one, they deal a lot in government and municipal bonds, which trade almost entirely over the counter. Second, they are also involved in distributions of new issues, both primary and secondary, which, again, take place in the over-the-counter market. Finally, large block transactions can be executed over the counter in such a way as to avoid unduly affecting the price of the security. (Attempting to sell too much stock on an exchange might depress the price.)

THE NATIONAL ASSOCIATION OF SECURITY DEALERS (NASD)

The National Association of Security Dealers (NASD) was organized under the Maloney Act, an amendment (Section 15A) to the Securities Exchange Act of 1934. Although established by Congress and supervised by the SEC, the NASD operates not as a government agency but as an independent membership association.

Purposes of the NASD

The NASD's certificate of incorporation, listing its purposes and objectives as shown in Figure 15-3, empowers the association to set operating standards to promote just and equitable principles of trade and to require adherence to high standards of commercial honor and integrity.

The NASD's power to regulate lies in its ability to deny membership to any broker/dealer operating in an unethical or improper manner. Because only NASD members have the advantage of price concessions, discounts, and similar allowances, the loss of membership

Figure 15-3. *Objectives of the NASD.*

To promote the investment banking and securities business.
To standardize principles and practices.
To promote high standards of commercial honor.
To promote the observation of federal and state security laws by members.
To provide a medium through which members may consult with government and other agencies.
To enable members to cooperate with governmental authority in the solution of problems affecting the securities of the industry and investors.
To adopt and enforce rules of fair practice.
To promote just and equitable principles of trade for the protection of investors.
To promote self-discipline among members.
To investigate and adjust grievances between the public and NASD members, as well as between NASD members.

privileges all but prevents a firm from competing in the marketplace. In addition, NASD members are permitted to do business only with other members, although they may deal with foreign banks and dealers.

How the NASD Is Organized

Board of Governors. The NASD Board of Governors is comprised of 31 members. Some of the members are elected by the board itself, but most are elected by the membership. Each of the NASD's 13 districts elects one or more governors as representatives on the board for three-year terms. The board as a group administers and manages the affairs of the NASD.

District Committees. The members in each of the 13 districts elect a committee, which supervises NASD programs in the district. In addition, it serves as a business conduct committee by doing the following:

• Reviewing the reports of NASD examiners.

• Investigating complaints against members.

• Conducting disciplinary proceedings.

• Imposing penalties for violations of federal and state laws and the NASD's Rules of Fair Practice.

The chairman of each district committee also serves as an advisor to the Board of Governors.

Bylaws. The NASD's bylaws spell out the terms and conditions of everyday operation of the NASD, as well as the classification, qualification, and responsibilities of its members, including the Rules of Fair Practice. The bylaws also deal with such key issues as membership, registration, and qualification standards.

Membership. Membership in the NASD is open to all properly qualified brokers and dealers whose regular course of business is transacted in any branch of the investment banking or securities businesses in the United States. A *broker* is defined as a legal entity (individual, corporation, or partnership) that effects transactions for the accounts of others. A *dealer* is a legal entity that engages in the buying or selling of securities for its own account. All broker/dealers must be registered with the SEC and the state authorities, as required by law, to be eligible for membership in the NASD. By definition, banks are not broker/dealers and are therefore not eligible for NASD membership.

Some broker/dealers may not become members of the NASD, according to the bylaws. Because the main purpose of the NASD is to promote high standards of commercial conduct, broker/dealers convicted of violations of law are barred from membership in the NASD. Specifically, membership is denied to the following:

1. Broker/dealers that have been suspended or expelled from a registered securities association or exchange for acts inconsistent with just and equitable principles of trade.
2. Broker/dealers whose registration with the Securities and Exchange Commission has been revoked or denied.
3. An individual who has been named as a "cause" of a suspension, expulsion, or revocation, or one whose registration as a registered representative has been revoked by the NASD or a national securities exchange.
4. An individual who has been convicted within the preceding ten years of any crime arising out of the securities business and involving embezzlement, fraudulent conversion, misappropriation of funds, or the abuse or misuse of a fiduciary relationship.
5. A broker/dealer whose partner, officer, or employee is not qualified for NASD membership.
6. A broker/dealer with officers, partners, or employees who are required to be registered representatives but who are not.

NASD RULES OF FAIR PRACTICE

The Rules of Fair Practice are a part of the NASD bylaws designed to promote and enforce the highest ethical conduct in the securities business. The most basic of the rules is Section 1, Article III, which states the fundamental philosophy of the NASD: "a member in the conduct of his business, shall observe high standards of commercial honor and just and equitable principles of trade."

The broad-based Rules of Fair Practice include specific rules on many areas of the securities business. Some of the areas addressed by the rules are as follows:

NASD Member Firm Advertising

The Rules of Fair Practice consider it a violation for a member to publish, circulate, or distribute any advertisement, sales literature, or market letter that a member knows to contain untrue, false, or misleading statements. Similarly, no material fact or qualification can be omitted from advertising material if such an omission causes the material to be misleading. In short, all advertising, sales, and market literature must be based on the principles of fair dealing and good faith.

Execution of Retail Trades

So that all customers may benefit from a free and open market, NASD members must use "reasonable diligence"—that is, consider all pertinent factors—to make sure that the customer gets the best possible price under prevailing market conditions. The rules also state that a member's obligation to do the best for customers is not fulfilled by channeling business through another broker/dealer, unless using a third party reduces costs to the customer.

Receipt and Delivery of Securities

No member may accept a customer's purchase order for any security without first making sure that the customer agrees to receive those securities against payment. On the sell side, no member may sell securities for a customer without being reasonably sure that the customer possesses the securities and will deliver them within five business days. To satisfy the requirement of "reasonable assurance," the broker/dealer or registered representative should note on the order ticket the present location of the securities to be sold.

Figure 15-4. *Sections in the Rules of Fair Practice.*

Section 1: *Business Conduct of Members.* The broad directive is to "observe high standards of commercial honor and just and equitable principles of trade." Outlined here are the conditions for accepting buy orders in a cash account, sell orders, or short sale orders, as well as directions for handling proxy materials.

Section 2: *Recommendations as to Customers.* This section stresses (1) knowing your customer and (2) obtaining the essential facts about a customer on a new account report form. The purpose is to provide the customer with *fair treatment* and intelligent counsel.

Section 3: *Charges for Services Performed.* Any fees must be reasonable and not unfairly discriminatory. Fees may include charges for collecting dividend or interest payments, tendering securities, registering certificates, subscriptions for new securities offered via rights or warrants, and so on.

Section 4: *Fair Prices and Commissions.* Members are directed to establish *fair and reasonable* markups, markdowns, or commissions. This section contains the 5-percent guidelines policy.

Section 5: *Publication of Transactions and Quotations.* False quotations and prices are forbidden. Nominal subject or nonbinding quotations, if used, must be identified as such. Using nominal quotations to force the contraparty to reveal a position—as a buyer or seller—is not permitted.

Members may not quote securities in newspapers, on the radio, or on television except under certain conditions. Only interdealer quotations (the inside market) may be published, not retail markups, markdowns, or commissions. Nominal quotations or quotations without bid prices may not be published for public information under any circumstances.

Section 6: *Offers at Stated Prices.* A dealer who makes a firm quotation for a security must be prepared to transact business at that price in the security's normal trading unit. Reneging, or backing away, violates principles of fair practice.

Section 7: *Disclosure of Price in Selling Agreements.* Underwriting syndicate and selling group agreements must disclose (1) the public offering price and (2) to whom and under what circumstances any price concessions may be allowed.

Section 8: *Securities Taken in Trade.* This section is designed to discourage dealers from swapping at artificial prices. A member offering securities at a fixed price, through either a syndicate or a selling group, may purchase other securities in trade (swap) from customers only (1) at fair market prices prevailing at that time or (2) if the member acts as agent in the transaction, charging a normal commission.

Example: If a member pays an inflated price for another issue in a customer's portfolio, the customer than has enough funds to purchase another security being offered by the members at a high public offering price. Although the member loses some money disposing of the customer's issue at the low prevailing market price, the markup on the public offering is high enough to make an overall profit. But because the customer

Figure 15-4. (*contd.*)

receives an artificial price for the first security, this practice, often referred to as *overtrading* or *highballing,* violates this section.

Section 9: Information Obtained as a Fiduciary. Anyone serving as a transfer agent, disbursement agent, trustee, or in a similar capacity has access to information about the ownership of securities. These agents may not use such information to induce purchases, sales, or exchanges in the issues, unless requested to do so by the issuing corporation.

Section 10: Influencing or Rewarding Employees of Other Firms. Members or their employees may not give any gift of more than $50 per person, per year (in cash or merchandise) to someone representing or associated with a customer, if the gratuity is related to business accepted from the recipient or from the recipient's employer. Bona fide employment contracts for services rendered are not subject to this limitation.

In some cases, registered representatives are paid commissions after they leave the employ of a broker/dealer: even after their deaths, survivors may be paid their commissions. Commissions may be paid, however, *only* if a bona fide contract was drawn up and signed by the rep while employed with the paying firm.

Section 11: Payment to Influence Market Prices. Except for legitimate paid advertising practices, members may not give anything of value to someone to influence or to reward comment in a public medium that may affect the market price of a security.

Section 12: Disclosures on Confirmations. Upon or before the completion of a customer's transaction, a member must furnish the customer with a confirmation that, among other things, states (1) whether the member acted as principal, as agent for the customer or for another person, or as agent for the customer and another person; (2) on principal transactions, whether the member is a market-maker in the issue; (3) on agency transactions, the contraparty's name and all commissions on the transaction.

Members who execute orders in listed securities in the third market and who act as brokers in such transactions are frequently charged an ⅛-point fee over the going price on the exchange by the market-maker. If the member intends to pay the fee out of the commission charged on the transaction, the member must notify the customer in a legend on the confirmation.

Section 13: Disclosure of Control. Broker/dealers who control, or who are controlled by, the issuer of a security must disclose that fact in writing to the customer before completing any transaction in the issue.

Section 14: Disclosure of Participation in Primary or Secondary Distributions. If a broker/dealer participates in or has a financial interest in the primary or secondary distribution of any security offering, the representative must tell the customer in writing before completing the transaction.

Section 15: Discretionary Accounts. Registered representatives may not exercise discretionary power in any account unless (1) they have written authorization from the customer and (2) written acceptance is evidenced by the

Figure 15-4. (*contd.*)

initials of a registered principal of the member firm. Even then, each discretionary order must be initialed promptly by a registered principal, and the account must be reviewed at frequent intervals to ensure against churning or transactions beyond the customer's financial capability.

The restrictions on "discretion" do not apply to the use of judgment regarding the price or time of execution, when the customer, either orally or in writing, requests such discretion.

Section 16: Offerings at the Market. Sometimes a member participates or has a financial interest in the primary or secondary distribution of a security that is not trading on a national securities exchange. In this case, the firm may represent the security as a *market offering* or as an offering *at the market*, if the member is the only market-maker for the issue. "Market" terms imply a competitive situation, and only one market-maker does not constitute such a situation.

Section 17: Solicitation of Purchases on an Exchange to Facilitate Distribution of Securities. When a broker/dealer participates in the distribution of a security or has a financial interest in a security, it may not offer any *special* compensation or inducement to get the security bought and sold on a national exchange.

Section 18: Use of Fraudulent Devices. Manipulative, deceptive, or other fraudulent devices are specifically prohibited. A *boiler room* is a high-pressure sales set up with many canvassers using telephone books and purchased mailing lists to solicit customers for securities of little value, such as those issued by asset-less shell corporations. A *bucket shop* is a brokerage firm that accepts but does not immediately execute customers' orders, hoping that market values will fluctuate against the customers' interest. The firm bills the customers at the unfavorable prices while executing at profitable prices, pocketing the difference for itself.

Section 19: Customers, Securities, and Funds. NASD members and employees are forbidden to make improper use of a customer's securities or funds. Specifically prohibited are (1) pledging or lending a customer's securities improperly, (2) improperly holding fully paid securities in cash accounts or excess collateral securities in margin accounts, (3) guaranteeing customers against loss in any securities transactions, (4) sharing in the profits or losses in any customer account, except under certain circumstances.

Section 20: Installment or Partial Payment Sales. Customers may not pay for their purchases in installments, or even over a period of time, unless (1) Reg T requirements are satisfied and (2) the member firm possesses or controls the securities while the obligation is outstanding.

Section 21: Books and Records. Each member has to keep and preserve any records applying to account information, in addition to a complaint file.

Section 22: Disclosure of Financial Condition. Broker/dealers must send their customers certain annual financial statements dealing with, among other points, the firm's subordinated loans, its required and actual net capital, and material deficiencies (if any). Every six months, the firm must send its customers an uncertified balance sheet and a statement of the firm's net and required net capital.

Figure 15-4. (*contd.*)

This section also defines *customer* as any person for whom, or with whom, the firm (1) has executed a transaction or (2) holds or owes money or securities.

Section 23: Net Prices to Persons Not in Investment Banking, or Securities Business. When dealing with someone who is not in investment banking or the securities business, members may not offer any discount, concession, or other allowance.

Section 24: Selling Concessions. Selling concessions, discounts, or other price allowances are permitted only for services rendered in the distribution of securities. So they may be granted only to broker/dealers engaged in investment banking or the securities business.

Section 25: Dealing with Nonmembers. Members must deal with nonmember broker/dealers at the same prices, commissions, fees, terms, and conditions accorded to the general public. This rule does not apply to (1) foreign broker/dealers, under certain conditions, (2) transactions on a national securities exchange with exchange members, or (3) transactions in certain exempted securities.

This last exception does not extend to municipal securities. Banks and the municipal securities departments of banks, however, are not defined as "broker/dealers." So they can and often do get favorable treatment from NASD members in municipal securities activities.

Section 26: Investment Companies. This section stipulates what members may or may not do in the offering and distribution of open-end managementries (mutual funds).

This section also requires that mutual fund sales charges should be "fair and reasonable." Although the markup is exempted from the 5-percent guideline, a sales charge higher than 8.5 percent of the offering price is considered excessive.

Section 27: Supervision. Members must maintain written procedures to ensure their employees' compliance with securities laws, regulations, and NASD policies. At least one office in the firm, called Office of Supervisory Jurisdiction (OSJ) and managed by a registered principal, must be responsible for reviewing the firm's compliance activities.

Section 28: Transactions for Personnel of Another Member. To accept an order for an employee or principal of another NASD firm, the executing firm must have written approval to open and maintain an account from the employer or fellow principal.

Section 29: Variable Contracts of an Insurance Company. A *variable contract* is an investment program whose value varies according to the performance of a portfolio maintained by an insurance company. This type of program is sold by broker/dealer affiliates of insurance companies or by broker/dealers licensed to sell insurance. The guidelines for marketing and sales charges for these programs are similar to those for mutual funds.

Section 30: Margin Accounts. This section establishes minimum initial and maintenance margin requirements, which may be more stringent than the Fed's

Figure 15-4. (*contd.*)

Reg T requirements. NASD members that are also members of a principal U.S. stock exchange are exempted from the NASD rule.

Section 31: Failed-to-Deliver Contracts. An *aged fail-to-deliver contract* is a transaction between brokerage firms that has not settled by delivery and payment for a 60-day period after the settlement date. (For foreign securities, the period is 90 days. Exempted securities are not affected by this section.) When a member has an aged failed-to-deliver contract, its registered representatives may not buy as agent for customer accounts or sell the security as principal for proprietary accounts.

Section 32: Blanket Fidelity Bond. If a member has employees and is required to join SIPC, it is subject to SEC net capital rules and must purchase and maintain fidelity bond insurance.

Section 33: Securities Options. The NASD Board of Governors is authorized to adopt, alter, amend, supplement, or modify rules relating to transactions in OTC options, as well as any listed options displayed on the NASDAQ system.

Section 34: Direct Participation (Tax-Sheltered) Programs. Direct participation programs refer to such investments as oil and gas drilling ventures, real estate syndicates (except REITs), citrus grove development, or cattle breeding programs. This section prescribes standards for such programs.

Section 35: Communication with the Public—Advertising Practices. Sales literature, market letters, and recruiting materials (except in-house intrafirm materials, tombstones, personal recommendations to clients) may not contain false or misleading statements of any material facts. Nor may such communications purposely omit important information. The section prescribes guidelines for acceptable content and approval procedures in preparing these communications.

Section 36: Transactions with Related Persons. Distributors of fixed-price offerings, such as corporate security underwritings, may not sell those issues to "related persons" unless all public demand has been satisfied. A "related person" is an entity that owns, or is owned by, an NASD member.

Section 37: Best-Efforts Underwritings (Proposed). The effect of this section is to eliminate price manipulation in secondary market activity while the security offering is still in progress. It further ensures the availability of enough certificates to reduce potential for premium prices and fail-to-deliver contracts between members when trading is permitted.

Section 38: Underwriting Inquiry Standards (Proposed). Because investment banking members must "perform due diligence" before underwriting a securities issue, this section contains guidelines to ensure adequate investigation. The investigation of tax-sheltered programs call for additional steps.

Forwarding of Reports and Proxy Material

When securities are held for a customer by a brokerage firm, they are usually held in *street name* (that is, in the name of the

Figure 15-5. *Violations of the Suitability Rule.*

1. Members should not recommend low-priced, speculative securities if they do not know the customer's other holdings, financial situation, and other relevant information. For example, a low-priced security may be suitable for a wealthy investor with large holdings who understands the risk. The same investment would not be suitable for a person of modest means on a fixed income with no other investments.
2. Creating excessive activity in a customer's account to generate commission is a violation known as *churning* or *overtrading*.
3. Trading in mutual fund shares is a violation of the Rules of Fair Practice. Mutual fund shares are considered long-term investments, and many funds charge a sales commission (or "load") on purchase. They are therefore clearly not trading vehicles, and trading these shares does not benefit the customer.
4. Members may not establish "fictitious" accounts to execute trades that would otherwise be prohibited, such as purchases of hot issues.
5. Members may not execute transactions that are not authorized by the customer.
6. Members may not use or borrow customers' securities without authorization from the customer.
7. Registered reps may not conceal transactions from the member firm that employs them.
8. No member can recommend the purchase of securities in amounts greater than the customer's financial ability to pay for them.

broker/dealer). In these cases, the issuer of the security sends all literature, including reports and proxies, to the brokerage firm, not to the customers. If NASD member firms do not promptly forward such material to customers, their conduct can be regarded as inconsistent with high standards of commercial honor.

Recommendations to Customers

According to the Rules of Fair Practice, all recommendations to a customer to purchase, sell, or exchange securities must be based on reasonable grounds and be suitable for the customer's account: The controlling factor is the best interest of the customer. To determine suitability, the member is expected to learn about the specific financial condition and needs of each customer. Specific violations of this section of the rules are listed in Figure 15-5.

NASD UNIFORM PRACTICE CODE

The Uniform Practice Code (UPC) is a part of the NASD bylaws whose purpose is the uniformity of the customs, practices, and trading

257

techniques used among all NASD members. The code includes rules for trade terms, the delivery of securities, payment, rights, stamp taxes, computation of interest, and due bills.

The administration of the UPC is the responsibility of the National Uniform Practice Committee and the District Uniform Practice Committees. Any changes in the rules by district committees must be approved by the board. Any contract between NASD members (except transactions in exempt securities or on national exchanges) is subject to the Uniform Practice Code.

If a situation arises that is not specifically covered by the written code, it is referred to the appropriate District Uniform Practice Committee for action. Controversies about an interdistrict trade are referred to the National Uniform Practice Committee.

Some of the important sections of the UPC are as follows:

Delivery of Securities

For each security transaction, there are two key dates: the trade date and the delivery date.

Trade Date. The transaction takes place on the trade date. The NASD code requires that all ordinary transactions be confirmed in writing on or before the first full business day following the trade date.

Delivery Date. The delivery date is the date on which payment is due. There are several types of delivery:

- *Cash:* Settlement occurs on the same day as the trade itself. Cash settlement is used when the client has to settle a transaction before a certain date, such as year end for tax purposes.
- *Next day:* The contract is settled the first business day after the trade date.
- *Regular way:* The seller agrees to deliver the securities to the office of the buyer on the fifth full business day following the transaction date.
- *Seller's option:* For securities other than U.S. government securities,

this type of delivery allows the seller to have the securities at the buyer's office on or before the business day that the seller's option expires.

Example: If securities are sold "seller's 30," the seller can deliver up to 30 days from the trade date, as long as one day's notice is given and five business days have elapsed from the trade date.

- This type of delivery is often requested by sellers who have difficulty getting possession of their securities.
- *Buyer's option:* This type of delivery gives the buyer the option to receive securities on a specific date.

Five-day (regular way) delivery applies to most trades in over-the-counter securities and securities listed on an exchange. All corporate, municipal, and most federal agency securities trade the regular way. United States government securities are usually settled on a next day basis.

Don't Know (DK) Procedures

After a trade, each broker/dealer sends the other a notice to confirm the details. If both parties recognize and acknowledge the trade, it is *confirmed,* or *compared.* Sometimes, however, the contrabroker (the broker/dealer with whom the trade was made) sends back a signed *DK,* a *don't know* notice, telling the confirming broker that the contrabroker does not "know"—or recognize—the trade. (Figure 16-5 in the next chapter shows an example of a DK notice.) If the contrabroker does not respond to the confirming broker by the close of four business days from the trade date, the following procedures can be used:

1. Not later than the fifteenth calendar day after the trade date, the confirming member sends a DK notice to the contrabroker.
2. The contrabroker then has four business days after the notice is received either to confirm or to DK the transaction.
3. Failure to receive a response from the contrabroker by the close of four business days constitutes a DK, and the confirming member has no further liability.

4. All DK notices sent by either party must be signed by authorized persons.

A DK is sometimes referred to as a *questioned trade* (QT).

Dividends

When a corporation declares a dividend, there are four significant dates as follows:

1. The *declaration date* is the date on which the corporation declares a dividend to common or preferred shareholders.
2. The *record date* is the date on which the corporation's recorded shareholders are listed for purposes of paying the declared dividend.
3. The *ex-dividend date* is the date on or after which the buyer of stock is *not* entitled to receive a declared dividend.
4. The *payment date* is the day on which the dividend is actually paid to shareholders.

Securities normally go *ex-dividend* (that is, without dividend) on the fourth business day preceding the record date. *Anyone purchasing the securities on or after the ex-dividend date is not entitled to receive the dividend.*

Example: Gyrus Corporation declares a dividend to be paid to holders of record on February 10, a Monday; this is the record date. Anyone buying the stock has to buy it at least five days before the record date in order to take delivery and be recorded as the owner. To be the holder of record, you have to purchase Gyrus on or by February 3 (seven calendar days or five business days before delivery). Gyrus starts trading ex-dividend on February 4.

Due Bills

Occasionally, a security is sold before the ex-dividend date but is delivered too late for the buying broker to record ownership and get the dividend. In this case, the selling broker receives the dividend but is actually not entitled to keep it. At the time of the sale, the buyer can demand a promise from the seller to pay the dividend. This claim on dividends is called a *due bill.*

Good Delivery

To assure clear ownership, the NASD Uniform Practice Code requires that all transactions must be for *good delivery*—that is, the security must be in proper form so that the record of ownership may be readily transferred. The qualifications for good delivery are as follows:

1. Stock certificates must be accompanied by an assignment. For example, if a stock certificate is registered in the name of John A. Smith, the owner must endorse the certificate exactly that way.

   The assignment (endorsement) can be made in the appropriate space on the back of the certificate. Or if a registered stockholder does not have the certificate available, a stock power can be used.

   If a certificate is issued in the name of joint tenants or tenants in common, the delivery is good only if the certificate is signed by all co-tenants. Sometimes a *power of substitution* is used, in which the owner assigns power of attorney to the broker to facilitate transfer.

2. The certificate must be in good condition.

3. When a contract is for more than 100 shares, the delivered certificates must be in denominations from which units of 100 shares can be made. For example, a trade for 300 shares can be satisfied by three certificates for 100 shares or six certificates for 50 shares. But four certificates for 75 shares are not good delivery because the pieces cannot be bunched into lots of 100 shares. For odd lots, the exact number of shares must be delivered.

4. A certificate in the name of a deceased person is not good delivery, even if it is properly assigned. Such certificates must be transferred to the executor of the estate or to street name.

5. A bond or preferred stock that is called for redemption is not good delivery unless the entire issue has been called.

6. Temporary certificates are not good delivery if permanent certificates are available.

7. Delivery of bonds should be in denominations of $1,000 or in multiples adding up to $1,000.

THE NASD CODE OF PROCEDURE

The Code of Procedure is a part of the NASD bylaws providing the rules for administering disciplinary action to members for infractions of the Rules of Fair Practice.

Complaints about violations of the NASD's rules can be filed by any member of the public, by an NASD member, by the district committee itself, or by the Board of Governors. All complaints must be made in writing and must cite the rule or interpretation allegedly violated. The respondent is allowed 10 days to answer or refute the accusation. Either party in a complaint has the right to request a hearing at which legal counsel may be present. All trade practice complaints are heard and passed upon first by the District Business Conduct Committee (DBCC), in whose district the respondent's main office is located or where the violation was purported to have taken place. The committee decides the case and determines the appropriate action. The DBCC has the power to censure, fine, suspend, and even expel members.

For minor offenses, the DBCC may offer the accused member a summary complaint proceeding. If the accused member accepts, the member agrees to admit guilt, waive a formal hearing, accept a penalty of censure and/or a fine up to $2,500, and waive all right of appeal before the Board of Governors.

More serious violations are adjudicated by the district committee through a regular procedure involving formal hearings and a trial. The committee's judgments are subject to review by the Board of Governors upon appeal by any participant or on the board's own initiative. The Board of Governors can either uphold, decrease, increase, or modify penalties.

Members not satisfied with the decision of the Board of Governors have the option of appeal outside the NASD, first to the SEC and finally to the public court system.

16

Operations—Order Processing

Until the late 1960s, securities transactions were processed on a "cash and carry" basis. For every transaction, the selling firm, on the trade's settlement date, delivered the securities by messenger to the purchasing firm. This delivery usually occurred before 11:30 A.M. The messenger delivering the securities was given a receipt for the securities and then moved on to the next delivery.

The firm receiving the securities then checked them to make sure that the delivered securities were the same ones that were purchased and that all of the other paperwork was complete. Once it determined that everything was in order, the receiving firm "cut a check" to the selling firm and arranged for the securities to be reregistered in the new owner's name.

Around 2:30 P.M. the same day, the delivering firm's messenger came back to the purchasing firm, presented the receipt, picked up the check, and returned it to the selling firm in time for the firm to:

• Verify that the check was for the correct sum.
• Deposit the check in the firm's bank.

This system left very little time for trades to be verified for accuracy and for errors to be corrected. It also required separate paperwork, messenger pickups, check cutting, and security re-registrations to be done for every single securities transaction. No matter how hard the brokerage firms' employees worked, there was a limit to how many transactions they could correctly process in a day. This became abundantly clear in the early 1970s when the New York Stock Exchange had to shorten its trading hours in an attempt to reduce the number of transactions occurring in a day—just so that the firms could keep up with the paperwork.

During this time, many firms went out of business not because they ran out of money, but simply because they couldn't keep up with the mountains of paperwork created by the cash and carry system of settlement. Clearly a new system was needed.

The system that evolved from this mayhem is still used today. The cornerstone of the system is a *securities depository* that acts as a central depot for most firms' securities. A depository holds in its vaults most of the actual security certificates owned by the firms that use the depository's services, as well as the securities owned by those firms' clients. In addition most firms maintain a cash balance at their depository.

To process a trade, the selling firm electronically instructs the clearing house to transfer the securities from its account at the depository to the purchasing firm's account there. The purchasing firm notifies the clearing house to pay the selling firm from the cash reserve in its account. When the clearing house has instructions from both firms, it verifies that they are correct and then transfers the securities and the money. With this system, no messengers need to be sent and no checks between firms need to be cut.

To simplify matters even further, the clearing house (discussed later in the chapter) "pairs off" trades.

Example: For their respective clients, Firm A sells 100 shares of XYZ, Inc. to Firm B, and Firm B sells 100 shares of XYZ to Firm C. The net effect is that Firm A has 100 shares less and Firm C has 100 shares more. The total for Firm B does not change because it has both bought and sold 100 shares of XYZ. Because Firm B has both bought and sold 100 shares of XYZ, these trades can be paired off. The clearing house simply instructs Firm A to deliver 100 shares to Firm C to settle all three transactions, thus reducing the number of transfers from three to one. Any price differentials are subtracted from, and/or added to, the firms' cash accounts, and each firm has the securities re-registered in the new owners' names.

Brokerage firms can process today's incredible volume of transactions only because of this depository/clearing house arrangement.

OPERATIONS DEPARTMENTS

The departments within a firm that collect, store, process and maintain all the paperwork associated with a securities transaction are collectively referred to as the *back office* or as *operations* (Figure 16.1). These departments support the sales department, which interacts with the firms' clients, and the trading department, which executes the buying and selling of securities. The operations departments and their functions are as follows:

New Accounts (Name and Address) Department

When a registered representative (account executive) in the firm's sales department establishes a relationship with a new client, at least three forms must be completed:

1. The *new account agreement* contains information on where the client's statements are to be sent, the client's investment objectives, usually some information about the client's employer, and/ or some credit references. (See Figure 16-2.)
2. In the *W-9 form*, clients disclose their social security numbers or tax identification numbers for the firm's and the government's tax records.
3. The *client agreement* authorizes the firm to act as the client's representative in the marketplace and establishes the terms and conditions of the client-firm relationship.

To expedite business, the new account form can be filled out over the phone by the salesperson asking the new client questions and recording the answers on the form itself. The other two forms

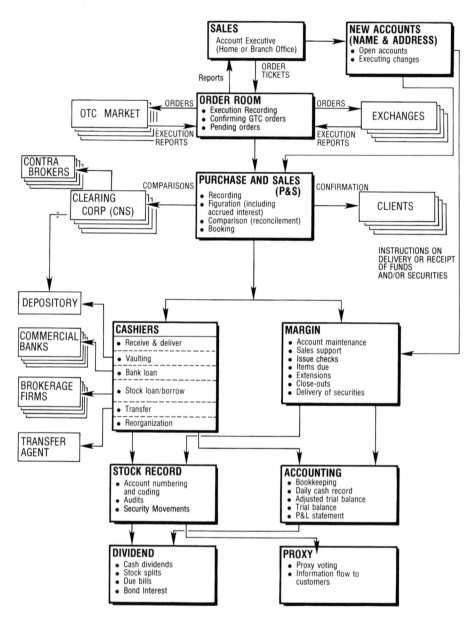

Reprinted with permission from David M. Weiss, *After the Trade Is Made: Processing Securities Transactions* (New York Institute of Finance, 1986).

Figure 16-1. *A Typical Back Office Setup.*

SF&L
Incorporated

New Account Information (Confidential)

ACCOUNT NUMBER

Branch	Account	Type	Ck.	RR

RR REGISTERED IN STATE OF
CUSTOMERS RESIDENCE   ☐ YES ☐ NO

ACCOUNT TITLE (in full as it should appear on billings; if JT Acct. specify JT/WROS or Ten. in common)

NAME _____

_____

_____

ADDRESS _____

CITY _____ STATE _____ ZIP _____

SOCIAL SECURITY OR
TAX IDENTIFICATION # |_|_|_|_|_|_|_|_|_|_|_|

RESIDENT OF N.Y. STATE

CITIZENSHIP (Country) _____ AGE _____   ☐ YES   ☐ NO

INSTRUCTIONS (SEE EXPLANATION ON BACK) CHECK ONE   DIVIDENDS

☐ HOLD SECURITIES IN FIRM NAME AND HOLD FUNDS (3/7)   ☐ PAY MONTHLY

☐ TRANSFER AND MAIL SECURITIES AS BILLED. REMIT FUNDS (1/8)   ☐ HOLD

☐ SETTLE TRADES C.O.D. THROUGH CLIENT'S AGENT. (5/6)   ☐ SAME AS ABOVE
AGENTS NAME, ADDRESS, DEPARTMENT, CLIENT'S IDENTIFICATION NUMBER

_____

_____

_____

☐ FOLLOW SPECIAL INSTRUCTIONS ON BACK (Check appropriate instructions)

☐ ALTERNATE NAME – DUPLICATE STATEMENTS, CONFIRMATION: ALTERNATE TRANSFER NAME,
ALTERNATE DIVIDEND PAYEE (SEE BACK)
*INSTITUTIONAL A/C FILL IN SHADED AREAS ONLY

TYPE OF ACCOUNT

☐ CASH
☐ MARGIN
☐ EMPLOYEE RELATED
☐ DISCRETIONARY
☐ OPTION (PROSPECTUS FURNISHED
_____)
DATE

PAPERS NEEDED

☐ JOINT ACCT. AGREEMENT
☐ MARGIN AGREEMENT
☐ TRUST AGREEMENT
☐ ESTATE PAPERS
☐ CORPORATE RESOLUTION
☐ PARTNERSHIP AGREEMENT
☐ N.Y. NON-RESIDENT WAIVER
☐ FIRST PARTY TRADING AUTHORITY
☐ THIRD PARTY TRADING AUTHORITY
☐ OPTION AGREEMENT
☐ INVESTMENT CLUB AGREEMENT
☐ INVESTMENT ADVISOR
☐ OTHER

INITIAL TRANSACTION	AMOUNT OF DEPOSIT $	TRF of A/C ☐	FORMER BROKER

EMPLOYER NAME and ADDRESS (IF UNEMPLOYED, SOURCE OF INCOME)	OCCUPATION/POSITION OR TYPE OF BUSINESS
	BUSINESS PHONE
HOME ADDRESS (IF NOT ALREADY GIVEN)	HOME PHONE
NAME OF BANK REFERENCE (IF BRANCH BANK INCLUDE LOCATION)	TYPE OF BANK ACCOUNT
	☐ CHECKING ☐ SAVINGS ☐ COMMERCIAL ☐ OTHER

IS THIS ACCOUNT TO BE OPERATED BY ANY OTHER PERSON THAN THE OWNER? ☐ NO ☐ YES, NAME _____ A/C # _____

RELATION TO CUSTOMER _____ OCCUPATION _____

ADDRESS _____ EMPLOYER _____

EXPERIENCE OF PERSON HOLDING THIRD PARTY TRADING AUTHORITY if APPLICABLE

DOES CLIENT OWN ANY UNREGISTERED STOCK?   ☐ NO   ☐ YES, COMPANY _____

DOES CLIENT OR MEMBER OF IMMEDIATE FAMILY HAVE ANY DIRECT OR INDIRECT
CONTROL RELATIONSHIP WITH A PUBLICLY OWNED COMPANY?   ☐ NO   ☐ YES, COMPANY _____

HOW WAS ACCOUNT ACQUIRED?   ☐ SOLICITED   ☐ CALL IN   ☐ AD LEAD   ☐ RE-OPENED   ☐ PERSONALLY KNOWN TO RR _____ YEARS

REFERRED BY

MARITAL STATUS   ☐ M   ☐ S   SPOUSE'S NAME _____ AGE OF DEPENDENTS _____

SPOUSE'S EMPLOYER _____

APPROXIMATE NET WORTH $	ANNUAL INCOME $	APPROX. TAX BRACKET %	AMOUNT LIFE INSURANCE $

CUSTOMER'S MAIN INVESTMENT OBJECTIVES   ☐ SAFETY OF PRINCIPAL   ☐ INCOME   ☐ LONG TERM GROWTH   ☐ TRADING PROFITS

ADDITIONAL INFORMATION FOR CLIENTS INTENDING TO WRITE UNCOVERED OPTIONS

DOES CLIENT HAVE ANY PREVIOUS EXPERIENCE
IN OPTION/COMMODITY TRADING?   ☐ NO   ☐ YES HOW LONG?   ☐ CALLS   ☐ PUTS   ☐ SPREADS   ☐ COMMODITY

HAVE YOU DISCUSSED TO CLIENT'S UNDERSTANDING THE RISK
OF WRITING UNCOVERED OPTIONS?   ☐ NO   ☐ YES

ESTIMATED LIQUID NET WORTH	CASH $	SECURITIES $	OTHER $

OTHER RELEVANT FINANCIAL INFORMATION.

DOES CLIENT MAKE HIS OWN INVESTMENT DECISIONS?   ☐ NO   ☐ YES   ☐ OCCASIONALLY

THE ABOVE IS CORRECT TO THE BEST OF MY KNOWLEDGE AND BELIEF (SIGN FULL NAME)

DATE _____ SIGNED _____   DATE _____ SIGNED _____

REGISTERED REPRESENTATIVE   OFFICER/ROP

ORIGINAL

Figure 16-2. *A New Account Information Form.*

Stone, Forrest & Rivers   INCORPORATED   **Customer Margin Agreement / Loan Consent**

Gentlemen:

In consideration of your accepting and carrying for the undersigned one or more accounts (whether designated by name, number or otherwise) the undersigned hereby consents and agrees that:

1. Applicable Rules and Statutes

All transactions under this agreement shall be subject to the constitution, rules, regulations, customs and usage of the exchange or market, and its clearing house, if any, where the transactions are executed by you or your agents, applicable provisions of the federal securities laws, and the rules and regulations of the United States Securities and Exchange Commission, and the Board of Governors of the Federal Reserve System.

2. Liens

Any and all monies, securities, or property belonging to the undersigned or in which the undersigned may have an interest held by you or carried in any of my accounts (either individually or jointly with others) shall be subject to a general lien for the discharge of all of the undersigned's debts and obligations to you, wherever or however arising and without regard to whether or not you have made advances with respect to such property, and irrespective of the number of such accounts you shall have the right to transfer, and you are hereby authorized to sell and/or purchase any and all property in any such accounts without notice to satisfy such general line. You shall have the right to transfer monies, securities, and other property so held by you from or to any other of the accounts of the undersigned whenever in your judgment you consider such a transfer necessary for your protection. In enforcing your lien, you shall have the discretion to determine which securities and property are to be sold and which contracts are to be closed.

3. Authority to Pledge

Any or all securities or any other property, now or hereafter held by you, or carried by you for the undersigned (either individually or jointly with others), or deposited to secure the same, may from time to time and without notice to me, be carried in your general loans and may be pledged, re-pledged, hypothecated or re-hypothecated, separately or in common with other securities or any other property, for the sum due to you thereon or for a greater sum, and without retaining in your possession and control for delivery a like amount of similar securities.

4. Authority to Borrow

In case of the sale of any security or other property by you at the direction of the undersigned and your inability to deliver the same to the purchaser by reason of failure of the undersigned to supply you therewith, then and in such event, the undersigned authorizes you to borrow any security or other property necessary to make delivery thereof, and the undersigned hereby agrees to be responsible for any loss which you may sustain thereby and any premiums which you may be required to pay thereof, and for any loss which you may sustain by reason of your inability to borrow the security or other property sold.

5. Maintenance of Margin

The undersigned will at all times maintain margins for said accounts, as required by you from time to time.

6. Payment of Indebtedness upon Demand

The undersigned shall at all times be liable for the payment upon demand of any debit balance or other obligations owing in any of the accounts of the undersigned with you and the undersigned shall be liable to you for any deficiency remaining in any such accounts in the event of the liquidation thereof, in whole or in part, by you or by the undersigned; and, the undersigned shall make payment of such obligations and indebtedness upon demand.

The reasonable costs and expenses of collection of the debit balance and any unpaid deficiency in the accounts of the undersigned with you, including, but not limited to, attorney's fees, incurred and payable or paid by you shall be payable to you by the undersigned.

7. Designation of Orders

It is understood and agreed that the undersigned, when placing with you any sell order for short account, will designate it as such and hereby authorizes you to mark such order as being "short," and when placing with you any order for long account, will designate it as such and hereby authorizes you to mark such orders as being "long." Any sell order which the undersigned shall designate as being for long account as above provided, is for securities then owned by the undersigned and, if such securities are not then deliverable by you from any account of the undersigned, the placing of such order shall constitute a representation by the undersigned that it is impracticable for him then to deliver such securities to you but that he will deliver them as soon as it is possible for him to do so. It is understood that such delivery is due on or before the settlement date of the transaction.

8. Capacity

In all transactions between you and the undersigned, the undersigned understands that you are acting as the brokers of the undersigned, except when you disclose to the undersigned in the confirmation that you are acting as dealers for your own account or as brokers for some other person.

9. Presumption of Receipt of Communications

Communications may be sent to the undersigned at the address of the undersigned or at such other address as the undersigned may hereafter give you in writing, and all communications so sent, whether by mail, telegraph, messenger or otherwise, shall be deemed given to the undersigned personally, whether actually received or not.

10. Reports and Statements

Reports of executions of orders and statements of the account of the undersigned shall be conclusive if not objected to in writing, the former within five (5) days, the latter within ten (10) days, of the date on which such material was forwarded by you or your agents to the undersigned, by mail or otherwise.

11. Free Credit Balances

It is understood and agreed that any free credit balance in any account in which I have an interest is maintained in such account solely for the purpose of investment or reinvestment in securities or other investment instruments.

12. Margin Interest Charges

The undersigned acknowledges receipt of   Truth-in-Lending Disclosure Statement. It is understood that interest will be charged on debit balances in accordance with the methods and procedures described in this statement or in any amendment or revision thereto which may be provided to me. Unless otherwise noted hereon, or unless I am provided notice to the contrary in accordance with the relevant provisions of this agreement, the following schedule shall set forth the maximum charges to be made on debit balances in the undersigned's accounts:

Average Debit Balance for Interest Period	Interest Charge Above Broker Call Loan Rate
$ 0—15,000	2.0%
15,001—50,000	1.5%
50,001—and over	1.0%

13. Agreement to Arbitrate Controversies

It is agreed that any controversy between us arising out of your business or this agreement shall be submitted to arbitration conducted under the provisions of the Constitution and Rules of the Board of Governors of the New York Stock Exchange or pursuant to the Code of Arbitration of the National Association of Securities Dealers, as the undersigned may elect.

Figure 16-3a. *A Margin Account Agreement. (front).*

268

Arbitration must be commenced upon service of either a written demand for arbitration or a written notice of intention to arbitrate, therein electing the arbitration tribunal. In the event the undersigned does not make such designation within five (5) days of such demand or notice, then the undersigned authorizes you to do so on behalf of the undersigned.

14. Extraordinary Events

You shall not be liable for any loss caused directly or indirectly by government restrictions, exchange or market rulings, suspension of trading, war, strikes or other conditions beyond your control.

15. Representation as to Capacity to Enter into Agreement

The undersigned, if an individual, represents that the undersigned is of full age, that the undersigned is not an employee of any exchange, or of any corporation of which any exchange owns a majority of the capital stock, or of a member of any exchange, or of a member firm or member corporation registered on any exchange or of a bank, trust company, insurance company or of any corporation, firm or individual engaged in the business of dealing either as broker or as principal in securities, bills of exchange, bankers' acceptances or commercial paper or other forms of credit securities or instruments. The undersigned further represents that no one except the undersigned has an interest in the account or accounts of the undersigned with you.

16. Joint and Several Liability

If the undersigned shall consist of more than one individual, their obligations under this agreement shall be joint and several.

17. Rights under Agreement

Your failure to insist at any time upon strict compliance with this agreement or with any of its terms or any continued course of such conduct on your part shall in no event constitute or be considered a waiver by you of any of your rights or privileges. The undersigned hereby expressly agrees that you shall not be bound by any representation or agreement heretofore or hereafter made by any of your employees or agents which in any way purports to modify, affect or diminish your rights under this agreement, and that no representation or advice by you or your employees or agents regarding the purchase or sale by the undersigned of any securities, or other property bought or sold on the undersigned's order or carried or held in any manner for the undersigned's account shall be deemed to be a representation with respect to the future value or performance of such securities, or other property.

18. Continuity of Agreement

This agreement shall inure to the benefit of your successors and assigns, by merger, consolidation or otherwise, and you may transfer the account of the undersigned to any such successors or assigns.

This agreement and all the terms thereof shall be binding upon the undersigned's heirs, executors, administrators, personal representatives and assigns. In the event of the undersigned's death, incompetency, or disability, whether or not executors, administrators, committee or conservators of my estate and property shall have qualified or been appointed, you may cancel any open orders for the purchase or sale of any property, you may place orders for the sale of the property which you may be carrying for me and for which payment has not been made or buy any property of which my accounts may be short, or any part thereof, under the same terms and conditions as hereinabove stated, as though the undersigned were alive and competent without prior notice to the undersigned's heirs, executors, administrators, personal representatives, assigns, committee or conservators, without prior demand or call of any kind upon them or any of them.

19. Headings are Descriptive

The heading of each provision hereof is for descriptive purposes only and shall not be deemed to modify or qualify any of the rights or obligations set forth in each provision.

20. Separability

If any provision or condition of this agreement shall be held to be invalid or unenforceable by any court, or regulatory or self-regulatory agency or body, such invalidity or unenforceability shall attach only to such provision or condition. The validity of the remaining provisions and conditions shall not be affected thereby and this agreement shall be carried out as if such invalid or unenforceable provision or condition were not contained herein.

21. Written Authority Required for Waiver or Modification

Except as herein otherwise expressly provided, no provision of this agreement shall in any respect be waived, altered, modified or amended unless such waiver, alteration, modification or amendment is committed to writing and signed by an officer of your organization.

22. The Laws of the State of New York Govern

This agreement and its enforcement shall be governed by the laws of the State of New York, shall cover individually and collectively all accounts which the undersigned may open or reopen with you, and shall inure to the

benefit of your successors and assigns whether by merger, consolidation or otherwise, and you may transfer the accounts of the undersigned to your successors and assigns.

23. Acknowledgement of Receipt of Agreement

The undersigned has read this agreement in its entirety before signing, and acknowledges receipt of a copy of this agreement.

Dated _____

INDIVIDUAL OR JOINT ACCOUNT SIGNATURE

_____

(Second Party, If Joint Account)

PARTNERSHIP SIGNATURE

_____

(Name of Partnership)

By _____
   (A Partner)

CORPORATION SIGNATURE

_____

(Name of Corporation)

By _____

Title _____

Lending Agreement

You are hereby specifically authorized to lend to yourselves, as principal or otherwise, or to others, any securities held by you on margin for any accounts of the undersigned or as collateral therefore, either separately or with other securities.

This agreement shall inure to the benefit of your successors and assigns, by merger, consolidation or otherwise, and you may transfer the account of the undersigned to any such successors or assigns.

Dated _____

INDIVIDUAL OR JOINT ACCOUNT SIGNATURE

_____

(Second Party, If Joint Account)

PARTNERSHIP SIGNATURE

_____

(Name of Partnership)

By _____
   (A Partner)

CORPORATION SIGNATURE

_____

(Name of Corporation)

By _____

Title _____

Figure 16-3b. *Margin Account Agreement (back).*

must be mailed to the client who must sign them and return them promptly.

In addition:

- To open a margin account, the client has to sign a *margin account agreement*. (See Figure 16-3.)
- To authorize the broker to make the decisions on what to buy and sell, and/or when to buy or sell, *without* first having to check with the client, the client has to sign a *discretionary account agreement*.
- To trade options, futures, or commodities, additional forms have to be completed.
- If the client is a corporation, partnership, charity, or any entity other than an individual, still more forms need to be completed.

All these forms are then sent to the new accounts department, which checks to be sure the forms are completed properly, stores the paperwork, and opens an electronic file for the client on the firm's computer system.

The new account department also makes sure that the information is kept up to date. It changes the client's file information whenever the client moves, gets a new phone number, changes employer, and so on.

Order Department

The order department acts as a "go-between" for the firm's salespeople and its traders. All orders solicited by the firm's sales force are sent to the order department. If the firm is a small one, the orders may simply be carried to the order department as they are received. In a large firm, with offices all over the country, the brokers forward their orders via an electronic mail system call a *wire*. (For these reasons large firms with multiple offices, are often called *wirehouses*.)

If a branch office sends an order to the order room via the electronic mail system, the order quickly prints out in the order room on a teletyper. The order department quickly checks the orders for any obvious errors (missing account numbers, missing office numbers, and the like). Then, since speed is of the essence, it quickly forwards the order (either electronically or via a phone) to the right person in the trading department so it can be executed.

It is essential that the order be sent to the right person or exchange, because securities are traded on different exchanges or by different traders in the over-the-counter market. If the security is traded on the exchange, the order is sent to the floor clerk who passes it on to the firm's floor trader. If the security is traded OTC, the order is forwarded to the individual within the trading department who trades that security.

In the meantime, the order department keeps a copy of the order in its file. When the client's order is executed (which may take seconds or months depending on the type of security and the type of order), the floor clerk or trader then reports the execution price back to the order department. The order department then:

- Records the execution price on its copy of the order.
- Notifies the broker (via the same wire system) of the execution and of the execution price, so that the broker can, in turn, notify the client.
- Advises the purchase and sales department that the order was executed. (See Figure 16-4.)

Purchase and Sales Department

The purchase and sales department (P&S) performs several tasks when it is notified that a trade has been executed:

1. Records the trade.
2. Prepares the customer's confirmation.
3. Figures the total billing to the client.
4. Compares the trade with the contrabroker.

Recording. The P&S department records the trade on the firm's master records. These records are used by the firm as the basis for later notifying the clearing house of which securities have been bought and sold by the firm—so accuracy is a must.

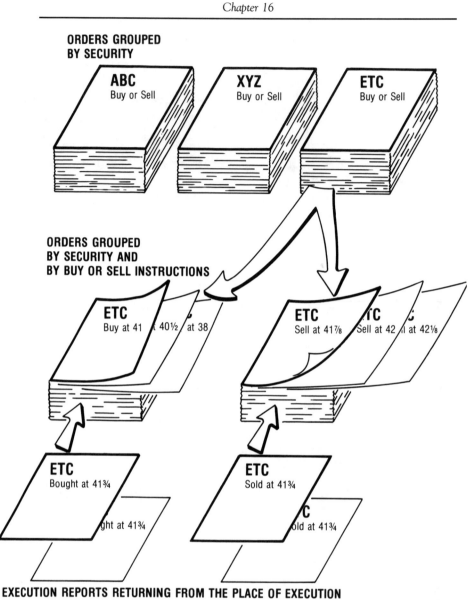

ORDERS GROUPED BY SECURITY

ABC Buy or Sell
XYZ Buy or Sell
ETC Buy or Sell

ORDERS GROUPED BY SECURITY AND BY BUY OR SELL INSTRUCTIONS

ETC Buy at 41 · 40½ at 38
ETC Sell at 41⅞ · Sell at 42 · at 42⅛

ETC Bought at 41¾ · ght at 41¾
ETC Sold at 41¾ · old at 41¾

EXECUTION REPORTS RETURNING FROM THE PLACE OF EXECUTION (Exchange or OTC)

Figure 16-4. *A Simplified System for Tracking Orders.* Reprinted with permission from David M. Weiss, *After the Trade Is Made: Processing Securities Transactions* (New York Institute of Finance, 1986).

Figuration. The P&S department computes (or figures) how much money the client owes the firm for a purchase or how much the firm owes the client for a sale. In deriving this total the department includes not only the sale or purchase price of the security but also:

1. Any commission the client owes the firm if the firm acted as the client's agent is *added* to the client's bill or *subtracted* from the client's sale proceeds.

2. Any accrued interest (if the security traded is a bond) is *added* to the client's bill or to the client's sale proceeds.

3. Any "ticket charges" (processing fees charged by some firms) are added to client's bill or subtracted from the sale proceeds.

4. Any applicable state and/or federal securities transfer taxes are added to the client's bill and/or subtracted from the sale proceeds.

The process of determining the total of all applicable charges is sometimes called *figuration.*

A statement called a *confirm* discloses each of these itemized charges, as well as the final total that the client owes the firm or the firm owes the client. *The confirm is prepared and mailed to the client the same day as the trade.* (See Figure 16.5.)

Comparison.. The P&S department also compares the details of the trade, from its firm's point of view, with the P&S department of the firm with which the trade was executed (the so-called *contrabroker*), to be sure that both firms' understanding of the trade is identical. Because of the sheer speed at which orders are executed and the number of trades performed each day, some misunderstandings are inevitable.

Example: Firm A thinks it sold Firm B 200 shares of a given stock, whereas Firm B thinks it bought only 100 shares of the stock from Firm A.

It's important that these disagreements be discovered, resolved, and corrected prior to settlement day. Otherwise the trade does not settle when it is supposed to settle.

Confirming the details of each and every trade with every other

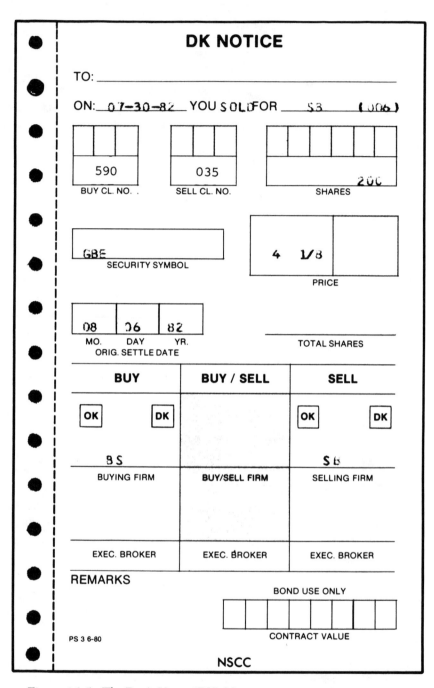

Figure 16-5. *The Don't Know (DK) Notice.* Reprinted with permission from David M. Weiss, *After the Trade Is Made: Processing Securities Transactions* (New York Institute of Finance, 1986).

firm would be an overwhelming task for any P&S department. So catching the majority of these disagreements prior to the settlement date is the responsibility of the appropriate clearing organization. Each day every firm submits to the clearing organizations (via various electronic means) its data on the trades it executed.

The four main clearing organizations are the following:

1. The Securities Industry Automation Corporation (SIAC) clears trades generated on the New York Stock Exchange.
2. The American Stock Exchange Clearing Corporation (ASECC) clears trades generated on the American Stock Exchange. [Note: Many of the computer operations of both the SIAC and ASECC are performed by the Stock Clearing Corporation (SCC), a wholly owned subsidiary of the NYSE.]
3. The National Clearing Corporation clears most OTC trades of NASDAQ securities.
4. The Option Clearing Corporation (OCC) clears most listed option transactions.

The trade is submitted to the clearing corporation, which pairs off the trades as reported. If there is no disagreement, there is no problem. However, after most of the trades are paired off, usually some trades are left over with no identical countertrade.

Example: Firm A reports a sale of 200 shares of XYZ at 43½, and Firm B reports a purchase of 200 shares of XYZ at 43⅜. There is no countertrade for either trade, which means that most likely one firm or the other made a price error.

In this case, both firms are notified that their trades do not match up, and it is left to them to decide how the error is going to be resolved. Perhaps one firm can prove to the other that it is right by comparing the price at which the transaction occurred to the price at which the stock was trading in the market at the time the order was executed. Or maybe one firm finds that it made a paperwork error and corrects the report it sent to the clearing corporation. If neither firm can prove it is right, then the two traders of the firms involved negotiate a settlement. Either each trader or firm assumes half the difference, or the firms take turns assuming errors.

While anyone can (and does) make an occasional mistake, if a trader or a firm gets a reputation for making too many "errors," the risk is of being ostracized by the rest of the traders and firms on the street. A trader that no one will trade with is of limited usefulness to anyone.

It's important to note that the firm, not the client, suffers the loss resulting from an error.

Example: A firm reports a purchase to a client at 43⅜ when it actually bought the stock for 43½. The client pays only 43⅜. The extra eighth of a point comes out of the firm's pocket (or the trader's annual bonus).

Trades that are not submitted to a clearing house are called ex-clearing house trades (XCH) and must be compared manually. This means one firm, usually the seller, must contact the other firm and verify the security traded, the quantity traded, the price, and the settlement terms. This is typically done by means of a written confirmation that the selling firm delivers to the buying firm and that the buying firm signs to signify its agreement on the details.

Cashiering Department

One of the departments that receives a copy of the firm's confirmation notices is the cashiering department, which is sometimes referred to as the *cage*. This department has a number of duties:

1. Receiving securities sent to the firm by other firms or by the firm's clients.
2. Delivering securities to other firms or to the other firm's clients.
3. Transferring the name on the security from the old owner to the new owner.
4. Borrowing and loaning shares of stock for short sales.
5. Arranging to borrow money from banks to support the firm's margin activities.
6. Reorganizing, that is, converting one security into another.

Receive or Deliver. The receive and/or deliver section of the cashiering department receives or accepts delivery of certificates from customers, other firms, or depositories. When receiving or delivering the securities, the firm must make sure that they are in *negotiable form.* To be negotiable, the securities must either be:

1. Signed on the back of the actual certificate by the owner. If a certificate has more than one owner (such as a husband and wife), both must sign the certificate just the way their names appear on the front of the certificate. Without the appropriate signatures, the securities cannot be delivered to the new owner.

2. If the stock certificate is held by the broker, the client(s) must sign a separate form (called a *stock power*), which the firm must attach to the actual certificate.

3. If the security is a bearer certificate (that is, there is no name on it), the person delivering the security must provide proof, such as a purchase confirmation, that he or she acquired the certificate legally.

Transfer. Every time a security changes hands, it has to undergo *transfer.* That is, the existing certificate, which carries the name of the former owner, must be cancelled and a new certificate, which reflects the name of the new owner, must be issued. This is the job of the *transfer agent,* usually a bank or other organization outside the brokerage firm.

Another outside agency, often a trust company or bank, acts as *registrar.* Its duty is to keep track of the number of shares or bonds an issuer has in circulation. It verifies that no more shares are issued than are destroyed, so that the total number of outstanding shares remains constant. (Often, the transfer and register duties are handled by the same bank or agency.)

When a brokerage firm receives securities that have been sold, it passes them on to the transfer agent so that they can be re-registered in the name of the new owner.

If the firm has the old certificates at a depository, the depository sends them to the transfer agent to be re-registered.

Vaulting. When a brokerage firm receives securities, it must place them into a vault or depository. Actively traded securities are usually placed in the depository. Thinly traded securities are typically held in the firm's own vault, or "box."

Whether held at the depository or in the vault, the securities must be divided into two groups: (1) securities that are owned outright by the firm's clients and (2) securities that the firm itself owns or that the firm's client's have borrowed against (that is, margined). By law securities that are owned outright by the firm's clients must be segregated from the other securities, regardless of whether the certificate is registered in the client's name or in the broker's name. For that reason these securities said to be *in seg* (short for "segregation").

Lending and Borrowing Stock. The securities that the firm itself owns, as well as the margined securities owned by clients, can be lent out by the firm to short sellers. The short sellers can be either clients of the same brokerage firm or other firms. The stock loan clerk arranges to lend surplus securities and to borrow, from other firms and sources, the securities that the firm's clients want to sell short.

Bank Loan. The bank loan section of the cashiering department arranges to borrow money from the firm's banks. The employees of this section arrange to borrow money from commercial banks, either to finance the purchase of securities for the firm's own account and/ or to provide funds for margin loans to customers.

Margin Department

The margin department supervises all the money in all of the firm's accounts, regardless of whether or not they are margin accounts. (In this respect the name "margin department" is something of a misnomer.) The margin department is responsible for ensuring that the firm's accounts meet all the financial requirements required by the various regulatory bodies. (See the chapter on margin and cash accounts.)

In addition to supervising cash and margin accounts, the margin staff has the following responsibilities:

- It instructs the cage to issue checks or to deliver securities.
- It files for extensions.

• It closes out positions when necessary.

Dividend Department

The dividend department is responsible for accepting, allocating, paying, and/or claiming dividends and interest distributions on securities held by the firm. The clerks in this department must be sure that the firm and its clients receive all the interest and dividends to which they are entitled. This task is complicated by the dividend-paying process.

Cash Dividends. For cash dividends the dividend process depends on four dates:

1. The *declaration date* is the date on which the company's board of directors announces that the company will pay a dividend. On this date, the company also declares the size of the dividend payment and the record date.
2. The *record date* is the date when the company asks its registrar to provide a list of its current shareholders so that it knows who is entitled to the dividend checks. To receive the dividend, the stockholder has to be on the company's books as a shareholder as of this date.
3. On the *payment date*, the company actually cuts the dividend checks. This date is usually about two weeks after the record date, so as to give the company time to generate all the dividend checks.
4. The *ex-dividend date* comes four business days before the record date, when the investors who purchase the stock for regular way (five-day) settlement are no longer entitled to receive the dividend. Because an investor who buys the stock on the ex-dividend day does not show up on the company's books as a shareholder until the day after the record date, the dividend is mailed to the stock's previous owner. As a result, the market value of the stock generally drops by the value of the dividend when it opens for trading on the ex-dividend date.

Example: Consider the following calendar:

```
              May
  S    M    T    W    T    F    S
       1    2    3    4    5    6
  7    8    9   10   11   12   13
 14   15   16   17   18   19   20
 21   22   23   24   25   26   27
 28   29   30   31
```

The board of directors puts out a press release on May 2 saying that it will pay a $0.50 dividend to the owners of record as of May 17, with checks to be mailed as of May 26. Then:

• May 2 is the declaration date.
• May 17 is the record date.
• May 26 is the payment date.

The ex-dividend date is May 11. If an investor buys the stock on May 11 for regular way settlement, the trade does not settle until May 18. The investor is not recorded as the owner of the stock on the company's books (maintained by the registrar) until May 18. Thus the *seller* is still entitled to receive the dividend.

Of course, other settlement options have other ex-dividend dates, but the vast majority of stock trades are regular way trades. For example, for cash settlement the ex-date is the day after the record date since a cash trade on the record date would entitle the new owner to receive the dividend.

Sometimes, however, the dividend check is mailed to the wrong person. Either the firm does not get the information about the new owner to the registrar in time, or the registrar does not process the information in time, or there is simply a human error somewhere along the line. If the dividend check is inadvertently mailed to the wrong party, that party must return it so it can be correctly routed.

Stock Dividends. For large stock dividends (20% or larger) and all stock splits, the sequence of these dates is different. The ex-dividend date, now called the *ex-distribution date,* is positioned after the payment date instead of after the declaration date. Thus the sequence for a stock distribution is as follows:

1. Declaration date.
2. Record date.
3. Payment date.
4. Ex-distribution date.

The ex-distribution date is usually the business day following payment by the corporation.

Example: Use the following calendar:

			May			
S	M	T	W	T	F	S
	1	2	3	4	5	6
7	8	9	10	11	12	13
14	15	16	17	18	19	20
21	22	23	24	25	26	27
28	29	30	31			

If the company declares a 25% stock dividend on January 2, for payment on January 24, then the stock starts to trade ex-distribution on January 25. Anyone who buys the stock so as to receive delivery before January 25 is entitled to receive the stock dividend.

Thus any trades entered into after the record date and settled before the payment date must have *due bills* attached. These due bills entitle the buyer to claim the additional shares when they are distributed. Shares without due bills attached cannot be delivered to settle a trade during this period.

The dividend department is responsible for checking every security in every account to make sure that all clients receive the dividends to which they are entitled (*and* to make sure clients do not keep any dividend to which they are not entitled).

The dividend department also allocates dividend payments paid to the firm by the company to their rightful owners. Many clients do not have their securities registered in their own name but instead have them registered in the name of their brokerage firm. By so registering the securities, they do not have to worry about signing the securities or a stock power when they want to sell. Instead all they have to do is call their broker and say "sell," and an officer of the firm endorses the certificate.

Of course, if a hundred clients, each of whom own 100 shares of a given stock, should decide to register their stock in their broker's name, then the company's books show that the firm "owns" 10,000 shares, even though those shares are actually being held for the benefit of the firm's clients. (The clients' claims are called *beneficial owner-ship.*) When it's time to pay a dividend, the company makes one check payable to the firm, since the company has no way of knowing the actual beneficial owners. The firm, when it receives the check, must then distribute the proceeds on a proportional basis to all of the actual owners. This task falls to the employees of the dividend department. The dividend department also allocates interest payments that it receives on bonds held in the name of the firm, or *street name.*

Proxy Department

The proxy department is closely related to the dividend depart-ment. The proxy department distributes corporate publications (in-cluding financial reports), notices of meetings, and voting information to the beneficial owners who have their securities in street name.

Proxies. The most important of these distributions is an "advisory and voting solicitation," which is mailed at least once a year. It gives the shareholder the right to elect the members of the board of directors and decide on other important matters brought before an annual, or special, meeting of the company. Owners, whose shares are in street name, cannot cast their votes directly. The company recognizes only the brokerage firm as its shareholder because that's the name on the stock certificates according to the firm's registrar.

To allow the real owners of these shares to vote on these matters, the proxy department sends a request form, called a *proxy*, to each of the beneficial owners. As the real owners return their proxies, the firm tallies the owners' votes and reflects the owner's wishes when it votes its shares at the annual meeting.

Example: Two owners leave their stock in street name. The first owner has 200 shares, and the second owner has 100 shares. The firm receives the right to cast 300 votes at the annual meeting. The firm sends proxies to the owners, collects their responses, and votes as they would have voted if they had actually attended the annual meeting and voted for themselves. If Investor A votes yes and investor B votes no on a certain proposal, then the firm casts 200 yes votes and 100 no votes at the annual meeting.

Sometimes the beneficial owners do not bother to advise the proxy department about their preferences. This can be a waste. Exchange regulations prevent a firm from voting on crucial issues unless it receives instructions from its clients. (However, firms can vote unreturned proxies on routine matters.)

Solicitations of Stockholders. The proxy department also acts as agent for anyone or any group that wishes to communicate with the beneficial owners whose shares are in the firm's custody, providing the group has registered its proxy statement or solicitation with the SEC, per Section 14 of the Securities Exchange Act of 1934, and agrees to reimburse the brokerage firm for postage and other out-of-pocket expenses connected with a mailing.

A stockholder solicitation may be a simple plea for a vote to effect a reform or to change the company's present management. Or it may be a request for the beneficial owners to tender their shares in response to a purchase proposition. The latter often leads to another function of the proxy department, although in larger firms it is assigned to a separate unit known as the reorganization department.

Reorganization Department

The reorganization department (reorg) is responsible for handling:

1. Redemption calls.
2. Conversions.
3. Exchanges.
4. Rights offerings (subscriptions).
5. Tender offers.

Redemption Calls. A *redemption call* is the exercise by the issuer of a call privilege on a stock or bond. An *absolute,* or *full,* call requires all holders to submit their bonds or shares for redemption. In a *partial call,* only the holders of specific certificate numbers must respond; these certificate numbers are chosen at random by the company, often by electronic means. If the called securities are held in safekeeping and segregated by owner through individual identification methods, reorg simply submits the appropriate certificates to the company and credits the customers with the cash received. But if the securities are segregated in bulk form, the firm must either (1) record the specific certificate numbers for each customer account, or (2) adopt an impartial lottery system.

Conversions. The reorganization department processes requests to convert convertible bonds into the underlying common stock, which sometimes results from a full or partial call in a convertible issue. The issuing company forces the holders to exchange their securities for the common stock or accept the call price, which is typically lower than the market value of the comparable common shares. In a typical bond call, the bondholder is advised that, unless some personal action is initiated before the close of business on a given day, (1) the conversion privilege is revoked, (2) accrued interest on the bond ceases, (3) the holder must accept the redemption price.

In the meantime, the reorganization department must contact the beneficial bond owners and solicit instructions from them.

Exchanges. When one class of security is exchanged for another of the same issuer, it is called *reorganization.* Sometimes, if a corporation is in dire financial straits, bondholders may accept an equity security in exchange for their debt instruments to avoid prolonged and expensive bankruptcy proceedings. Or such an exchange may be directed as a result of a decision in bankruptcy court. Either way, the reorg department submits the old certificates on behalf of the owners and accepts the new ones in satisfaction. If the exchange is voluntary, reorg needs a voluntary exchange request—that is, written instructions from the beneficial owner. In an involuntary exchange, no instructions are needed.

When one company's securities are exchanged for those of another, it is known as a *merger.* In a merger, reorg submits its customers' shares for shares in the surviving company or for shares of a newly organized third company. Records of the holdings of the firm and its customers are adjusted at the completion of the exchange. If the merger is an outright acquisition for cash, the customers' accounts are credited with the funds received after the reorganization department submits the old shares and obtains payment.

Preemptive Rights (Subscriptions Privilege). In a preemptive rights offering, the reorganization department uses these rights and supplementary funds from a customer's account to subscribe to the new stock from the company. If additional rights are needed to satisfy the customer's written instructions, they are purchased, either from the issuing company's agent or in the open market. Conversely, if certain customers decide not to subscribe or if they own rights in excess of the amount needed to subscribe for the number of shares they want to buy, the reorganization department disposes of the extra rights before they expire. It may either sell them to the company's agent bank or standby underwriter, or accept someone else's bid in the open market. Either way, the appropriate customer accounts are credited with the net proceeds of that sale.

Purchases by means of subscription *warrants* are handled similarly. Reorg needs written instructions from the beneficial owner before taking action. These purchases also entail a ratio formula set by the company.

Tender Offers. A *tender offer* is a formal solicitation by means of a proxy statement to shareholders to induce them to sell their shares. A tender offer can be a successful method for acquiring large amounts of stock without upsetting the supply/demand equilibrium in the marketplace. It is often used by corporations or large institutions to effect a merger with, or to gain control of, another company at reasonable cost. If not enough shares are submitted for sale, the offering company is denied its desired objective. Under these circumstances, the offerer usually reserves the right to refuse the purchase of any shares tendered—a valuable privilege not available in open-market transactions. Similarly, if a tender offer produces more than enough shares to satisfy the offerer, the offerer can accept all the shares, any portion of them, or only the amount specified in the proxy statement. If only some of the shares are to be purchased, they can be bought either on a first-come/first-served basis or on a prorated basis.

Stock Record Department

The position lists used by the dividend, proxy, and reorganization departments are a part of the records that are prepared and maintained by the stock record department. This part of operations serves as a control and reference source for monitoring securities under the brokerage firm's jurisdiction. Although its title is "stock record," it keeps records of all securities—stocks and bonds alike. An individual record is maintained for each issue. For financial and regulatory reasons, these records must be unquestionably current and accurate. The stock record ledger shows the following:

• Name of the security.
• Owner of the security.
• Location of the certificate.

In terms of location, the stock record has to identify whether that security is in one of the following:

• Safekeeping.
• Segregation.
• A loan arrangement at a bank.
• A loan to another broker/dealer.
• Reregistration proceedings at the transfer agent.
• Transit to the customer's agent bank or broker versus payment.
• Fail-to-receive status from a contrabroker/dealer or customer.

During the course of trading each day, the status of the securities under the firm's care changes constantly. Certificates arrive from and go out to customers and other brokers. Others go to the transfer agent, and still others come back. Book-entry changes of ownership occur, even though the certificates do not change hands.

Throughout all this change, the stock record has to remain balanced at all times. A *break* in the record indicates that a mistake has been made. Given the amount of activity surrounding this document, errors must be corrected immediately—or they might never be corrected at all.

To ensure that record books are kept to a minimum size and corrected as soon as possible, the stock record department issues a daily report and a weekly report. The *daily stock record* reports the movement of all securities involved in any kind of movement: sale, purchase, transfer into or out of the vault, received from a customer, and so on. The *weekly stock record* is a balance sheet of all securities under the supervision of the firm, whether or not they were involved in a transaction the preceding week. Both of these reports must balance—like a balance sheet. Stock may not be removed from a part of the record without being accounted for in some way or another.

Accounting Department

The accounting department in a brokerage firm performs all the tasks that it would in any other type of company. Basically, its responsibilities are as follows:

- Keeping the firm's journals and ledgers.
- Preparing periodic trial balances.
- Issuing the firm's balance sheet and income statement.
- Generating reports for management as necessary.

In addition to its quarterly and annual reports to stockholders, the accounting department also issues special reports for regulatory bodies such as the SEC or NASD. Sometimes the regulatory authority calls for a report as the result of a special audit. Other reports are generated periodically, such as the *Financial and Operational Combined Uniform Single (Focus) Report*. This statement gives regulators vital statistics regarding the financial health of the brokerage firm that might not be available from the company's other reports.

Customer's Statement. The accounting department is also involved in the very last step in customer operations activity—the preparation of the statements of account. Under federal law, if there has been any transaction activity, security position, or money balance in an account within the preceding calendar quarter, the customer must receive a statement of account. Many firms comply by sending their customers (particularly margin account customers) monthly statements instead of the mandatory quarterly report.

Whether monthly or quarterly, the statement summarizes all that has occurred in the customer's account during the period. All purchase expenses are debited to the account, and sales proceeds are credited. However, each purchase and/or sales transaction is posted on the contract settlement date, whereas all other activities are posted on the day they occur.

Example: A check received from a customer is credited to the account on the day it is received, and money delivered out of the account is debited on the actual day of reimbursement. But a regular way sale of a corporate security on June 26 is not posted until July 3, five business days later.

This difference is often a point of confusion for customers, especially when they receive their monthly statements of account without certain month-end trades posted on it.

Despite the best efforts and intentions of the accounting department, mistakes occur. Perhaps an issue is not carried forward to the following month's position listing, or duplicate entries are processed accidentally and both items posted in the account. A typical customer statement, therefore, carries a self-protective legend, *"E&OE,"* which means, *errors and omissions excepted.* This statement allows the brokerage firm an opportunity to correct the mistake without legal liability.

The statement may also carry a legend advising customers of financial protection afforded them under SEC Rule 15c3-3. Free credit balances must be maintained in a "special reserve bank account for the exclusive benefit of customers," a rule that denies the brokerage firm the right to use those funds in the speculative conduct of its own business. The accounting department, employing a formula approved by a stock exchange or the NASD, supervises the firm's compliance with this rule and ensures that customer money is used only for customer purposes.

IN CLOSING . . .

When they think of the securities industry, many people call to mind the busy floor of the stock exchange, the electronic trading screens, and the Wall Street area. Not many can picture the sometimes feverish backoffice work that is necessary to keep the records and books straight, to comply with regulations, to protect the interests of customer and firm alike, and, through it all, to make a profit.

17

Government Regulation

The American people have never been fond of restrictions on their freedoms. For that reason laws and regulations are generally enacted only after a disaster has made the need for legislation readily apparent. Thus, during the late 1800s, excessive borrowing by both individuals and corporations led to the Banking Panic of 1907 and, as a result, to the establishment of the Federal Reserve System (the Fed) in 1913. Similarly, in the years following World War I, excesses in issuing and trading securities brought on the disastrous market crash of 1929, followed by the Great Depression of the 1930s, the worst depression the country ever endured. This disaster made it clear that the securities markets were of such crucial importance to the country's financial well-being that they could no longer remain completely unregulated.

At the same time, lawmakers realized that an over-regulated market cannot be an efficient market. Historically, the efficiency of the United States' capital markets has made it very easy for companies to raise the capital needed to expand, and this has given the U.S. an edge in world markets. Thus lawmakers were faced with the task of walking a fine line between under-regulation and over-regulation, either of which could be equally destructive to the U.S. economy.

In response to this dilemma, Congress passed legislation that regulated the securities and financial markets and that created the

Securities and Exchange Commission (SEC) to enforce its rules. One of the most significant developments of this legislation is the requirement that the rules and procedures of any nationwide securities association and/or self-regulatory organization, from then on, have to be approved by the SEC.

In an attempt (so far successful) to forestall any further major direct intervention by the government into the capital markets, the securities industry formed self-regulatory organizations (SROs) to police itself and to correct many of the abuses of the past. Each securities "market" has its own SRO:

1. The *exchanges*, by adopting rules and regulations that conform to federal law, police the listed securities marketplace.
2. The *National Association of Securities Dealers* (*NASD*) assumes that role in over-the-counter stock and corporate bond trading. (Discussed in Chapter 15.)
3. The *Municipal Securities Rulemaking Board* (*MSRB*) regulates the trading of municipal bonds.
4. The *National Futures Association* (*NFA*) and the *Commodities Futures Trading Commission* (*CFTC*) monitor futures trading.

The standards and requirements of these SROs are generally *more stringent* than the minimum standards required by federal and state law.

Although these regulatory bodies—the Fed, the SEC, the SROs—are the primary agents of regulation for the financial markets, other regulatory bodies exert control over certain sectors or niches of the financial industry.

For example, the depository institutions in this country fall under the sway not only of the Federal Reserve, but also of the Comptroller of the Currency, the Options Clearing Corporation (OCC), the Federal Deposit Insurance Corporation (FDIC), the Federal Home Loan Bank Board (FHLBB), the National Credit Union Administration (NCUA), and the Federal Savings and Loan Insurance Corporation (FSLIC). In addition, a whole host of state regulators exert control over the depository institutions.

Over the years, the duties of all these agencies have become so intertwined and overlapped that Congress established another interagency body in 1978, the Federal Financial Institutions Examination Council, to coordinate their efforts.

Part of the problem within the regulation community is simply one of definition of roles. In simpler times:

1. A commercial bank accepted deposits and made loans.
2. An investment bank underwrote, sold, and traded stocks and bonds
3. An insurance company underwrote and sold insurance policies and annuities.

Today banks sell insurance, brokers offer checking accounts, and insurance companies offer stock trading. So it's sometimes hard for regulators to know which regulations should apply to which institutions.

THE FEDERAL RESERVE (THE FED)

In passing the Federal Reserve Banking Act of 1913, Congress' aim was to provide a banking system that would reduce the likelihood of major bank failures and related economic ills that occurred regularly during the 1800s. From the beginning, however, it was clear that the Fed would have to recognize broader economic objectives, specifically:

1. To stimulate noninflationary growth.
2. To promote full employment.
3. To maintain a stable value for U.S. currency.
4. To promote a favorable balance of trade with foreign countries.

Unfortunately, these objectives are often mutually exclusive. Promoting full employment is often inflationary. Maintaining a stable value for the currency can adversely affect our trade balance. Thus, the Fed must walk a tightrope with regard to balancing these objectives and periodically re-ranks them in order of priority as it sees fit. For example, Federal Reserve Chairman Paul Volcker's primary concern was squeezing the high rate of inflation out of the economy, even though doing so resulted in sharply higher unemployment.

Organization

The Federal Reserve System attempts to balance centralized control with local autonomy. Accordingly, the United States is divided into twelve districts, each of which has its own federal reserve bank and is under the guidance of a local board of governors. The district board reports to the Board of Governors of the Federal Reserve, located in Washington, D.C. Another important entity in the Fed organization is the Federal Open Market Committee, which has become the chief means of implementing monetary policy. At the base of the organization are the member banks, which represent many of the largest commercial banks in the country. (See Figures 17-1 and 17-2.)

Monetary Policy

The Fed's monetary policy is designed to ensure that enough money and credit will be available to meet the long-term needs of a growing economy. The short-term goal is to dampen cyclical inflationary and deflationary pressures.

The Fed implements its monetary policy chiefly in three ways:

1. Modifying member banks' reserve requirements.
2. Raising or lowering the "discount rate."
3. Performing "open market operations."

Modifying the Reserve Requirements for Member Banks. Most major commercial banks in this country are members of the federal reserve system. To be part of this system, a bank must deposit a certain percentage of its assets into its local Federal Reserve Bank. This deposit at the Fed cannot be loaned and is effectively money taken out of circulation. By raising or lowering the percentage of a bank's assets that must be held in this reserve, the Fed can dramatically alter the amount of money that banks have available to lend. The scarcity or availability of loan monies drives interest rates up or down, respectively.

Raising or Lowering the "Discount Rate." Banks that do not have enough assets to meet their reserve requirements at the Fed (because they lent more money than they should have) can borrow the cash

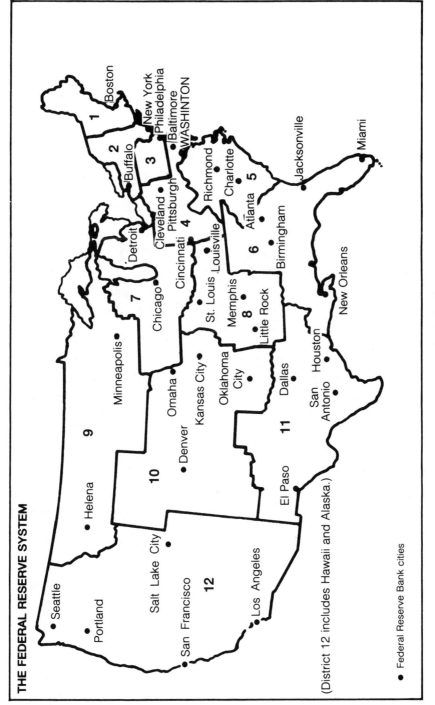

Figure 17-1. *Districts of the Federal Reserve System.*

THE FEDERAL RESERVE SYSTEM

(District 12 includes Hawaii and Alaska.)

• Federal Reserve Bank cities

they need to pay the Fed—from the Fed itself. Banks pay interest to borrow from the Fed, and the interest rate is called the *discount rate*. By raising this rate, the Fed makes borrowing from itself (called "borrowing at the discount window") less attractive. That, in turn, makes banks think twice before they make a loan that may put them in the position of having to borrow from the Fed.

Performing "Open Market Operations." In *open market operations*, the Fed buys government securities from, or sells them to, its primary dealers (the forty or so government securities dealers authorized to deal directly with the Fed). Among these dealers are most of the largest banks and brokerage firms. If the Fed buys securities, then the primary dealers have more money, which is injected into the banking system, thereby increasing the money supply. If the Fed sells securities, the dealers have to pay for the securities, thereby reducing the amount of money in the banking system and the money supply. The Fed can also enter into repo contracts with its dealers in order to adjust the money supply. Thus open market operations are often used to "fine-tune" the money supply.

Federal Open Market Committee (FOMC)

The task of deciding whether to increase or decrease the money supply falls primarily to the Federal Open Market Committee (FOMC). This committee, which is composed of all of the members of the board of governors as well as the presidents of several of the twelve district banks, meets eight times a year. At these meetings, the committee members assess the state of the economy, along with reports on the long- and short-term capital markets. On the basis of these assessments, and given the Fed's current monetary policy, the FOMC may elect to either increase or decrease the money supply to keep it in line with the country's current need for capital.

Other Controls

The Fed may exert control over the supply of available credit in other ways. For example, it is empowered:

• By *Regulation W* to set minimum down payment levels and the maximum loan maturities for consumer credit (such as car loans,

ORGANIZATION OF THE FEDERAL RESERVE SYSTEM

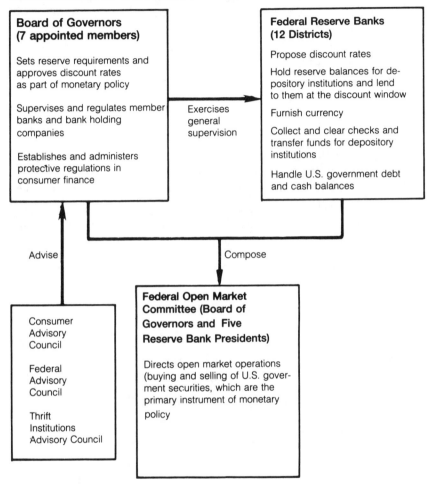

Figure 17-2. *Organization of the Federal Reserve System.*

charge cards, and the like). The board has exercised this power only during wartime and during a short period following World War II.

- By *regulation U* to regulate the terms and conditions of bank loans.
- By *Regulation G* to regulate the terms and conditions of loans by all other creditors.

To enforce compliance among its member banks, the Fed may also use *moral persuasion.* Since the board may elect to examine bank practices or even close a bank, it is in a position to exert pressure on uncooperative members to comply with its directives. The potential influence of the Fed on its bank members is tremendous, and the banking industry feels it keenly.

Fed Watching

The Federal Reserve has such a great effect on the money supply, credit availability, interest rates, and other facets of the economy that financial institutions employ staff economists to monitor Fed activity and, as far as possible, forecast its future policy. These specialists, as well as anyone who keeps a weather eye on the Fed, are known as *Fed watchers.* Their numbers are evidence of the essential role of the Fed in the day-to-day activities of the securities industry.

SECURITIES AND EXCHANGE COMMISSION (SEC)

Two major laws emerged from the backwash of the 1929 stock market disaster: the Securities Act of 1933 and the Securities Exchange Act of 1934. The 1933 Act was designed to protect the public against fraud in the new issues market (when a company first sells securities to the public). The Act of 1934 safeguards against abuses in securities trading after the original issuance, regardless of whether the security is exchange-listed or OTC-traded. The 1934 Act also established the Securities and Exchange Commission (SEC). It empowered the SEC to supervise and enforce not only the 1934 law but also the 1933 Act and all future legislation relating to the securities industry.

The Securities Act of 1933

If the thrust of the 1933 Act can be summed up in one word, it is "disclosure." The Securities Act of 1933 required that, before a company may sell securities to the public, it must first disclose to the public all of the relevant information that an investor needs to make an informed decision about an investment opportunity. (For a complete description of the Securities Act of 1933, see Chapter 17.)

The Securities Act of 1934

Fundamentally, the Securities Act of 1934 states that all of the securities that trade on an exchange and all the exchanges themselves must be registered with the SEC. For a security to be traded or for an exchange to conduct trading without being registered, it must be specifically exempted from registration by the SEC. All other sections of the law serve or otherwise center around this requirement.

Figure 17-3. *Section-by-Section Summary of the Securities Exchange Act of 1934.*

Section 1: Title

Section 2: Objectives

Section 3: Important Definitions. In addition to defining such terms as "broker" or "dealer," the Act defines *exempted securities* as obligations that are issued by, or whose principal or interest payments are guaranteed by, the United States, any state or commonwealth in this country, or any municipality.

Section 4: The Securities and Exchange Commission. The SEC's executive body is composed of five commissioners, including the chairperson, who are appointed by the President of the United States, with the consent of the Senate, for five-year terms of office. No more than three commissioners may be members of the same political party, and all must devote their full time to the job during their tenure in office.

Section 5: Transactions on Unregistered Exchanges. All exchanges must be either registered with the SEC or exempted. No broker/dealer may use the U.S. Postal Service and or engaged in interstate commerce to employ any facility of an exchange unless that exchange is registered or exempted.

Section 6: Registration of National Securities Exchanges. Registered exchanges are the American Stock Exchange, Boston Stock Exchange, Chicago Board Options Exchange, Cincinnati Stock Exchange, Instinet System, Intermountain Stock Exchange, Midwest Stock Exchange, New York Stock Exchange, Pacific Stock Exchange, Philadelphia Stock Exchange, and Spokane Stock Exchange. The Honolulu Stock Exchange is exempted because its activity is minimal.

Section 7: Margin Requirements. The Federal Reserve Board derives its authority to regulate margin from this section.

Section 8: Borrowing Restrictions. A broker/dealer may pledge securities that are registered on a national stock exchange only if it borrows the money from (1) a Federal Reserve Bank member, (2) a nonmember that has agreed to comply with the 1934 Act, *or* a broker/dealer and exchange member permitted by the Federal Reserve Board.

Figure 17-3. (*contd.*)

Hypothecated customer's securities may not be commingled with the securities of any other customer—or with those of anyone else except a bond fide customer—without the owning customer's written consent. Also, a broker/dealer may rehypothecate a customer's securities for an amount needed to finance the debit balance in the customer's account and no more.

Finally, the broker/dealer may not lend a customer's securities to anyone without the customer's written consent.

Section 9: Manipulation of Security Prices on Exchanges.   This section prohibits the following:

1. *Wash sales*—the purchase and sale of the same security at the same time and price, by the same customer, through the facilities of the same brokerage firm.
2. *Matched orders*—the purchase and sale of the same security, at the same time and price, by the same customer, through the facilities of different brokerage firms.
3. *Dissemination of false or misleading statements.*
4. *Use of tip sheets or touts* to promote the purchase or sale of securities in which the writer or sponsor has a personal interest.
5. *Pegging or fixing prices* of securities.

Section 10: Use of Manipulative and Deceptive Practices.   This section prohibits the use of misleading and fraudulent means to influence prices on securities exchanges.

Plus-Tick Rule—a short sale in a listed security, whether executed on the exchange or over the counter, must be sold at least $\frac{1}{8}$-point higher than the previous different-priced transaction in that issue. This rule prevents short sellers from depressing the price of the security.

Some other sanctions are the following:

1. Churning, or overtrading, in discretionary accounts.
2. Repurchase agreements used to manipulate securities prices, such as:
   a. *Daisy chains* consist of continuous buying and/or selling in the same issue by the same person, or with the same broker, at successively higher or lower prices.
   b. In *warehousing*, a sale made between a broker/dealer and a customer (or another broker/dealer) carries a proviso for repurchase on a future date at a preset, artificially fixed price.
3. A broker's use of a customer's securities and monies for personal use without the customer's written consent.
4. Confirmation of transactions for customers without proper disclosure of the essential facts or concealment of essential information in promoting purchases or sales of a security.
5. Boiler room sales—the use of high-pressure sales tactics to trade securities of questionable value.
6. Secret transactions in fictitious accounts.

Figure 17-3. (*contd.*)

7. Using nonpublic material information by an insider for personal financial gain.
8. Short-tendering—that is, tendering securities that are not owned in response to a public offer.
9. Stabilizing transactions contrary to specific procedures set forth in SEC Rule 10b-7.
10. Extensions of credit unless the borrower is furnished with a written explanation of the terms and conditions at the time the arrangement is made.

Section 11: Limitation of Functions of Exchange Members. Broker/dealers may not extend credit to customers on the purchase of a new issue if they have participated in a primary distribution of that issue within the past 30 days.

Section 12: Securities Registration Requirement. To be listed on an exchange, a security must be SEC-registered. Also, if the corporate issuer of an OTC stock has at least 500 stockholders of record and at least $1 million in total assets, then its security must be registered with the SEC.

Section 13: Periodical and Other Reports. Registered corporations must submit to the SEC reports on any changes in their financial condition, which then become available for public inspection. One of the most important is *Form 10K*, the annual report with certified financial statements attached.

Section 14: Proxies. This section spells out the type of information required for proxy solicitations or for offers to tender securities. The dominant feature of this section and its accompanying SEC rule is full and complete disclosures to facilitate an intelligent voting judgment by the shareowner.

Section 15: Over-the-Counter Markets. A securities firm must register with the SEC unless it deals exclusively in intrastate business or in government/government agency securities, commercial paper, or bankers' acceptances. If a firm does not register with an exchange or the NASD, it is called a *Securities and Exchange Commission Organization* (SECO). This section also spells out the requirements for registered broker/dealers with regard to supervision of employees, bookkeeping, customer accounts, and minimum net capital.

Section 16: Reports of Officers, Directors, and Principal Stockholders: All officers, directors, and persons holding 10 percent or more of an equity security of a registered issuer must file (1) a statement of beneficial ownership with the SEC and (2) a notice with any exchange on which that security is registered. The identified "insiders" may not retain a profit realized through the purchase and sale of these securities in any six-month period.

Section 17: Books, Records, and Reports of Brokers/Dealers. Broker/dealers must maintain specific books, records, correspondence, and memoranda. Among the most important are employment applications, periodic financial reports, and exchange notices of proposed rule changes.

In amending this section of the Act in 1975, Congress required securities clearing agencies and transfer agents to register with the SEC. The law

Figure 17-3. (*contd.*)

also directs the SEC to use its authority to end the physical movement of securities certificates in connection with transactions between brokers and dealers.

Section 18: Liability for Misleading Statements. People who file misleading statements, applications, reports, or documents with the SEC may be liable for civil legal action.

Section 19: SEC Powers over Self-Regulatory Organizations. This section allows a self-regulatory body to represent registered clearing associations and transfer agents if one should ever be organized. But all self-regulatory bodies must submit their rules and regulations to the SEC for approval; until they are approved, the rules are neither effective nor enforceable.

Section 21: Investigations, Injunctions, and Prosecutions of Offenses. The SEC has authority to conduct investigations into alleged violations of the Act. The Commission may also obtain injunctions enjoining further violations and prosecute offenders. Even if an action simply appears to violate this act, the SEC, at its discretion, is empowered to bring court action to enjoin that action or to seek a restraining order or injunction against that practice.

Section 22: SEC Hearings. The manner and location at which public and private hearings may be held is included here.

Section 23: Rules and Regulations: Annual Reports. This section empowers both the SEC and the FRB to make up whatever rules and regulations they need to protect the public interest, short of anything that would restrict competition.

Section 24: Information Filed with the SEC. Reports and documents submitted to the SEC become public information unless the party who files the material requests confidential treatment for all or part of it. Requests for privacy are considered on their individual merits.

Section 25: Court Review of SEC Orders. Anyone disciplined by the SEC may obtain a judicial review of the order by filing a petition in a district court of appeals of the United States within 60 days after notice is handed down by the SEC.

Section 26: Unlawful Representation. No action or failure to act by the SEC or FRB constitutes an approval or guarantee of any registration statement or report filed with either agency.

Section 27: Jurisdiction of Offenses and Lawsuits. The federal district courts of the United States and of the District of Columbia have exclusive jurisdiction in Act-related matters.

Section 28: Effects on Existing Law. The 1975 amendments prohibit state and local governments from levying securities transfer taxes under certain conditions.

Section 29: Validity of Contracts. Any contract, arrangement, or agreement that binds someone to waive compliance with or protection offered under this law is null and void.

Figure 17-3. (*contd.*)

Section 30: Foreign Securities Exchanges.   No one may use the U.S. Postal Service or any sort of interstate commerce to make a transaction on a foreign exchange that is contrary to SEC rules if the issuer of the security (1) is a resident of the United States, (2) is organized under the laws of the United States, or (3) has its principal place of business in the United States.

Section 31: Registration Fees.   The annual fee for registration is 0.03% of the total value of the equity securities available for sale on an exchange in the preceding calendar year. Bonds and exempted securities are not included. The charge applies to OTC transactions in equity securities that may be traded on national securities exchanges, whether or not the transactions are actually effected on those exchanges.

Section 32: Penalties.   Violators are subject to a $10,000 fine and/or five years' imprisonment for each violation.

Section 33: Separability of Provisions.

Section 34: Effective Date of the Act.

Section 35: Authorization of Appropriations.

The Maloney Act

The Securities Exchange Act of 1934 originally applied only to listed exchange transactions. It was first amended in 1938. The amendment, commonly referred to as the Maloney Act, expanded its provisions to include the OTC market and led to the registration of the NASD and its members with the SEC. It also provided for the registration of any association that establishes standard operation rules and trading procedures for its members (such as SROs) in the conduct of its securities business. Registered associations are accorded self-regulatory and disciplinary powers similar to those accorded registered securities exchanges. Yet under this act the SEC retains the right to review and to deny new rules and regulations.

Municipal Securities Rulemaking Board (MSRB)

The 1975 amendment to the Securities Act of 1934 mandated the SEC to appoint a Municipal Securities Rulemaking Board (MSRB). This board formulates entry standards, operating rules, and procedures for municipal securities firms that are obliged to register with the SEC. Because the MSRB's rules parallel those of the NASD, the NASD enforces compliance with MSRB rules by all municipal securities firms that are also NASD members (which includes most dealers). Supervision of the banking industry's municipal broker/dealers remains the responsibility of various bank regulators.

Glass-Steagall Act of 1933

The Glass-Steagall Act was passed to protect bank depositors against the type of widespread collapse of banking that occurred in the early years of the Great Depression. Two of the law's provisions are key: It authorized deposit insurance and prohibited commercial banks from owning brokerage firms.

Deposit Insurancee. Today, two agencies provide deposit insurance:

1. The *Federal Deposit Insurance Corporation* (*FDIC*) guarantees deposits of up to $100,000 (principal and interest) in commercial banks. All of the money held in one bank in one name is considered to be one account for FDIC insurance purposes. However, a family of four can easily exceed this maximum by opening one account in the husband's name, one account in the wife's name, one account in joint name, one account where the father is trustee for the first child, and so on.
2. *Federal Savings and Loan Insurance Corporation* (*FSLIC*) provides comparable safeguards for noncommercial bank deposit accounts, such as those held in insured savings and loan institutions.

Separation of Banking and Brokerage Operation. For approximately half a century, since its adoption, the Glass-Steagall Act prohibited banks from engaging in brokerage activities. Then, in the mid-1980s, Glass-Steagall was amended, and banks were permitted to offer money market funds, discount brokerage services, and other secondary market investment services. Today Glass-Steagall continues to prohibit banks from acting as investment bankers in the primary underwriting of corporate securities and many municipal securities.

NEW YORK STOCK EXCHANGE

Regulation and Surveillance Department

The Regulation and Surveillance Department deals with the conduct of its members, of its member organizations, and of the employees of those member organizations. The department assures that a customer's financial interests are properly safeguarded when the customer deals with a member organization.

Fidelity Bond Insurance and Broker's Blanket Bond Coverage

Exchange member organizations that do business with the public must carry insurance policies to protect against the loss of money or securities resulting from fraudulent practices or from misplacement of client securities. The type of policy dealing with losses from criminal activity is called *fidelity bond insurance*. The policy insuring the firm against fraudulent trading, check and/or securities forgery, and unexplained shortages of money and securities is known as a *broker's blanket bond*. Generally, the minimum coverage ranges from $200,000 to $5 million per firm.

Because insurance is no guarantee against mismanagement, each member organization has to maintain net capital in amounts prescribed by SEC Rule 15c3-1. If a firm's ratio of indebtedness reaches dangerous levels, the regulatory authorities require an immediate infusion of additional capital, or else the company could be closed down.

Early Warning System

The NYSE has implemented an early warning system to forestall a member firm's possible dissolution. When a member organization's ratio of indebtedness to net capital is more than 10 to 1 for fifteen consecutive business days, the firm may not expand its business activities until that ratio declines. If the ratio is more than 12 to 1, it must reduce its business to maintain a ratio that does not exceed 10 to 1. Furthermore, if at the end of a month indebtedness is more than 12 times capital, or if the firm's net capital is less than 120 percent of the capital required, other action becomes necessary. A special report must be filed promptly with the SEC, and the report must be continued for each month until the deficiency is remedied and remains so for three consecutive months.

Securities Investor Protection Corporation (SIPC)

Established in 1970 as a government-sponsored private corporation, SIPC (pronounced "sip-ick") offers financial protection to brokerage firm customers from broker/dealer bankruptcies. SIPC funds its guarantees by levying annual assessments on broker/dealer firms.

Upon notification of a brokerage firm's imminent bankruptcy, SIPC requests a federal court to appoint a trustee to assume management of the concern. The trustee advises customers and creditors of the firm's insolvency, liquidates the firm's assets in an orderly manner, distributes the proceeds to customers and creditors, and compensates customers according to the net values of their accounts.

SIPC insures and guarantees repayment of money and securities in customer accounts valued up to $500,000 per customer ($100,000 of which can be cash). The term, *separate customer*, as used by SIPC, does not mean the separate accounts of each customer but rather the total of the various accounts of a customer at the brokerage firm. Different types of accounts by the same person do not constitute separate accounts.

Example: A single customer has a cash account, a margin account, and a bond account at Colonial Brokerage Corp. For SIPC purposes, these accounts must be combined to determine the $500,000 insurance responsibility. As much as, but not more than, $100,000 of SIPC insurance may be used for the repayment of a cash credit balance in the account. The $100,000 cash credit insurance is included within the $500,000 amount.

If a financial crisis in the investment community were to grow into a calamity, SIPC has the authority to employ up to $1 billion from the U.S. Treasury to restore customer accounts held by the affected broker/dealers.

Regulation of Personnel

The regulation and surveillance department also oversees the qualification and conduct of all "registered persons" within the financial industry. Included in this category are the following:

1. *Registered representatives,* often called account executives or stockbrokers, are the firm's sales force. They solicit buy and sell orders from the public and dispense investment advice. To become registered representatives, individuals must:
   - Devote a major portion of their time to the business.
   - Be of legal age (18 in most states).
   - Have a minimum of four months "on-the-job training" if the firm for whom they work is a member of an exchange.
   - Pass a six-hour exam administered by the NYSE and the NASD.
   - Be licensed in each and every state in which they solicit business.
2. *Registered principals* include most senior managers within a brokerage firm. Again an individual must successfully complete an exam in order to become a registered principal.
3. *Financial principals* are responsible for making sure that the firm meets the capital requirements required by the exchange and for filing the required periodic financial reports. Successful completion of an exam is required to become a registered financial principal.

In addition, if the firm does any options or futures business, it must have at least one options or futures principal who's responsible for making sure that all of the applicable rules and regulations are observed.

Chief Examiner's Department

Annual Audit. To ensure that NYSE member firms have sufficient capital on which to operate, they must submit to an annual audit by the exchange as well as to several examinations of their operating condition during the course of the year. Member organizations also employ independent public accountants of their own choice and make arrangements for them to conduct formal audits of the firm's books and financial activities.

Monthly Focus Report. Supplementing the annual audit is a series of internal examinations by the member firm itself. Its results are reportable to the exchange and to other supervisory bodies in a document known as the *Financial and Operational Combined Uniform Single Report (FOCUS)*. This is actually two reports: an abbreviated form prepared monthly and a more detailed analysis filed quarterly. The FOCUS reports probe deeply into the details of a member firm's capital structure, aggregate indebtedness, operating activities, profitability, and, in general, its continuing efficiency.

Annual Statement to Customers. In keeping with the NYSE policy of financial disclosure and in accordance with SEC Rule 17-5, member organizations must send customers an annual statement of their financial condition determined at the time of the formal audit. Furthermore, within 40 days after each calendar (or fiscal) semiannual period, the firm must also send its customers an uncertified balance sheet, along with a statement of its current net capital and required net capital (computed in accordance with SEC Rule 15c3-1).

Marketing Department: Public Relations

The Marketing Department of the Regulation and Surveillance Committee oversees guidelines for the approval of the following:

1. All market letters and sales literature issued by member organizations.
2. All research reports or statistical analyses issued by member organizations.
3. All other forms of advertising, including newspaper, magazine, radio, television, and telephone market reports.

This NYSE department scrutinizes copies of all documents used in communications with the public to make sure they are accurate and not misleading.

Arbitration

Industry-related disputes between NYSE members must be decided by arbitration, not by the public court system.

Each year, the chairman of the NYSE Board of Directors appoints a Board of Arbitration comprised of members and allied members. From time to time, as needed, the chairperson also appoints two panels of arbitrators. In all controversies over money or securities that are brought to arbitration, the board's majority decision is final and binding; there is no appeal to the NYSE Board of Directors or to the public courts. The exchange's arbitration facilities are also made available to hear claims between the following:

1. Members and allied members.
2. Allied members and allied members.
3. Registered representatives and member organizations (or allied members in the organizations).

Because these individuals are registered by the exchange, they may be compelled to resolve a controversy before the arbitrators if the other party to the dispute so wishes. But if both disputants agree otherwise, they may seek satisfaction in court instead.

NYSE arbitration is also available to nonmembers, such as customers. Nonmembers cannot be required to use the arbitration facilities, but they can compel members, member organizations, or registered representatives to appear before an arbitration panel concerning their claims. All the nonmember has to do is sign an agreement to abide by the decision without further recourse in a public court. There are several advantages to using arbitration to settle disputes, including:

1. It is *faster*. Arbitration proceedings usually take less than three months from the time the paperwork is filed until the time a decision is rendered. Court cases can take years.
2. It is *cheaper*. Neither party needs to be represented by a lawyer although both parties have that option.
3. It is *fairer*. The panel deciding a case are industry professionals

who are familiar with acceptable practices. In a public court, the case may be decided by a jury composed of two beauticians, one waiter, two engineers, three homemakers, and so on.

MUNICIPAL SECURITIES RULEMAKING BOARD (MSRB)

Created in 1975, the Municipal Securities Rulemaking Board (MSRB) is an independent, self-regulatory organization that acts as the primary rulemaker for the municipal securities industry. The MSRB regulates dealers, banks, and brokers, but its authority does not extend to municipal issuers.

Because MSRB is not a governmental body, it is financed not by the federal government but by the municipal securities industry itself. Its operations are supported by fees and assessments paid by firms engaged in the industry.

Municipal Bond Insurance Association (MBIA)

By purchasing insurance for a bond, a municipality may be able to lower the total amount of interest and principal that it has to pay. In 1974, the Municipal Bond Insurance Association (MBIA) was established to insure municipal bonds. The MBIA has five member underwriters: Aetna Casualty and Surety Co., Fireman's Fund Insurance Co., Aetna Insurance Co., Travelers Indemnity Co., and Continental Insurance Co. Each of these firms is liable for a fixed proportion of the MBIA's insurance obligations. Insurance premiums are based on the size of the principal and interest paymetns that can be paid by the issuer or underwriters.

18

Taxation

For tax purposes, securities—stocks, bonds, options—held by *investors* are classified by the U.S. tax code as "capital assets." Gains resulting from the trading of capital assets are subject to taxation, and losses resulting from the trading of capital assets are tax-deductible. Losses can be used to offset gains, making the gains effectively tax-free. If an investor has more gains than losses in a given year, then all of the *excess* gains are subject to capital gains tax.

However, if the investor has more losses than gains, there is a *limit* on the amount of capital losses that can be deducted in any one year. Currently, the maximum amount of capital losses that can be used to offset (or shelter) ordinary income (salaries, rental income, and the like) is $3,000 per year. Any losses in excess of $3,000 can be carried forward to the next tax year to offset future gains (in any amount) or future ordinary income (again up to $3,000).

Example: An unlucky investor loses $20,000 more in 1987 in the market than he made. His net loss is therefore $20,000. He can use $3,000 of that loss to offset his 1987 salary, effectively reducing his salary for tax purposes by $3,000. The remaining $17,000 in losses are carried forward to 1988.

In 1988 the investor fares better, and he makes a net profit in the market of $10,000. Because he has a tax loss carry-forward, he can offset this gain and shelter it from taxes. Additionally he can again offset up to $3,000 of ordinary income. Offsetting his 1988 gains and ordinary income uses up $13,000 of his tax loss carry-forward, leaving him only a $4,000 carry-forward into 1989.

In addition to the general rules on capital gains and losses, other rules affect investors in securities, including those on short sales, wash sales, options, and various types of dividends.

DETERMINING THE HOLDING PERIOD

The holding period is the amount of time that the investor has owned the investment. Historically, *short-term investments,* currently defined as investments that an investor owns for six months or less, have been subject to higher tax rates than "long-term investments." However, under the Tax Reform Act of 1986, both short-term gains and long-term gains are taxed at the same rate for most investors. This has led many investors to the mistaken assumption that determining the holding period for their investments is no longer important.

Nothing could be further from the truth. While it is true that for tax years starting after December 31, 1986, both short-term and long-term gains are, for most taxpayers, taxed at the same rate (that is, the investor's ordinary income tax rate), the Tax Reform Act of 1986 did not repeal the distinction between short- and long-term holding periods. By not repealing this distinction, Congress left the door open for a future increase in the tax rate applied to short-term capital gains.

As of this writing, raising the short-term capital gains taxes is one of the ideas under consideration as a way of reducing the huge federal budget deficits.

Long Positions

For long securities positions (positions in which the investor first buys the security), the holding period begins on the *day after the trade date that the securities are purchased* and extends to, and including, the *trade day when the securities are sold.* The holding period is determined in the same fashion regardless of whether the trade is done with a cash, next day, skip day, regular way, or seller's option settlement. The same rule applies for both exchange-listed and OTC transactions.

Example: An investor purchases 100 shares of stock through a broker. The confirmation shows that the trade is executed on August 14, 1987 and that the settlement date is August 21, 1987. Because the investor's holding period for the stock begins on August 15, the investor must hold the stock until February 15, 1988 to have the transaction classified as "long term." If the investor sells the stock on or after February 15, the transaction is considered long term regardless of when the investor actually delivers the security to the buyer.

The major exception to this rule applies to securities purchased on the last day of the month (regardless of how many days there are in the month). If a security is purchased on the last day of a month, the security must be held to the first day of the seventh month in order for the holding period to be considered long term.

Example: Stock acquired on February 28 (in a nonleap year) must be held until September 1 of the same year to be considered long term. However, in a leap year February 28 is not the last day of the month and thus the investor satisfies the long-term holding period requirement by holding the security until August 29.

Securities Acquired by Exercising
Options, Warrants, Rights, and When-Issued Contracts

If a security is acquired through exercising an option, the holding period of the acquired security begins the day after the *option* is exercised. The holding period of the security does *not* include the holding period of the option itself. Options and their underlying securities are considered separate securities for purposes of calculating the holding period.

The holding period rules for when-issued transactions are similar to those for options. The purchase of securities on a when-issued basis is treated as the purchase of a contract to buy the underlying securities (that is, as an option). This "contract" has its own holding period, and the holding period for the underlying securities does not begin until the securities contracted for are actually issued.

Securities acquired by exercising rights or warrants have a holding period that also begins when the right or warrant is exercised. The rights and warrants are again considered to be separate securities with their own holding period, which begins the day after the rights or warrants are purchased.

Convertible Securities

The holding period of convertibles securities is calculated the same way as other securities, from the day after the purchase trade date up to and including the sale trade *if* the security is not converted. If an investor buys a convertible bond and then later sells the bond, the holding period is calculated just like any other security. However, if the security is actually converted into another security, then the holding period of the *new security* depends on whether or not the investor has to pay any money to effect the conversion.

- If the investor *does not* pay any money to effect the conversion, then the holding period of the new security begins on the day after the *original convertible security is purchased.*
- If the investor *does* pay money to effect the change, then the holding period for *the portion of the newly acquired security attributable to the additional payment begins on the day after the payment.* For the portion not attributable to the additional payment, the holding period begins on the day after the trade date on which the original convertible security was purchased.

GIFTS, INHERITANCES, TAX-FREE EXCHANGES, SECURITY DIVIDENDS

Securities acquired by a descendant as part of an inheritance are always treated as having a long-term holding period regardless of how long the securities were actually held by the deceased.

Gifted securities have a holding period that includes the time the securities were held by the donor. If the donor held them for only a month before gifting them and the donee sold them immediately, the resulting gain or loss would be short term.

Securities acquired in a tax-free exchange (resulting from a merger or acquisition) have a holding period that includes the holding period of the exchanged securities.

Securities acquired as a result of a tax-free dividend (such as a stock split or stock dividend) have a holding period that includes the holding period of the stock on which the new stock is issued.

DETERMINING THE AMOUNT OF GAIN OR LOSS

In addition to knowing whether the gain or loss is long or short term, there are rules for determining the amount of the gain or loss. At first glance, the "obvious" amount of gain or loss is the difference between the purchase price and the sale price. However, a number of factors can cause the reportable gain or loss to be different from the "obvious" one.

The reportable gain or loss for any transaction is the difference between the "amount realized" and the "cost basis" with both adjusted to reflect the expenses involved in buying and selling (such as commissions, processing fees, and ticket charges.) In addition, any state and/or local transfer taxes may be either included as an expense of the purchase or sale, or deducted separately as part of an investor's itemized state and local tax deductions.

Example: An investor buys 100 shares of a stock at a price of $10 per share. In addition to the cost of the stock the investor also pays a $50 commission, a $10 processing fee, and a $5 ticket charge. This brings the total cost to the investor for the 100 shares up to $1,065, which is the investor's *cost basis.*

The investor later sells the stock for $13 a share. At the time of the sale the investor incurs another $50 commission, another $10 processing fee, another $5 ticket charge and a transfer tax of $1.30. The net proceeds to the investor are therefore $1,233.70. The reportable gain for tax purposes is therefore $168.70 ($1,233.70 − $1,065.00), not $300 ($1,300 − $1,000).

Securities Acquired as a Gift

For individual investors the general rule is that the recipient of a gift (the donee) has the same cost basis as the giver of the securities (the donor).

Example: A grandfather gives his grandson stock that is currently worth $50 per share. If the grandfather's cost basis is $6 a share, the grandson's cost basis is $6 a share (not $50). Thus, if the grandson later realizes $70 a share upon selling the stock, he is subject to tax on $64 of gain per share, not just $14 of gain per share.

There are two major exceptions to this rule.

First, if the donee sells the securities at a loss, the amount of the loss must be calculated by using the fair market value of the securities at the time the gift is made *if* this fair market value is lower than the donee's cost basis.

Example: The grandfather's cost basis is $30 a share, and the market value of the shares is $20 at the time the shares are gifted. The grandson later realizes $10 per share from the sale of the stock, the grandson's reportable loss is $10 ($20 − $10) a share, not $20 ($30 − $10) per share.

Second, if the amount of the gift is so large that the donor incurs a gift tax, the donee's cost basis may be adjusted to reflect the portion of the gift tax attributable to any appreciation in the value of the securities while they were held by the donor.

Securities Acquired by Inheritance

The cost basis of securities acquired through an inheritance is the fair market value of the securities on the date that the executor chooses for estate valuation purposes. Usually this date is either the day of the decedent's death or the day that is exactly six months after the decedent's death. Thus the recipient's cost basis is the same as the security's value for estate tax purposes.

IDENTIFICATION OF SECURITIES

If an investor purchases the same security at different times, then the chances are that the investor also purchases it at different prices.

Example: An investor buys 50 bonds in 1982 for $650 each, and then, in 1984, she buys 50 more of the same bonds. Very likely, the investor will pay more or less than $650 for the second order of bonds. Let's assume that the bond's market value has risen and that the investor has to pay $800 per bond in 1984.

Later, in 1986, the bond's market value rises so that the bonds are worth $1,000 each. If the investor wants to sell 50 of her bonds, she has to specify whether she is selling the 50 bonds bought for $650 each or the 50 bonds bought for $800 each. The reason is that the realized gain is different depending on which bonds she sells.

The investor must make this indication before the trade is executed or else the government automatically assumes that she is selling the first bonds purchased and assesses taxes accordingly. (In other words, the government assumes first-in first-out, unless otherwise specified.) To indicate which bonds are being sold, investors can either:

1. Specify on their sales order the identification number of the actual bond certificate they want to sell.

2. Or specify on the sale order the date on which the bonds they wish to sell were purchased and/or the price paid for them, such as "Sell 50 bonds purchased on date ＿＿＿＿＿＿ for ＿＿＿＿＿＿ price."

WASH SALES

A wash sale occurs whenever an investor sells securities at a loss and, within 30 days before or after the sale, purchases securities that are identical or "substantially identical." For tax purposes *losses on a wash sale are not tax-deductible,* although gains on a wash sale are fully taxable. The reason is that Uncle Sam does not want investors to accelerate their losses.

Example: An investor buys a stock in 1987 for $20 per share. By 1988 the value of the stock falls to $10 per share, but the investor believes the stock will recover and rise to $30 per share by 1989. By selling and then immediately repurchasing the stock in 1988, the investor has a reportable loss of $10 per share in 1988 and a $10-a-share cost basis going into 1989. If the market value does rise to $30 a share in 1989, the investor has a capital gain of $20 per share in 1989 (that is, the investor loses $10 a share in 1988 and gains $20 a share in 1989 for a net gain of $10.)

If, instead, the investor does nothing but buy the stock in 1987 for $20 and sell it in 1989 to realize $30, the investor has the same gain of $10 per share. Although the total gain is the same, the investor, if allowed to do a wash sale, is able to claim a loss in 1988 despite the fact that the investor is still optimistic about the stock's investment prospects.

Basis Following a Wash Sale

Although deducting losses resulting from a wash sale is not allowed, special cost basis rules allow investors to reflect this disallowed loss in the cost basis of the newly acquired security. Essentially, the basis of the newly purchased securities is the basis of the securities sold *adjusted for the difference between the sale and repurchase price.*

Example: An investor owns 100 shares of stock, for which he paid $1,000. He sells the stock on May 1 for $800 and buys 100 shares of the same stock on May 15 for $900. Although he is not allowed to take the $200 tax loss because of the wash sale rule, his basis on the new stock is $1,100 ($1,000 basis on the old stock plus $100). Because the basis on the new stock is $200 higher than the stock's current market value, the investor incurs no tax liability on the first $200 of appreciation in the value of the stock. This break partially offsets not being able to take the tax loss.

TAX SWAPPING

In direct contrast with wash sales are tax swaps. In a *tax swap*, an investor sells one security on which there is a loss and buys a *somewhat* similar security to take its place. In doing so the investor realizes a tax loss and seeks to replace the security on which there is a loss with another security that is a better performer. Tax swaps are not subject to the wash sale rule and are therefore very valuable tax planning tools.

SHORT SALE RULE

In a short sale the sale takes place before the purchase. Since the profit or loss on the position is not known until the offsetting purchase, there is no tax liability until the offsetting purchase is made. As with long transactions, the profit or loss on the transaction is the difference between the sale price and purchase price including all fees and commissions. Profitable short sales always generate short-term capital gains or losses, regardless of the holding period.

If the short seller must pay any dividends on the borrowed stock to the party from whom the stock is borrowed (as compensation for missed dividends), the short seller may deduct the payments if and only if the short position is closed:

1. More than 45 days after it is opened in the case of regular dividends.
2. Or more than one year after it is opened in the case of an extraordinary dividend.

If the holding period is such that these deductions are allowed, they reduce the basis of the stock used to close the short position, thereby reducing the gain or increasing the loss for tax purposes.

SHORTING AGAINST THE BOX

With a substantial profit on a long position, investors often want to sell the security and take their profits. Unfortunately, if the investor sells the security, the resulting gain becomes taxable in the year in which the stock is sold. If it is near the end of the year, the investor faces the choice of taking the profit and paying the tax in the current year, or holding off on the sale until the following year so as to delay incurring the tax liability. Of course, by delaying the sale, the investor risks losing some or all of the profit on the security. After all, the price of the security might fall before the next year comes.

Fortunately, when faced with this situation, the investor has a third option: "shorting against the box." *Shorting against the box* means simply shorting the same number of shares that the investor is long. Being long 100 shares of a stock and short 100 shares of the same stock is a perfect hedge. The investor holds both positions until the following year. When the next year starts the investor closes out both positions and takes the profit.

This strategy is sound if the investor's goal is merely to delay paying taxes. However, shorting against the box *cannot be used to turn a short-term gain into a long-term gain* because the holding period for the long position is frozen when the investor establishes the offsetting short position.

PUT AND CALL OPTIONS

Options are taxed only when they are exercised, sold by one holder to another, or expire.

1. If an option expires worthless, then *upon the expiration date* the writer has a short-term taxable gain equal to the option premium. The buyer has a capital loss.

2. If an option holder resells an option prior to its expiration, then the holder has a capital gain or loss equal to the difference between the option's cost and the amount realized upon the subsequent sale.

3. If an option is exercised, both the writer and the holder adjust the basis of the underlying security to account for the option's premium.

Upon receiving the exercise notice for a call, the writer sells the underlying security at the strike price. The buyer then *adds* the amount of the option's price to the securities purchase price to determine the cost basis for the security. On the other side of the transaction, the call writer determines the amount realized on the sale of the security by *adding* the price received for the option to the amount paid for the security (that is, the strike price).

Example: Investor A, the writer, receives a $500 premium for a call option on a given stock with a strike price of $100 per share. Investor B, the holder, later exercises the option. Both Investor A and Investor B add the option premium to the stock's strike price. Thus both investors use $10,500 for the transaction. $10,500 is A's cost and B's sale proceeds.

Upon receiving an exercise notice for a put, the writer must purchase the underlying security at the strike price. The writer then *deducts* the amount of the option's price from the security's purchase price to determine the cost basis for the security. On the other side of the transaction, the put holder determines the amount realized on the sale of the stock by deducting the price paid from the amount received for the security.

Example: Investor A, the writer, receives a $500 premium for a put option on a stock with a strike price of $100 per share. Investor B, the holder, later exercises the option and forces investor A to buy the stock at $100. For both Investor A and Investor B, the price is the same. $9,500 ($95 × 100) is A's cost and is B's sale proceeds.

DIVIDENDS

A corporation may pay dividends in the form of cash, property, or additional shares of its own stock.

1. Cash dividends are usually taxed as ordinary income except when the dividends paid do not represent a distribution of profits. If a company has no earnings and no profits, then its distributions to shareholders are not considered dividends for tax purposes. Instead,

the dividends are considered to be a return of the investor's capital and, when received, reduce the investor's cost basis in the stock. (Investors are informed whenever a dividend is not currently taxable.)

Example: An investor owns a share of stock in which her cost basis is $10, and she receives from that corporation a $1 dividend that is not taxable because the company has no earnings or profits. The investor can pocket the dollar without any tax liability but must, at the same time, reduce her cost basis by the same $1. If one year later the investor realizes $20 from the sale of the stock, she reports a long-term gain of $11, not $10.

2. Property dividends are often called *property in kind dividends* and often take the form of stock in a separate company, such as when a company spins off a division of itself to its shareholders as a second company. These dividends are taxed at their fair market value in the year in which they are received. Whatever value is reported becomes the initial cost basis for the security.

3. Stock dividends are not usually a taxable event. Instead, they cause the investor's cost basis to be adjusted accordingly.

Example: An investor owns 100 shares of a stock that has a current market value of $80 per share and in which the investor's cost basis is $40 per share. The company announces a dividend of one share for every share the investor already owns. After the dividend the investor owns two shares, each of which has a cost basis of $20.

Example: An investor owns 100 shares of a stock with a cost basis of $50 per share. If the company issues a 5% stock dividend, the investor owns 105 shares—each with a cost basis of $47.62.

However, if the investor has the option of receiving the dividend either in cash or in stock and chooses to take the stock, the dividend is still taxable. Just having the right to receive the dividend in cash qualifies the dividend as a cash dividend, not as a stock dividend, even if the investor chooses to receive the stock.

Index

absolute redemption in call, 289
accounting department, 287–288
account executive, defined, 1, 5
    see also registered representative, stockbroker
accounting firms, 7
accrued interest:
    explained, 86–87
    in figuration, 273
    in U.S. government securities trading, 96–98
adjustable rate mortgages (ARMs), 119
advance-decline theory, 39, 41
advertising:
    NYSE requirements, 308
    requirements of Rules of Fair Practice, 256
ADRs, *see* American Depository Receipts
advance-decline/volume theory, 39, 42
aged failed-to-deliver contract, 256
agent, defined, 238
all or none (AON) order, 226
American Depository Receipts (CDRs), 67–68
    traded OTC, 237
American Stock Exchange (ASE), 3, 234
    and ASECC, 275
    registration requirement, 299
American Stock Exchange Clearing Corporation
    (ASECC), 275
Amex, *see* American Stock Exchange
analysis, of common stock, 23
annual reports:
    NASD requirements, 256–257
    of NYSE member firms, 308
    SEC requirements, 302
AON, *see* all or none order
arbitrage:
    in futures trading, 193
    with options, 157, 161
arbitrageurs, and stock prices or different exchanges,
    234
arbitration procedure in NYSE, 309–310
ARMs, *see* adjustable rate mortgages
articles of incorporation, 10–11
ASE, *see* American Stock Exchange
ASECC, *see* American Stock Exchange Clearing Cor-
    poration
ask price, in U.S. government securities quotation, 96
assets, in determining book value, 36
assignment, in good delivery, 261
assignment of options, 120
at-the-money option, defined, 160
at the open/close order, 226
auction day, 116
audit, as regulatory tool of NYSE, 307–308
Australian dollar, options on, 171
authorized shares, defined, 10
average multiple of stocks, 38

BA, *see* banker's acceptance
back-end sales charge, 140

back office, *see* operations
balanced (mutual) funds, 136
banker's acceptance (BA), 101, 103–105
    in repo, 105, 107
bank and finance companies, as issuers of bonds, 80
banks, changing role of, 2
Banks for Cooperatives, 98
BANs, *see* bond anticipation notes
banking operations, separated from brokerage opera-
    tions, 304
Banking Panic of 1907, 291
bank loan, compared to underwriting, 201–202
bank loan section, 266, 278
bankruptcy:
    of broker/dealer, 306
    claims of bondholders, 51–52
    claims of common stockholders, 19
    claims of preferred stockholders, 51
    reorganization as result of, 284
bar chart, explained, 48–49
Barrons, 24
    as source of information on mutual funds, 142
basis, in wash sale, 317–319
bearer certificate, in good delivery, 277
bear market, characterized by odd lot buy orders, 40
beneficial owners, 282
best efforts underwriting, 201–202
    requirements of Rules of Fair Practice, 256
bid price, 221
    duty of specialist, 218
    example of order execution on exchange floor, 220
    in OTC trading, 240
    in U.S. government securities quotation, 96
blanket fidelity bond, 256
block transactions, in fourth market, 248
blue chip:
    defined, 13, 16
    mutual funds, 136
blue room, of NYSE, 216
blue skying, 206
Board of Arbitration, NYSE, 309
Board of Directors,
    of a corporation, 1, 17–18
    of NYSE, 309
Board of Commons:
    of Fed, 294
        duties of, 297
    of NASD, 249
        handling of complaints, 262
boiler room sales, 300
bond anticipation notes (BABs), 108
Bond Buyer, The, 116
bonds, 73–92
    compared to preferred stock, 51–52
    futures trading on, 191
    illustration, 74–75
    options on, 171
    as vehicle for raising capital

332